The Sermon as Symphony

The Sermon as Symphony
Preaching the Literary Forms
of the New Testament

Mike Graves

Judson Press ® Valley Forge

The Sermon as Symphony:
Preaching the Literary Forms of the New Testament
© 1997 Judson Press, Valley Forge, PA 19482-0851

Bible quotations in this volume are from the New Revised Standard Version of the Bible, copyright © by the Division of Christian Education of the National Council of the Churches of Christ in the United States of America. Used by permission. All rights reserved.

"Cries in the Graveyard" by Eugene Lowry from DAEMONIC IMAGINATION edited by Robert Detweiler and William Doty. Used by permission of Scholars Press.

"Figs Out of Season" by Thomas Long from PREACHING BIBLICALLY edited by Don Wardlaw. Used by permission of Westminster John Knox Press.

"I Am Who I Am" from THE PREACHING LIFE by Barbara Brown Taylor. Used by permission of Cowley Publications, 28 Temple Place, Boston, Mass., 02111. Tel. 1-800-225-1534.

Excerpts from PREACHING TO STRANGERS by William H. Willimon and Stanley Hauerwas. Used by permission of Westminster John Knox Press.

"Down the Up Staircase" by Eugene Lowry. Used by permission of *Preaching Today.*

Library of Congress Cataloging-in-Publication Data
Graves, Mike.
  The sermon as symphony : preaching the literary forms of the New Testament / Mike Graves.
    p. cm.
  Includes bibliographical references.
  ISBN 0-8170-1257-5 (pbk. : alk. paper)
  1. Bible. N.T.—Sermons. 2. Bible. N.T.—Language, style. 3. Preaching. I. Title.
BS2341.3.G72 1997
251—dc21   96-49361

Printed in the U.S.A.
05 04 03 02 01 00 99 98 97
6 5 4 3 2 1

To Al Fasol,

my first professor of preaching,

ὁ κύριος μετὰ ὑμῶν

Contents

Genre: The Revelation of John

Foreword

A generation ago the great New York preacher Harry Emerson Fosdick could zing his famous one-liner: "Nobody except the preacher comes to church desperately anxious to discover what happened to the Jesbusites." Beneath that clever quip, though, there lurked an impoverished notion of the Bible as mainly a book of ancient religious history, and not a very interesting one at that. Jesbusite, Ammonite, Levite, Sadducee, Pharisee, Dead Sea—the whole biblical text whirled by in a mind-numbing blur, leaving behind a dusty cloud of forgotten tribes, moldy laws, enigmatic pronouncements, and quaint customs. Of course the Bible was important—it did, after all, record the involvement of God with the world—but if the preacher was looking for excitement and imagination, then inside one's head or outside in the street were more promising locales than down deep in the mire of some biblical text.

Indeed, many recent developments in homiletics can be attributed to the loss of confidence in the liveliness of Scripture expressed in Fosdick's crack. When the voltage drops in the Bible, preachers desperately plug the sermon into any outlet that promises a jolt of energy: psychotherapy, narrative, image, communication theory, personal disclosure—the list goes on. Even some preachers who proclaim that they are "Bible preachers" and loudly trumpet the claim that while others may have strayed from the Scripture they alone have not bent the knee, upon analysis turn out to preach sermons long on dogmatics and moralisms but innocent of any serious interaction with a biblical text.

Fortunately, both in and out of season, the cause of creative and faithful biblical preaching has never lacked able advocates. In recent times, one thinks of such names as O.C. Edwards, Leander Keck, Ernest Best, Haddon Robinson, Walter Brueggemann, Fred Craddock, and others, who, from their own distinctive theological and hermeneutical vantage points, summoned preachers to serious engagement with biblical texts and their textures. Now to this list we can add the name of Mike Graves.

In recent years, the cause of lively biblical preaching has gained an ally in literary-critical and rhetorical approaches to the Scripture, and it is this new friendship between homiletics and biblical studies that Mike Graves develops in this book. The idea that the biblical writers were not just trying to *say* something with words but also to *do* something opened up exciting avenues of textual understanding. The writers of the Bible were no mere chroniclers; they were, in a way, preachers who chose and arranged language not only for its content but also for its impact. If this is so, then the contemporary preacher's task of interpretation involves far more than cracking open a text's shell and prying loose some idea that will "preach." Preachers must place the exegetical needle in the grooves of the text, track its movements and contours, and think about sermons as regenerations of the textual event.

To understand the relationship between text and sermon this way, one must develop an eye for the small details, the odd shifts, the subtle ironies, the delicate patterns of biblical literature. Mike Graves teaches us, through explanation and example, to "look small" before we "preach large," to examine the intricate textures and microscopic patterns of aphorisms and parables, pronouncements and discourses as a means to discover and extend their impact.

Preachers will be both more cautious and more bold because of this book. On the side of caution, preachers will be mindful of the differences in biblical literary forms, careful not to throw every text thoughtlessly into the homiletical blender, thus turning the multiflavored biblical witness into a bland vanilla milkshake. On the side of boldness, preachers will discern anew the excitement of biblical texts and hear within them promptings of the Spirit that evoke urgent proclamation.

Thomas G. Long
Princeton Theological Seminary

Preface

A few years ago some friends of ours invited my wife and me to a performance of Mozart's best-loved pieces by the Kansas City Symphony. The orchestra and symphony chorus were going to be performing, among other things, selections from Mozart's *Requiem Mass*. It was a beautiful Sunday afternoon in early autumn, and after everyone had filed in and quieted down, the choir entered to polite applause. After that the concertmaster entered, followed by William McGlaughlin, the conductor. Both were greeted with enthusiastic applause. McGlaughlin tapped his baton and the orchestra struck up a most majestic noise, accompanied by the chorus.

After the first piece the chorus exited along with the concertmaster and McGlaughlin, since the second piece was for orchestra only. We had probably heard about six minutes of the performance thus far. Then the man behind me complained to his wife, "You mean it's already over? I gave up football for this?" Obviously the man was not a lover of the symphony, or at least was not acquainted with its ways.

This book uses the metaphor of a symphony (and music in general) to discuss preaching, a kind of proclamation that is a moving and majestic experience. You do not have to be involved with the fine arts to understand these concepts, although it would not hurt (and it is never too late to get involved). In every culture and every age it is the artists who speak the truth. Over and over again I have been struck by the artistry and the poetry of the New Testament. But the poets in the New Testament speak on behalf of God.

My hope is that this book will be useful to you in your preaching ministry as you strive to be the poet-prophet who speaks on behalf of God today. I do not envision you reading this work from cover to cover, although you might want to read the three introductory chapters first. These chapters address the ideology, methodology, and ecclesiology of form-sensitive preaching respectively.

I envision a preacher who has before her an open Bible and a couple of good commentaries, but feels a need for more as she considers Paul's use of a hymn in the lectionary readings for Palm Sunday. Or I envision a seminary student who longs for more resources to help him understand Jesus' parables and how to preach from them. Those who do read this work from cover to cover will encounter some repetition, although I have tried to keep it from being the equivalent of reading through Kittel's *Theological Wordbook.*

As a preacher myself and as a teacher of preachers, I am most at home in shaping sermons, not in analyzing the role of characterization in the Fourth Gospel. I know much more about gathering stories and organizing sermon materials than I do about the influence of the crowds on Luke's view of the triumphal entry or the preexisting literary forms behind Paul's epistles. In short, I am not formally trained in literary form, or rhetorical criticism. I have found, however, that not many biblical scholars—who are trained in these areas—adequately address my practical concerns about preaching a given text. Tragically, we preachers often unfairly malign these scholars, accusing them of answering questions that no one is asking. I have heard ministers ask things like, "Who has the time to do in-depth research on the difference between ancient hymn forms and confessions?" The answer is obvious—biblical scholars. Preachers in local church ministry obviously do not have the time, but we ought to be eternally grateful that others do. These scholars have provided us with rich resources for preaching, but we have not always known how to incorporate their scholarship into our sermons.

The idea for this work came from another book—*Literary Forms in the New Testament: A Handbook,* by James L. Bailey and Lyle D. Vander Broek. Theirs is an example of biblical scholarship with implications for the teaching and preaching ministries of the church. This book is an attempt to mobilize homiletics to meet them halfway—to try to bridge the gap between serious biblical criticism and homiletics.

I hope to show how sermons can be shaped in light of the New Testament's literary forms. Depending on how you classify forms, there are roughly thirty different forms in the New Testament alone, so perhaps it would be good to say something about the forms that have been omitted, as well as those that have been selected. Some forms, though crucial in New Testament studies, are simply too few in number to warrant a thorough look at how they might be preached. The genealogies of Jesus, for example, are rich in theological insights and preaching material. Matthew's genealogy (Matthew 1:1-17) is a wonderful advent text, but there are only two genealogies in the entire New Testament (Luke 3:23-38 being the other). Likewise, Paul's use of diatribe (conversations with imaginary opponents) has much to offer the preacher who wishes to take seriously the role of literary form in shaping the sermon, but it occurs only once in its complete form (Romans) and partially in James.

Other forms are plentiful, such as the speeches in Acts. Scholars continue to investigate the speeches and sermons that make up roughly 20 percent of the book of Acts, material that helps us understand the development of the narrative. I became intrigued, however, by the lack of attention paid to the other 80 percent of the book—adventure stories that include jailbreaks, shipwrecks, and all the other types of adventure that held my attention as a child. I wondered how those adventure stories could be captured in sermon and retold.

The ten forms that we will consider are categorized within the four major genres of the New Testament: gospel, acts, epistle, and apocalypse. These genres are presented in canonical order. In order to assist readers who are unfamiliar with the more technical terms for the various forms, I have attached a subtitle to each of the form chapters.

In my attempt to wed biblical studies and homiletics, I am not so naive as to think that I am constructing a great concrete bridge that you can just drive over without any special thought or concern. Perhaps it is more like a shaky human bridge made up of biblical scholars on one side and homileticians on the other, all standing with arms raised and hands joined while you, the preacher, gingerly cross over and back. It is an exciting endeavor, one that I liken at times to being asked to stand and sing before a congregation, or, even more unlikely, being asked to join the symphony orchestra.

Speaking of the symphony, on one occasion I heard conductor William McGlaughlin speak glowingly about three of his musicians who were retiring. Their collective years of service performing with the Kansas City Symphony added up to 139 years. In a very informal and touching moment McGlaughlin waved his baton and said, "See, it really doesn't make any noise. I am dependent on the musicians." That is where I find myself in the writing of this book. I am dependent on several persons who have shown me how to make music in my preaching and who have supplied encouragement along the way: Al Fasol, my first professor of preaching and my good friend; Grant Lovejoy, a friend from graduate school days who offered perceptive comments early on in this project; Bill Stancil, a former colleague whose proofreading skills and theological insights were most helpful; many former colleagues at Midwestern Baptist Theological Seminary; my present colleagues at Central Baptist Theological Seminary, the administration and faculty, especially David May who offered rich insights and timely encouragement; my colleagues in the Academy of Homiletics; Robin Sandbothe and David Eaton, who shared ideas with me during the writing of the final draft; my students, of course, who over the years heard these ideas often, including some who even helped with last-minute editorial work; the staff at Judson Press who made the whole project worthwhile and treated me so kindly; and, finally, my family—my wife, Carol, and my three children, Michael, Melissa, and Michelle. They have taught me more than they will ever know.

Part I

An Introduction in Three Movements

CHAPTER 1
First Movement

Text and Tune: The Shapes and Sounds of Sermons to Come

Prelude

I am a baby boomer. In terms of chronology that means I was born between 1946 and 1964. In terms of music that means I grew up listening to the songs of artists such as Elvis Presley, the Beatles, the Rolling Stones, and Led Zeppelin. My generation cranked our stereos all the way up, producing shock waves among most law-abiding citizens and sound waves that shattered more than a few eardrums along the way.

My mother grew up listening to Frank Sinatra and Mel Tormé. Her dad was a fan of Lawrence Welk. I realized that the generation gap was insurmountable the time my grand-dad heard me talking about Alice Cooper and asked, "Who's she?"

I used to pride myself on being current musically, but I don't any longer. What happened? Besides the fact that I grew older, mellowed, and fell in love with classical music, there arose a generation that knew not Beethoven or the Beach Boys. Today's youth are currently infatuated with the rhythms of young country, alternative rock, rap, and grunge.

Is that stuff really music? Yet another generation gap seems to have developed.

Changing musical taste is hardly a modern phenomenon. My parents shocked their parents with the sounds of bebop and early rock 'n' roll. Music historians note that even classical artists were rebels in their day. At its debut in 1913 Stravinsky's *Rite of Spring* was considered scandalous. Now it is a classic.

Changes in taste should come as no surprise to those who know anything about the history of preaching. The homiletical top forty of all time is hardly a homogeneous group. Alongside the traditional sounds of Augustine, Martin Luther, and John Broadus, several others have broken into the business and climbed to the top of the charts.

Fred Craddock is to preaching what Elvis Presley was to music. "The things that man does with a biblical text shouldn't be done," some said. "It's just not proper." Others, however, were ecstatic. Craddock revolutionized preaching with the publication of *As One without Authority* in 1971, turning the world of preaching upside down, literally and figuratively. In the chapter entitled "Inductive Movement and Structure" he notes that while the Bible is rich in all sorts of literary forms (for example, poetry, saga, narrative, proverb, hymn, and parable), most sermons tend to take the same old form week in and week out.[1] With biting sarcasm Craddock asks, "Why should the multitude of forms and moods within biblical literature and the multitude of needs in the congregation be brought together in one unvarying mold, and that copied from Greek rhetoricians of centuries ago?"[2] Good question!

Although Craddock's voice has been the most influential, he was not the first to question the form issue in preaching. In 1958 H. Grady Davis was a voice crying in the wilderness. His book, *Design for Preaching*, was the first work solely devoted to sermon form.[3] Following in the footsteps of Davis and Craddock, in 1980 Eugene Lowry introduced us to the jazzy sounds of narrative preaching, sermons that move from tension to resolution through a prescribed loop.[4] In the mid-eighties Don Wardlaw put together an ensemble of varied voices—Ronald Allen, Thomas Troeger, Charles Rice, Gardner Taylor, and Thomas Long, to name a few—concerned with "creating sermons in the shape of Scripture." In the introduction Wardlaw describes traditional preaching as forcing a "straitjacket of deductive reason" over the forms of the Bible, resulting in sermons more akin to legal briefs than a living word of God.[5]

Craddock's influence persisted. In 1989 Thomas Long's book, *Preaching and the Literary Forms of the Bible,* was published. It was the first work solely devoted to the impact that the Bible's literary forms should have on preaching. In it Long reminds us that sermons can be biblical in form as well as content.[6] This book, like Long's, is *not* a call to a new way of preaching, but to consideration of a very old way that has been directly in front of us all the time—the way that the biblical texts present themselves. The very forms of the biblical texts can give us clues about how to preach them, resulting in an approach to preaching that I call "form-sensitive."

The terms "form" and "genre" are often used interchangeably, which can lead to misunderstanding. So allow me to clarify their usage here. The term "genre" will refer to the larger literary units within the New Testament, of which there are four: gospel, acts, epistle, and apocalypse.[7] The term "form" will refer to the smaller literary units within those broader genres, such as parables within the gospels, topoi within the epistles, and so forth.

This book builds on Long's work. One difference, however, is that whereas Long considered mostly the larger genres of both the Old and New Testaments (for example, psalms, proverbs, epistles) and only one of the smaller forms (parables), this work focuses exclusively on several New Testament forms, looking at ten distinct forms as found in the four major genres of the New Testament. In addition to genre and form, Randolph Tate notes the importance of subgenres or devices (such as hyperbole and euphemism) that function within the biblical texts.[8] Therefore, every text may be classified according to genre, form(s), and literary device(s). (Some texts combine literary forms and use more than one device.) A given passage, for example, could be analyzed as being the *genre* of gospel and the *form* of parable and using the *device* of hyperbole.

Form-Sensitive Sermons

Simply put, form-sensitive sermons are sensitive not only to the literary form but also to the genre and devices of a given text. They do not merely report the form of the text nor do they slavishly copy it. The reporting model is the more traditional of the two. All good preachers know that the literary form of a biblical passage should influence its interpretation. You do not interpret a parable like one of Paul's warning passages. They are different in form as well as content. Unfortunately, most preachers stop there. Having determined what a text means in light of its literary form (as well as its history, linguistics, and so forth), they simply report on it in the sermon: "This passage before us is a warning passage. There are several things you need to know about warning passages." These kinds of sermons are reports, not events.

This kind of reporting, however, can be quite sophisticated. For example, many preachers know that some narrative materials in the Bible are structured in the form of an *x*, which is known as a chiasm. A chiastic narrative is one in which the elements at the beginning of the story correspond roughly to the elements at the end, with everything in the story pointing to the center. A chiastic structure within a narrative should serve as a clue for how to focus the sermon. But the preacher need not specifically mention the chiasm any more than the tense of a Greek verb.

Others simply disregard literary form altogether. For instance, one recent book in preaching that addresses how to preach from various genres and forms suggests that preaching on miracle passages is no different from preaching on any other narrative material. The preacher must "describe it, explain it, and apply it." The writer adds, "For most miracle texts, the Analytical method is the usual and preferred approach as far as homiletical structure is concerned." He suggests that a sermon on the man born blind in John 9 might follow an outline such as this:

I. The case
II. The cure
III. The confession
IV. The consequences[9]

What is there about this outline that uniquely fits the miracle story of John 9? Could the same outline be used for just about any passage in the Bible? I think I have heard this one somewhere before. Form-sensitive preaching means more than just forcing the same old sermon structures onto the various literary forms. Form-sensitive sermons are more than reports.

Equally misguided is the notion that form-sensitive sermons must somehow copy the biblical forms. If that were the case, a sermon on the Lord's Prayer would have to be preached in the form of a prayer, and a sermon on a Pauline hymn would have to be sung. It is true that some forms of narrative preaching are essentially modified versions of the biblical text, an approach that can be valuable. One of the biggest limitations of narrative preaching is a tendency to restrict the canon to narrative passages alone. Some narrative preachers rarely preach from the epistles, although recent scholarship has shown that even Paul's epistles contain narrative elements.[10]

The ideal in form-sensitive preaching is maintaining the proper "respect" for the text and its literary form.[11] This volume attempts to bridge the gap between theory and practice by providing practical suggestions on how to respect the literary forms of biblical texts. Chapters 4-13 also include a sample sermon, a list of additional published sermons, and exercises from biblical passages.

A recent work in biblical studies, *Literary Forms in the New Testament*, offers much in regard to understanding and interpreting the specific forms.[12] What is needed is a homiletical companion. Preaching Paul's epistles, for example, means being sensitive to a whole host of forms within that genre. An understanding of how these forms work, as well as the implications for preaching them, is what this book attempts to communicate.[13] It offers practical advice for preaching from texts like the miracle stories in the Synoptic Gospels, the lengthy discourses in John's Gospel, and Paul's use of hymns. It discusses what it means, precisely and practically, to "respect" a text's form. But first, let us examine the hermeneutical and homiletical premises of form-sensitive sermons.[14]

Hermeneutical Premises

1. Form-sensitive sermons require exegetical integrity (as do all types of sermons). I refer here not to authorial intention, but to the abuses of what might be called "ministerial invention." While no interpreter can claim to possess *the* meaning of a passage, neither should *any* random meaning be allowed. Even reader response has limits. The biblical text is not a Rorschach inkblot test. Those who perceive the newer forms of preaching as being soft on biblical content do not understand the newer forms. "Expository" preaching or any other traditional understanding of sermon structure is just as

likely to be unbiblical. There is no sermon structure or approach to preaching that guarantees biblical content and exegetical accuracy. The goal in form-sensitive sermons, as with all good sermon structures, is to be hermeneutically sound, though bridging from what a text meant "then" to what it means "now" is never simple.

2. Form-sensitive sermons, like all types of sermons, should account for the literary form of the text in the interpretive task. As we have already noted, the form of a text and its content cannot be separated. This is true in all areas of life, not just preaching. Take, for example, the experience of receiving mail. You find a wide range of documents—different sizes, shapes, colors, textures—in your mailbox daily. A glossy travel brochure catches your eye with its gorgeous pictures of pristine waterfalls. You have always dreamed of going to Hawaii, and some enterprising travel agent hopes to cash in on your dream. Behind the brochure is a painful reminder of why you have not made it to Hawaii yet: a bill. It has to be a bill. The company logo, the name of a bank card you use regularly, is in the upper left corner. Your name and address, produced by a dot-matrix printer, appear in the envelope window. You choose not to open this one right away because behind it is a letter from a close friend. You know it is personal because this is the first letter you have received from him since his mother died. Your address and his return address are in his own handwriting. Behind the letter is a larger envelope, one with Ed McMahon's picture on it. On and on the list goes—every day an adventure.

The mere shape of the envelope tells you something about the letter inside—the packaging and the content go together. What if they did not? Imagine some creditor sending you a bill in personalized letter form. "Dear Mike: It was good to hear from you last month and to receive that payment. How are Carol and the kids? I hope things are going well at the seminary. By the way, you owe us more money this month.

Be sure to write. Sincerely ..." Or imagine a friend addressing you as "Occupant." Packaging and content go together. In the case of the biblical texts, however, the literary form is more than packaging.

Homiletical Premises

1. Form-sensitive sermons, unlike traditional sermons, should seek to be more experiential than expository. As Frank Lloyd Wright once quipped, "A house should be *of* the hill, not *on* the hill." In other words, the house should be an integral part of the environment. The same can be said for sermon and text. In the case of form-sensitive sermons, that means being more re-presentational than propositional. Propositional sermons address listeners primarily through the mind, teaching the lessons of the text. Propositional preachers are fond of expressions such as, "What I want us to see this morning is . . ." or "Let's consider the lessons this text has for us . . ." Propositional preaching places a premium on the information that a text conveys. This information is usually expressed in the form of points. A drawback with these preachers, as Craddock notes, is that they can sour the rich tastes and textures of the biblical texts by boiling them off, and they end up preaching the stain in the bottom of the cup.[15] Another writer has said expository preaching often fails to "communicate the experience" of a passage.[16]

Re-presentational preaching, on the other hand, seeks change through an encounter with the text. It seeks to *present again*, or *re-present*, the text. Propositional preaching is like watching a documentary on the Holocaust, while re-presentational preaching is like seeing the movie *Schindler's List*. This kind of preaching, like a touching piece of music, comes through the gut more than through the mind.[17] As Gustav Mahler put it, "What is best about music is not to be found in the notes." Sometimes it may even be hard to articulate what it was about the event that was so moving. That is because music is experiential. And so is re-presentational preaching. The goal of such preaching is to proclaim the text in such a way that what happened in those who first heard the text "then" happens in those who hear it "now." It is not so much talking *about* the text as talking *of* or *from* the text.

2. Form-sensitive sermons are oral events based on a biblical text that was originally oral (or aural) in nature.[18] Many of the biblical texts (the Gospels, for instance) were circulated orally before being written down, and are, therefore, oral. Other texts (such as the epistles) were written down first, but were intended to be read aloud, and are, therefore, aural. Both have a performance base. Thus we can see that the words of a biblical text are somewhat like a musical score.[19] They come back to life as they are played aloud. No musician would give a concert consisting of a lecture instead of music: "If you will look at the musical score with me, you will notice the first measure begins with four quarter notes. According to Bach, each note. . . ." What a preposterous image! Yet preachers frequently turn preaching into reporting. A text that once had an oral existence, having been written down, becomes an object to be dissected by lecture.

Nicholas Lash asks us to consider what we see when we leaf through the pages of the New Testament. "A letter from Paul to his friends in Corinth? Matthew's account of the passion of Jesus? . . . No, we don't see anything of the kind. All that we *see* is a set of black marks on white paper."[20] To interpret those black marks, whether letters or musical notes, is more than reading them or playing them accurately; it is "performing" them as a score that comes alive and catches up the listeners in an event.[21]

Richard Ward has tried to redeem the term "performance" as it relates to preaching. He notes that the word comes from an old French expression that meant to "carry through to completion" and also meant "form coming through."[22] What great images for preaching!

Preaching, like music, is a performance art. Eugene Lowry, an accomplished musician and homiletician, notes that "both music and preaching are temporal events, not constructions of space." A sermon is an "acoustical event."[23] Preaching that is sensitive to the orality of Scripture brings the text alive and produces an experience like Mozart's *Requiem Mass* or Handel's *Messiah* for those who hear it. I have come to think of sermon preparation in terms of composition, not construction.[24] What does it mean for a sermon to be more event than lecture? How can a sermon respect the literary form of the text? By paying attention to the mood and movement within that text.

Mood and Movement: Harmony in the Sermon

The two primary components of form-sensitive sermons are mood and movement.[25] The mood of a given biblical text is the state of mind or feelings that the text evokes when we read it. The movement of a passage is its progression, structural pattern, or divisions of thought. We will look at each of these factors separately.

Textual Mood

The mood of a piece, any kind of piece, is not easy to define. I think of Louis Armstrong's response when he was asked to define jazz: "Man, if you don't know, I could never tell you." Defining mood may not be easy, but identifying it is. As Fred Craddock notes, "Hearing some sermons, I think of seventy-six trombones coming down Main Street. Other messages make me picture a violin and a crust of bread."[26] Using musical analogies in referring to the mood of a sermon or text seems to be common. Preachers in the African American tradition have used it frequently.[27] Thomas Long writes, "Trying to decide whether the text is better accompanied by a flute or trombone can go a long way toward determining the text's mood."[28] For some time I have encouraged my students to imagine what music might best fit a given text. This relationship is not as far-fetched as you might think. Stories are often told through music, and not just at the opera: for example, Tchaikovsky's *Peter and the Wolf* and Walt Disney's *Fantasia*. A similar process can be applied to the Bible. "Listening to Scripture and its different forms is like listening to music and learning to hear with a trained ear."[29] Some tape recordings of the Bible include background music to help achieve mood.

Careful attention to mood is a basic element of form-sensitive homiletics. The preacher must identify the mood of the text. It might be the soft oboes of John 11:35-36: "Jesus began to weep. So the Jews said, 'See how he loved him!'" Or it might be the brilliance of Mendelssohn's "Wedding March" played on the piano when John says in Revelation 19:7 that "the marriage of the Lamb has come and his bride has made herself ready." It might be the sound of militant brass as Paul proclaims that God's peace "will guard your hearts and your minds in Christ Jesus" (Philippians 4:7).

It is important to note, however, that biblical texts often have mood swings within them. The somberness of Lazarus's death gives way to the glorious splendor of resurrection. The sermon must respect this mood swing. Some texts demonstrate several moods. At the crucifixion Jesus feels betrayed, his disciples feel forlorn, the Pharisees feel relieved, a centurion feels betrayed. The language, the delivery, the images, and the supporting material must all be sensitive to the mood(s) of the biblical text. Worship planning that is sensitive to the mood of the text can also be beneficial, especially what precedes or follows the sermon, although elements of worship should never be viewed merely as primers for preaching.[30]

Textual Movement

Textual movement refers to the progression, structural pattern, or divisions of thought within a text. In a narrative passage it might be the plot or scene changes. In a piece of biblical poetry it might be stanzas. In a Pauline passage it might be the rhetorical devices used to differentiate thoughts.

Movement is also important in music. It can refer to the complete divisions of a symphony and concerto, or it can refer to the suggestion of action. Good music implies movement. The same can be said for good preaching. Some sermons move toward crescendo, others drift into contemplation with only minor resolution, if any. Sensitivity to the movement in the text is essential to movement within the sermon.

Interlude

With this preliminary material before us, several practical questions still need to be answered. What is the relation between mood and movement? How do mood and movement figure into the preparation process? How do you go about preparing a form-sensitive sermon? Are there any unique factors involved in preparing this kind of sermon? These are some of the issues discussed in the next chapter.

CHAPTER 2
Second Movement

Listening to the Music: Preparing Form-Sensitive Sermons

Preliminary Considerations of Sermon Composition

On the wall of my office is a framed piece entitled "Music," composed of various quotes about music. A few years ago the seminary I attended was raising funds for the school of church music. My wife and I gave some money, and we received this piece as a gift. All of the quotes are in calligraphy, and it is signed by the artist Rachel Joy Colvin.

Several features of the piece stand out, such as color and artistic arrangement, but my eye is drawn toward two quotes in particular. The first is the line by Gustav Mahler that I referred to in chapter 1, "What is best about music is not to be found in the notes." What is best about Mahler's line, at least for me, is its reference to the mystery of music itself. You can write it down, just as you can write down a sermon, but you cannot really capture it on paper.

The second line comes from Leopold Stowkowski: "Music is created on the canvas of silence." Stowkowski's line also intrigues me. An awesome responsibility goes with the act of filling the void of silence with our own creative effort. When I consider that, awe gives way to fear. I suddenly remember that Sunday is coming, and I must create a sermon to fill the waiting silence every seven days. Order must come out of chaos each week. But we preachers do not speak on our own initiative; God has already spoken. P.T. Forsyth reminds us that we are not there to "astonish people with the unheard of." Rather, it is more like uncovering "a mine on the estate."[1] We inherit the biblical witness and thus are stewards of texts. But how do we use these texts to compose our sermons?

Form-sensitive preaching addresses three questions: What is the text saying? What is the text doing? How can the sermon say and do the same?[2] The first question relates to exegetical integrity, the second question to the role of literary forms in interpretation, and the third to both exegetical and homiletical integrity. Let us consider each of these separately.

What Is the Text Saying?

Finding the answer to this question is the goal of interpretation. It involves many disciplines of study, one of which is an analysis of the text's literary form.[3] Several good helps are available to assist with form analysis.[4]

Every good preacher knows the importance of doing hermeneutical homework as preparation for preaching. Unfortunately, many preachers begin and end with the question, What is the text saying? Their sermons are nothing more than a reporting of what Paul said to the church at Galatia or the distance between Jerusalem and Jericho. As one preacher so aptly put it, "You should never preach a sermon that could just as well have been preached in the first century."[5] Arriving at what the text is saying is only the first step. Biblical texts, like musical texts, not only say something, they *do* something.

What Is the Text Doing?

The answer to this question involves analyzing the text in order to determine the strategy (or strategies) being used to communicate the biblical truth.[6] Every literary form operates differently. Some texts are complicated, while others are very straightforward. Some make extensive use of imagery and story, others are prosaically pedantic. A preacher needs to move beyond the first question and struggle with the second question in order to compose a sermon that is all that it can be. Eugene Boring notes that attention to both of these matters is essential to the kind of preaching that hopes to transcend reportage and "release the meaning of a text for the congregation."[7]

For example, Fred Craddock preached a wonderful sermon entitled "When the Roll Is Called Down Here" based on the list of names in Romans 16.[8] If he had only examined the text's content (what it says), he probably never would have preached the sermon. It is a list of names of people whom Paul knew. Taking into account the literary function of that list, however (that is, what it was doing), Craddock's sermon reminds us of the importance of Christian community, both then and now. Form-sensitive preaching takes seriously the rhetorical impact of a text.

Or take Luke's record of the death of Ananias and Sapphira in Acts 5. The text says that they died when they falsely presented their offering in worship. That is what Luke says happened. But what is the text doing? Luke notes in verse 11 that "great fear came upon the whole church . . ." This is the first time in Luke's two-volume work that the word "church" is used. There is not one word about the church in his Gospel (only Matthew mentions it), and not a word about the church at Pentecost (although the King James Version uses the word "church"). Not until this couple dies does Luke use the word "church." What is Luke doing? He reminds us that the sin of Ananias and Sapphira was a violation of the commitment among fellow believers that was required in this group called the church. The text *says* that two people died. The text *functions* to remind us of the seriousness of commitment to each other within the church.

Form-sensitive preaching takes seriously the text's content and form, operating on the premise that both are inspired. The preacher does not have the luxury of taking the content seriously and ignoring the form. The text's rhetorical impact must be treated as well. It is the third question that presents the homiletical stumper.

How Can the Sermon Say and Do the Same?

The idea of a sermon *saying* what the text is saying is nothing new. Traditional homiletics has always focused on that task. Form-sensitive sermons, however, are more re-pre-sentational than propositional. Their primary concern is not with teaching the lessons of the text but with experiencing the message of the text. But that does *not* mean that re-pre-sentational preaching is devoid of biblical teaching. (We will say more about the importance of teaching and preaching in the life of the church in the next chapter.)

Form-sensitive sermons seek to *say* what the text is saying and *do* what the text is doing. How is the latter possible? How can a sermon *do* what the original oral/aural text was doing? What does it mean to "respect" the text's literary form and mood? For me, the answer is found in musical analogies.

To speak of the sermon as symphony is to think of the preacher as composer-conductor. Let's say someone approaches the composer with poetry to be put to music. The composer must be sensitive to more than just what the words say, giving attention to the mood of the piece and even to the movement within it. How will the musical composition work in harmony with the words? (Those who compose music for movies have similar concerns. What tune will best presage an imminent shark attack? How can the tenderness of a romantic scene be conveyed musically?) The composer must attempt to compliment[9] the text with music.

Once the composition is complete, however, the task itself is not. The piece must be played. Now the composer becomes conductor. Many instruments will be brought together, with their many different sounds, but they must be in harmony. One sound must emerge out of many sounds; and when everything comes together, the results are indescribable.

The sermon as symphony, then, consists of an interpretation of a text, a searching for its mood and movement, an artistic blending of text and tune, a moving performance, and an acoustical event in which something happens.

What happens, of course, varies from sermon to sermon, as well as from person to person. It is important to note that the persons in the pews on any given Sunday are more than passive listeners, or at least we hope they are. But all analogies break down if pressed too far, and so it is with the sermon as symphony. Our listeners make up a congregation (brothers and sisters in Christ), not an audience, though we must remember that unbaptized persons may also be present. We have ecclesiological concerns to consider.[10] Even so, we want our sermons to do things to our listeners.

I have attended musical performances during which the people in front of me counted the ceiling tiles in the concert hall. I have also attended musical performances that so exhausted me with delight that I was unable to move when they ended. It is the wonderfully mysterious wedding of words and music that fill people with delight and wonder, and that is, in a sense, what we want our sermons to do.

Composing the Form-Sensitive Sermon

What does it mean to think of sermons as compositions? How do we go about artistically blending text and tune? We have already noted that preachers must pay attention to the mood and movement within a biblical text. Both of these concerns are important musically as well. The poet writes with a certain mood in mind. The musician, therefore, must seek to wed the mood to the music harmoniously. The words, "I was sinking deep in sin, far from the peaceful shore . . ."

usually get sung at such breakneck pace and with such flippancy that they do not fit the tune. The best hymns of our faith wed tune and text in such a way that listeners are caught up in the presence of God. For instance, in Martin Luther's "A Mighty Fortress Is Our God," the tune and the text work together to produce a sense of security. Singing that text to the tune of "Happy Birthday" would not work because the tune is too light. The tune and the text must work together.

Composers must also be concerned with movement in the text, which occurs in poetry with the stanzas, or in prose and other forms with scene changes. But what, specifically, is the relation between mood and movement in composing the sermon?[11]

Identifying the Mood

Identifying and being sensitive to textual mood is of primary importance. The ideal in form-sensitive preaching is not slavishly copying the form of the text but respecting the mood of the text. So the place to start is with the determination of the mood. Imagining the appropriate music to accompany that passage is helpful, but the sermon itself does not actually consist of musical accompaniment. One preacher 1shared that she prefers to think in terms of colors. Another said that she actually sketches out the scene—the multitudes reclining on the hillside watching Jesus break the bread and pass it out. Others might prefer to imagine appropriate textures. Each of these approaches engages the preacher through various metaphors, various senses.

For me the musical analogy works best, although the mood must ultimately be translated into words.[12] Therefore, I have found it helpful to brainstorm adjectives and adverbs that best describe the text's mood. The marriage scene in Revelation 19 might be described as "wonderfully festive." Jesus' arrival at Lazarus's tomb could be described as "tragically somber," while Lazarus's resurrection might be "incredibly hopeful." These descriptive phrases serve to identify what kind of mood is most appropriate to the sermon. Is the text lighthearted, serious, reflective, joyful, fearful, supportive, confrontational, hopeful, despairing?

Noting the Movement

Having determined the mood, the preacher then focuses on the possibility of learning from the movement in the text as well. It is important to remember that not every text will lend itself to three rhetorical points. Not every text will lend itself to a narrative structure, either. Form-sensitive preaching entails discovering a text's own organic structure, not importing a synthetic form into it.[13] Interestingly enough, some contemporary sermon structures (particularly narrative and inductive) have much in common with these textual patterns.

Still, the idea is to begin with the text and to search for structural ideas from the text's literary form. Forcing forms onto the text that are actually foreign to its structure would mean violating textual movement in many cases, as well as textual mood in most cases. Singing the words of "A Mighty Fortress Is Our God" to the tune of "Happy Birthday" violates not only the mood but also the meter (movement).

Occasionally it may be possible to duplicate the movements of the text to some extent within the sermon. But there are some structural forms that simply do not lend themselves to being duplicated. A sermon on a prayer does not have to be delivered in the form of a prayer, though the sermon should respect the mood of that prayer. Besides, as Lowry notes, the sermon is not the same art form as the text. A picture of someone praying does not have to include the words of the prayer to be a valid portrayal of the act of praying.[14]

As Fred Craddock notes, it is more important to discern what the form of a text "achieves" than to copy its form, thereby answering the question, What is the text doing?[15] This relates directly to the mood of the text. Forms not only contain content but also convey mood. Consider, for example, a contemporary literary form—the newspaper obituary. Its structure or movement is predictable enough: last name, first name, date of birth, date of death, and surviving family members. The mood is apparent enough, too. This is an announcement of death, a note of sorrow for friends of the deceased. The form and content go together, but do they have to? No. The factual information conveyed in an obituary could be reported in story form (which often happens when celebrities die). The story would have to be sensitive to the mood of the death announcement. But sensitivity to mood does not require *duplicating* structure or movement.

On the other hand, form-sensitive sermons may draw upon the movement and structure in the text, even in some sense duplicating them. For instance, a sermon on John 9, the healing of the man born blind, could duplicate the sevenfold structure in the text. Using a narrative structure, the sermon might build on the seven scenes of a play. Most important, however, would be the need for the sermon to respect the mood of that passage, especially the irony of a blind man who sees and seeing people who do not. Form-sensitive sermons always respect the mood of the text; respecting the movement as well is optional.[16]

Shaping the Sermon

There is a pattern that has emerged in my efforts to prepare form-sensitive sermons, which you may find helpful in your own sermon preparation (three points—wouldn't you know it!):

1. Listing/brainstorming of possible sermon components. The issue here is determining what elements *might* go into the sermon. How much textual detail will you include? Will your treatment of the text be heavy on explanation or application—or both? Will you make use of other Scripture passages? How much contemporary material will you include?

Will you use any stories? Current events? Some of these ideas will already have occurred to you in the interpretive stage.

Remember that you are brainstorming at this point, not thinking critically. Creativity means never shutting off ideas or dismissing them prematurely. You will have time for editing later.

My own preference is to list on one side of a piece of paper the various textual and biblical images, and on the other side the various contemporary images that might go into the sermon. Once I have completed the initial brainstorming, I can begin to focus more specifically on the structure (or flow) of the sermon.

2. Determining the mood of the sermon and brainstorming possible metaphors and structures. What will the mood of the sermon be? The answer to this question depends largely on the mood of the text. For example, if the textual mood is lighthearted, somber materials probably will not work, although exceptions are always possible. This consideration relates directly to the music of the text and will determine what components get into the sermon as well as what structure or shape the sermon will take.

Determining sermon structure comes next. This is a matter of utmost concern to me. Once I have accomplished this, I can relax. The text often provides clues about shape. There are any number of shapes that a sermon might take. Form-sensitive sermons do not have to copy the form of the text. They do need to be consistent with the mood of the text, and they do need to do what the text did originally. The preacher determining sermon structure is like a hymn writer looking for the best tune to accompany a lyric.

3. Determining final structure and arrangement of components. Once the structure is set, the preacher must then determine which components will get in, and in what order. The strategic arrangement of materials is one of rhetoric's five classical canons, rhetoric being the study of how to speak

more effectively.[17] Sometimes the preacher will want to withhold material until the end of the sermon for the sake of impact. At other times the preacher might want to use material at the beginning. Rearranging the materials several times is a good idea. There are all kinds of possibilities in regard to how it might be ordered.

An analogy that I share with my students is that of a map. If someone asked a friend to draw a map, the first and most obvious response would be, "A map to where?" Destination is a crucial concern when drawing a map. The second question would be just as obvious: "Where are you coming from?" Origination and destination not only apply to drawing maps but also to good preaching as well.

Think of where the listeners need to go during the course of the message. That is the sermon's destination. A particular story or line might fit perfectly as the sermon's conclusion. Next, ask where the listeners will begin their journey. What do they bring to the topic and text at hand? That is the sermon's origination. Typically these designations will help determine the flow of the sermon between origination and destination.

Preparing form-sensitive sermons is akin to composing music. It is an artistic enterprise in many respects. Delivering form-sensitive sermons requires artistry as well. Preaching that is sensitive to the music of the biblical texts will use cadence and pausing, volume and pitch, word choice and imagery so that the preaching moment becomes pregnant with meaning the way Handel's *Messiah* does.

Interlude

Good preaching is like good music. The best sermons I have ever heard were more like musical events than lectures. Strategically located within a moving worship service, those sermons were works of art that caused me to get lost in the wonder of God's good news. That preaching occurs in worship reminds us that it occurs in community. The form a sermon takes must respect several aspects of community life. The next chapter deals with some of the practical issues involved in trying new forms within congregational life.

CHAPTER 3
Third Movement

Four-Part Harmony:
Form-Sensitive Preaching in
the Context of the Church

Occasionally I have been asked to sing in choirs, though never more than once in the same choir—for good reason. The scene usually unfolds like this. A musician or a friend in the choir approaches me with, "Hey, Mike, we need some male voices in the choir for the Easter cantata. How about joining us?"

"Oh, I don't sing, not really."

"Come on, it'll be fun. Besides, anybody can sing."

"No, I'd better not."

Eventually I give in to their urging. After all, I enjoy singing. The catch is that I am heavily influenced by those around me. If I am near the bass section, I sing bass. Seat me next to the altos, I sing alto. Luckily, no one ever allowed me to sit next to the sopranos. I sing whatever I hear, whatever comes along.

There are preachers like that. They have no idea what kind of preaching voice they really have. If they preach traditional three-point sermons, it is simply because that is what they have always heard. Then Fred Craddock comes along and asks them to preach inductively. Suddenly the people in their congregations are going home scratching their heads, "What was that sermon about?" Let these preachers hear about narrative, and the next thing you know they are stringing together a series of stories from the pulpit. Homiletically, these preachers are tossed to and fro by every preaching wind that blows.

No preacher should embrace form-sensitive preaching to the point of abandoning everything else. Preaching takes place in a specific context—the worship service of the local church. Certain concerns need to be dealt with in that context, issues such as the teaching function of the preacher, the relation between communication theory and textual move-ment, the congregation's preaching preferences, and the preacher's attitude toward new styles of preaching. Let us briefly examine each issue.

A Limited Repertoire?

Form-sensitive preaching is not a comprehensive homiletical theory. It is one valid approach (among many) to preaching. We need to avoid what Richard Bartlett calls "formal fundamentalism"—the insistence that all sermons be influenced by the shape of the text[1]—just as we would want to avoid the insistence that all sermons be shaped by Greek rhetoric or by narrative plots. The preacher's reper-toire must be larger than that, if for no other reason than the diversity of the forms included in the Bible.

In the early stages of sermon preparation the preacher needs to decide whether the sermon will be propositional or re-presentational. Form-sensitive sermons are clearly re-pre-sentational. The initial decision is actually a matter of pur-pose. Both propositional and re-presentational preaching seek change, the former through exposition and the latter through experience. The preacher needs to ask, What am I trying to accomplish with this sermon? For instance, the sermon might be on one of the Lord's Supper passages in the New Testament. Several key questions would have to be addressed. Do I want people to understand that the historical precedents for the Lord's Supper are found in Israel's Passover? Do I want the people to experience the power of remembrance as the early church experienced it in the Supper? Both are valid approaches to the text, but they are radically different in sermonic methodology. Both seek to change the listeners—the first through information and the second through encounter.

Since every aspect of worship is experiential, the emphasis that re-presentational preaching puts on encountering and experiencing the text makes it highly appropriate for the worship context. Worship consists of singing the hymns, not just talking about them, of praying the prayers, not just talking about them, of passing along the peace, not just talking about it. Why then does so much preaching that I hear spend more time talking about the text than experiencing it? The re-presentational nature of form-sensitive preaching makes it consistent with the rest of worship.

Perhaps that helps explain why recent homiletical trends have moved away from propositional models. Some propositional approaches have become lifeless and predictable. Traditional sermon structures certainly do a good job of communicating information, although sometimes information is all they communicate. Thomas Long notes that most of us have welcomed as good news the move away from cumbersome explanations and boring propositions to newer forms "irrigating" our sermons with "story, indirection, and poetic shock, with word pictures and fluid sermon forms." The bad news is that the teaching aspect of preaching has dried up.[2] In other words, while many congregations have begun to experience the power of remembrance in the Lord's Supper, for instance, fewer and fewer congregations know anything about its precedents or its theological significance.[3]

This matter is of crucial importance in contemporary homiletics. Form-sensitive preaching is concerned with the sermon's saying *and* doing what the text is doing. Getting a sermon to *say* what the text is saying is nothing new, but as sermons become more artistic and more narrative, the importance of enabling a congregation to name the world theologically must not be overlooked. Form-sensitive sermons must seek to *say what the text is saying*.

Eugene Lowry offers a wonderful model for contrasting the old and new models of preaching. He says that the old model consisted of the "sermonic envelope being governed by rhetorical principles with poetics [for example, story and images] inside," whereas the new model is governed more by poetics with some rhetorical elements inside.[4] In other words, the newer forms of preaching are more re-presentational with some teaching in them, as opposed to the older forms that were largely propositional with some illustrations in them. Sermons of the newer type can help listeners experience the power of the Lord's Supper and do some teaching at the same time. These sermons offer listeners a richer experience of the Lord's Supper than sermons that focus on the significance of the Lord's Supper and only hope to evoke some experience of the passage.

Form-sensitive preaching, therefore, is primarily an experiential approach to preaching, which briefly (sometimes indirectly) conveys biblical exposition. There are parallels to this in music. Classical music stations frequently supply listeners with the history of a piece before playing it, though the explanation is never substituted for the piece itself. The symphony provides printed programs that contain background information about the arrangements. This information has become more important as audiences have become less culturally literate. One well-known music critic lamented the fact that today's audiences do not even know when to clap and when not to. He added, "Maybe singers could save everyone some annoyance by making such announcements from the stage, right at the beginning. Hints, obviously, don't work." I recently attended a performance of the Lafayette Symphony Orchestra in Lafayette, Indiana, conducted by Anne Harrigan. Prior to the performance of a piece by Brahms, the conductor offered a brief explanation and demonstration of what to listen to in the performance itself. I thoroughly enjoyed it!

Perhaps as congregations become more biblically illiterate, ministers will have to rely less on hints and more on direct teaching. Where that becomes true, however, the explanations must never be used as substitutes for the event itself. The explanation and demonstration in Lafayette was followed by the actual performance. Form-sensitive sermons are largely experiential kinds of sermons. They are not, however, devoid of propositional biblical teaching.[5] Rather, they attempt to deal seriously with the text's content and form. But what if the form of the text conflicts with communication theory?

The Battle of the Bands

For well over a century, sermon structure has been dominated by forms that are foreign to the text itself. Preachers have dogmatically insisted on strong biblical content, while the shape of their sermons has been influenced most heavily by secular rhetoric, though that has not been all bad.[6] Something happened in homiletical studies, though, something that many have not heard about yet: the marriage of homiletics and rhetoric came on hard times. As Thomas Long put it, "It was a mixed marriage—homiletics being Jewish and rabbinical in background, and thus religious; rhetoric being Greek, gentile, and ideologically neutral."[7] Preachers began to think about the implications of taking their sermon content from the Bible and their sermon structures from rhetoric,[8] especially when the two were in conflict. Of course, even the most avant garde preachers among us still use rhetoric in their sermons. No preacher would ever think of mounting the pulpit some Sunday morning and saying, "I am going to preach a seventeen-part sermon this morning that will probably last two hours" because of rhetoric, the rules of speaking. In reply to Tertullian's age-old question, "What has Athens to do with Jerusalem?" today's preacher must declare, "Everything! Rhetoric has everything to do with biblical preaching!" [9]

Inductive and narrative preaching came to prominence, however, not only because rhetoric showed them to be effective forms of communication but also because the biblical texts employ these techniques. In this same vein, form-sensitive preaching seeks to be true to the text's content and form.

But what about cases where the text's form violates contemporary communication theory? For instance, it has often been noted that several of Jesus' parables are open-ended; that is, the meaning of the parable is left up to the listeners to determine. Communication theory, however, indicates that not all listeners are capable of receiving implicit messages. Regardless of gender, age, and education, some people cannot pick up on subtleties (though these studies did not consider the role of the Holy Spirit in communication).[10] What is the preacher to do?

My own conclusion is that when communication theory, or what the preacher knows about the congregation, or common sense seem to dictate otherwise, the preacher should not feel bound to follow slavishly the text's own structure. The primary emphasis in form-sensitive preaching is being true to the mood. Following the movement of the text is optional. One of Paul's texts, for instance, directly addresses the need for people to support the ministry financially. But that is not to say that a sermon on this text has to be just as direct. Inductive movement, where the sermon moves toward the thesis, is generally better when the listeners might resist the message.[11] Preachers would do well to exegete their texts and their listeners, remembering the part that both play in preaching.[12] We will address the role played by listeners next.

Congregational Acoustics

Every text has its own mood and movement, and so does every congregation. Any approach to preaching that fails to account for the listeners generally fails to count. Acoustical theory states that the room determines the sound as much as the one producing the sound. In fact, the two work together. In preaching, this means that the preacher is only one part of the equation. As P.T. Forsyth reminds us, it is the church's pulpit and not ours.[13] The preacher who wishes to introduce a new style of preaching will need to be sensitive to the expected norms of the congregation. Some church members are convinced that Paul himself preached "three points and a poem"—alliterated, of course. For those persons anything other than a rhetorical approach is simply not preaching. Church members with a different point of view might not consider the traditional approach to be preaching, but rather some kind of mental exercise appropriate in a seminary classroom, but definitely not in the pulpit on Sunday morning.

Experimenting with new forms can cause tension, but there are ways to ease it.

1. Educate the congregation about preaching. Through pastoral articles, small group settings, and informal times, let the people know what it means to preach. We teach people the seriousness of the sacraments and how they are to be understood. Why not teach them how to hear sermons and to understand their importance?[14] Let them know that sermon form is culturally conditioned, and more specifically,

that form-sensitive preaching is a return to the forms of the biblical texts themselves.

2. Ease the congregation into new styles of preaching. The preacher who has been preaching the same way for years should not mount the pulpit one Sunday and announce, with utter finality, "Never again will I preach points." Some will hear that as, "Never again will my preaching have any point to it at all." Violating a congregation's norms is a serious matter. The wise preacher will introduce new forms occasionally throughout the year, a Sunday here, a Sunday there. If the church has multiple services throughout the week, the preacher could introduce the newer forms in a setting other than Sunday morning at eleven o'clock, when all of the traditions are expected.

3. Prepare the people ahead of time for hearing something new. I have found over the years that if I make an announcement that next Sunday's sermon will be different, people seem to grant me more leeway than if I spring it on them without warning.

I tell my seminary classes that exposing a congregation to new forms of preaching brings the preacher "Rolaids and accolades." Some people resist innovation of any kind. Their greeting at the back door will be barbed. "Good, uh, story, preacher. Are you going to preach next week?" Others will experience the gospel as they have never heard it before, going on and on about how wonderful the sermon was. It is hard to say which is easier to handle, but the preacher should be prepared in either case. This points to another factor in relation to introducing new forms of preaching—the preacher's own comfort level with change.

The Preacher's Voice

The motion picture *Amadeus* is the story of Mozart, the child prodigy whose musical talent was surpassed only by his vulgarities and immoral behavior. You may recall that the story is told in the movie by Salieri, the court composer who became more and more jealous of Mozart's abilities. In the closing scene, Salieri finishes telling the story to a priest, who seems to be hearing the whole tale as some kind of confession. Salieri turns to the shocked priest and says, "I am the patron saint of mediocrity." As the senile old composer is wheeled through the asylum, he repeatedly proclaims, "I absolve you of your mediocrity. I absolve you of your mediocrity!"

The movie is a frank warning to any person who would dream of worshiping the creature over the Creator, no doubt.[15] It also seems to me to be a reminder that God is not honored with our half-hearted attempts. Preaching demands our best, our very best. Quality sermons can be our offering to God.

When preachers begin to consider new forms of preaching, their excitement is usually mixed with feelings of anxiety. Trying a new style of preaching can be a harrowing experience, especially for those who customarily stick to one specific model.

Occasionally students describe something new that they had tried on a recent Sunday and at which they failed miserably. They usually add, "That's the last time I'll try something like that." Then I ask, "Is that what you said after your first sermon ever?" I continue, "Isn't it interesting that when we first began to preach, we knew that we were not very good and that we would require time to improve, but now that we've been preaching for some time, we wouldn't dream of honing new skills?"

Postlude

Trying new forms of preaching is always an adventure, like learning to ride a bike for the first time without training wheels. It is a scary proposition, but an exciting and liberating one as well.

Or maybe it is more like standing up before the church to sing a solo for the first time ever, wondering whether or not anything resembling music will come out of your mouth. That is a scary thought, indeed, but the song must be sung, and the message must be proclaimed. And so we sing and so we preach!

PART II

The Literary Forms

CHAPTER 4

Parables:
Tales of God's Kingdom

Jesus said that the kingdom of God is like, among other things, a farmer throwing seed into the wind with reckless abandon, two brothers and their relationship with their father, a woman baking bread, a big tree filled with chirping birds, and a salesman coming upon an exquisite piece of jewelry. Jesus did not say that the kingdom of God is all-encompassing, filled with promise, surprisingly different, or nondiscriminating. Put simply, Jesus spoke in stories. When he spoke of the kingdom of God and what it is like, he more often than not spoke in parables.

He did so for a very good reason: stories may be the single best mode of talking about God. Some have suggested that it is the only adequate mode: "Story is the fundamental means of talking about and listening to God, the only human means available to us that is complex and engaging enough to make comprehensible what it means to be with God."[1] Ronald Sider and Michael King note that stories are "complex and engaging," mysterious and challenging. Stories are also able "to integrate the transcendent and the immanent, the sacred and the profane."[2]

The parables of Jesus, therefore, remind us that the Transcendent and Sacred One "became flesh and lived among us" (John 1:14). Most serious preachers have known for some time that good preaching must take on fleshly form—that listeners need illustrations (doctrine incarnated). The traditional wisdom of preaching has generally maintained that preachers must view life through the lens of doctrine and doctrine through the lens of life. This is not to say that abstract statements and propositions are the most important things in the world, which our life experiences and stories back up. It is quite the opposite. Our life experiences and stories constitute the stuff that life is made of, and abstract statements help us to make sense of our stories.[3] Parables demonstrate that life bears out the reality of God's encompassing love, and parabolic stories can communicate that truth more powerfully than any propositional statement. It is not the case that the theological abstraction of God's nondiscriminating love is of primary importance and that a story drawn from life can validate that truth; quite the opposite.

Applied to preaching, all of this means that the form and the content of the various texts deserve the preacher's special attention. Therefore, we will look at the three preliminary questions of sermon preparation as they apply to parables.

What Is the Text Saying?

The parables of Jesus are "preacher friendly," to borrow Thomas Long's phrase. On the surface they appear to be simple, certainly recognizable. Not every preacher would be able to identify midrashic forms in the Scriptures, but every preacher and probably most churchgoers would be able to identify a parable. Still, the apparent simplicity and familiarity of Jesus' parables can be a hindrance rather than an asset to the interpreter and preacher alike. The interpreter must first be clear as to what a parable is.

C. H. Dodd's classic definition has stood the test of time: "At its simplest the parable is a metaphor or simile drawn from nature or common life, arresting the hearer by its vividness or strangeness, and leaving the mind in sufficient doubt about its precise application to tease it into active thought."[4] Bernard Brandon Scott has offered a brief yet scholarly definition of a parable as "a *mashal* that employs a short narrative fiction to reference a transcendent symbol."[5] It could be argued that both definitions appear more complex than the parabolic form itself. Actually, the intricacies of these definitions point out just how complex parables really are. They are not mere illustrations that Jesus thought might help keep his listeners interested. Jesus' parables are highly complex literary forms. To understand them better, let us consider Scott's definition in detail.[6]

1. Jesus' parables are only one type of *mashal* (the Hebrew term for "riddle" or "parable"), one specific structure in which Old Testament wisdom was expressed. Thus the parables of Jesus are part of a larger literary family.

2. The phrase "short narrative fiction" distinguishes parables from other *meshalim*, such as proverbs and riddles. It reminds us that Jesus' parables are largely storylike materials, though not all of them are full-blown narratives.

3. Parables *refer* to more than their surface meaning. Jesus' parable about two boys and their dealings with their father was not about the rewards and trials of parenting but about something else altogether. The story *refers* to something else.

4. The symbol is what the parables refer to. Later rabbinic parables were used to reference the keeping of the Torah,[7] but Jesus' parables were given as reference to the kingdom (or "reign") of God. The Greek term from which we get our word "parable" means to "cast alongside." In Jesus' parables everyday situations are "cast alongside" what the transcendent reign of God is like.

Referring to Jesus' parables as "short narrative fiction" is something of an oversimplification, however. Jesus' parables take on many different forms, although the exact number is subject to debate.[8] Is parabolic allegory legitimate? How many meanings can a parable convey? Is the parable a simile or a metaphor? These are some of the questions scholars debate.

Robert Funk argues quite convincingly that metaphorical experience lies at the heart of all of Jesus' parables. For instance, Jesus likens the kingdom to a merchant in quest of fine pearls who finds one of unusual quality and sells everything to buy that one. In light of traditional approaches to interpreting this parable, Funk asks, "Who can say which item in the figure represents the kingdom?"[9] Is it the merchant? Is it the quest? Is it the one great pearl? Is it selling all? Citing the work of Jeremias, Funk contends that an even better translation for the phrase "the kingdom of God is like . . ." would be "it is the case with . . . as with . . ." Pursuing the metaphorical approach, David Stern refers to parables as "virtual experiences in themselves, linguistic and poetic events that go beyond the merely discursive stretch of conventional metaphysics and theology."[10] The parables do not illustrate a point; rather, they are a point unto themselves. They are story events.

Although opinions vary regarding the different types of parables, all scholars agree that the parables of Jesus are life-shattering, iconoclastic experiences. The parables invite us into a familiar world, only to shake up our familiarity. Jesus implicitly invites us to try on his world-view for size, in hopes that it will change us permanently.[11] In the parabolic world of Jesus, Samaritans are seen as heroes and Pharisees as villains. What was truly life shattering in its time still is today, once the Samaritans and Pharisees of our day are identified. Essential to the process of interpretation is determining how parables work, and this brings us to the next question of sermon preparation.

What Is the Text Doing?

Although each individual parable must be considered on its own, there are some characteristics common to all of the parables. We will consider five primary features.

1. The parables are vivid, concrete stories rooted in real-life experiences; that is, the characters and settings of Jesus' stories were lifelike. Parables are not propositional concepts, but rather "the natural expressions of a mind that sees truth in concrete pictures rather than conceives it in abstractions."[12] Jesus told parables to a people who lived in an oral culture. Stories were not substitutes for abstract thinking or illustrations of abstract thinking. Orality and story were central to their thinking. (The question for us is whether our contemporary society is an oral culture as well. That question will be addressed in the next section.)

2. Jesus' parables are full of surprises couched within the familiar. His stories are rooted in concrete life experiences, and yet those experiences get turned upside down. The parabolic story experience begins so innocently. The scene is familiar, and "everything is so simple and clear that a child can understand."[13] But then, without warning, Jesus' listeners are shocked at the conclusions. "The world of the parable," writes Funk, "is like Alice's looking-glass world: all is familiar, yet all is strange."[14] Funk goes on to note several ways that this shock is achieved.

Sometimes the shock comes in "a surprising development in the narrative"—Jesus' paying those who worked only one hour a full day's wages (Matthew 20:1-16). Other times the shock is expressed in "an extravagant exaggeration"—a merchant selling *everything* to buy just one pearl (Matthew 13:45-46). The shock can also come in the form of paradox—a tax collector commended (Luke 18:9-14). Or the shock "may lurk below the surface in the so-called transference of judgment for which the parable calls"—a Samaritan who is commendable (Luke 10:25-37).[15] It is this surprising aspect of parabolic experience that leads hearers to exclaim, "Oh, my God, I never imagined."[16] Rather than the listener interpreting the parable, the parable interprets the listener.

3. The characters in Jesus' parables are detailed enough to make them realistic but open-ended enough to allow all listeners to identify with them.[17] Although parables, like all narratives, are open-ended enough for hearers-readers to identify with any character they choose, listeners typically identify with "sympathetic" characters, such as the man in the ditch who fell among thieves.[18]

Typically, however, only two or three characters are actually mentioned in a given parable. Nothing is said, for instance, about the prodigal son's mother or any of the relatives of the woman who lost one coin.[19] In addition, a character's description is not intended to be psychologized.[20]

4. Jesus' parables are open-ended experiences that force listeners to make application to themselves. Parables have the capacity both to reveal truth and to obscure it.[21] It seems likely that Jesus' listeners, upon hearing the parable of the farmer who stumbled on buried treasure, might respond in two entirely different ways. Some might have exclaimed, "Oh, my God, I never imagined." Others, however, might have gone home thinking, "Well, I never really thought about finding a treasure out in my field." Parables are for those who have ears.

The parabolic experience entails "an inductive and open-ended form of communication."[22] We are not told whether the elder brother ever joined the party in honor of the prodigal. As the story ends, the father is pleading with his eldest on the porch. The familiarity of the parable's material was obvious enough to Jesus' listeners. Whether or not the religious implications were perceived depended on them.[23]

5. Jesus' parables employ a range of miscellaneous techniques that enhanced their impact on listeners. For instance, six of the parables in Luke's Gospel use the narrative device

of interior monologue, where the characters speak to themselves. This device gives us direct insight into crucial moments of decision within those parables.[24]

Some parables make use of "end stress," an emphasis on the final episode that is crucial to the entire parabolic experience.[25] The identity of the man (a Samaritan) who stopped to help is only revealed well into Jesus' story. He had good reason not to begin with something like, "Let me tell you experts in Jewish law a story about a Samaritan helping someone." Other parables utilize the "law of repetition," in which phrases are repeated for emphasis and even irony.[26] In the parable of the unforgiving servant, for instance, the forgiven servant makes the same speech as the fellow servant (Matthew 18:26, 29). The irony is apparent.

Attention to detail is one of the hallmarks of Jesus' parables. Unnecessary or distracting details are omitted, while many lifelike details are retained.[27] We know that the Samaritan paid the innkeeper two denarii, but we are not told if the man ended up spending more. How can all these observations be incorporated into a strategy for preaching the parables?

How Can the Sermon Say and Do the Same?

The parables of Jesus may well be the one literary form least in need of explanation. After all, parables are events, and they are some of the most familiar passages in the New Testament. Yet familiarity can be a hindrance. The preacher may need to explain how parables function or how traditional interpretations have missed the point entirely, for example, by asking, "If the parable of the good Samaritan is simply about the need to be neighborly, then why does Jesus make a despised half-breed out to be the hero?" Such a question could help prepare listeners for a new hearing. The explanation would not have to be overstated, especially since the sermon can usually reproduce the impact, both in mood and in movement.

Sermonic Mood

Since the parables are largely storylike materials from an agrarian, oral culture, we must briefly examine the kind of culture we are preaching in today. Is the learning style of those who are listening to us literate or is it oral? The answer to this question will dramatically affect our strategy for preaching the parables.

A recent work on preaching, *Thinking in Story* by Richard Jensen, argues quite convincingly that in the United States a new kind of oral culture is emerging—a postliterate culture. The first oral culture was a storytelling culture in which no written forms of communication were in use. The invention of the phonetic alphabet and eventually the printing press gave way to a literate culture that dominated until very recently. In this literate communication culture the task of preaching was seen as information and exposition. Sermons were about explaining biblical texts. What has begun to emerge in recent times is a secondary type of oral culture, one largely shaped by new electronic forms of communication, especially television.

Jensen's work is a homiletical follow-up to Neil Postman's *Amusing Ourselves to Death*. Postman laments that our nation may be losing the ability to think critically, that we are becoming conditioned by television to expect to be entertained. As my son, Michael, would say: "I hate boring sermons." This emerging communication culture is called postliterate, not in the sense that people cannot read, but in the sense that people no longer want to read. In 1985, for the first time ever, the number of videos rented surpassed the number of books checked out from public libraries. That trend continues at a staggering pace.

Jensen notes that in the transition from oral to literate culture the church responded marvelously. Printed tracts,

Bible distribution, and Sunday school lessons were initiated to minister to a literate world. Jensen ultimately posits two key challenges for the church and for preachers as we enter the next century: (1) preaching that is in touch with postliterate, television-glutted Christians and (2) preaching that reaches congregations made up of both literate and postliterate Christians.[28]

In response to these challenges, form-sensitive preaching seeks not only to "do" what the text was doing, but also to "say" what the text was saying. Most congregations are largely heterogeneous in their preferences regarding communication modes. A thirty-six-year-old baby boomer sits next to an eighty-year-old widow. The one was raised on "book learning," the other on *Sesame Street* and MTV. Times are changing rapidly, however. American culture in general and the church subculture in particular are quickly becoming postliterate and story based. How do we preach parables in this context?

1. The effective preacher will base a sermon on the experiences in concrete stories, not on vague abstractions. The task of *interpreting* a parable is to determine the theological meaning of a given text, but the task of *preaching* a parable is to package the meaning in a narrative format that will generate an impact on today's listeners that is the same as the impact generated by the original story on the original listeners.[29] It is one thing to speak about the hypocrisy of well-intentioned religious people; it is quite another to tell the story of social misfits banqueting in heaven while the Pharisees are locked outside (Luke 14:1-24). That is what Jesus did. He told a story. The task of the preacher is to retell Jesus' story so as to flesh it out.

The homiletical process does not stop there, however. The preacher also needs to discover some contemporary story (or stories) that might produce the same impact as the biblical story did in its day. This is essential to the preaching of parables, since it is the analogous nature of parables that causes them to work on us.[30] For example, Douglas Oakman notes that peasants probably would have heard the Samaritan parable differently from the aristocracy.[31] If stories about farmers, peasants, and Pharisees could communicate life-shattering news in Jesus' day, what kinds of stories can do that in our day?

It might be a story about a respected husband and father who always does the right thing and keeps his life neat and organized. Then he misses his daughter's birthday party for the second year in a row. On the morning of her birthday his daughter had asked, "Daddy, you'll be there, won't you?" In reply, he gave her a big hug—the best of intentions. The kingdom of heaven, so it is said, is like a person who receives an invitation to which that person responds with the best of intentions, but . . . . The sermon could juxtapose the contemporary story and the biblical story so that listeners begin to detect parallels.[32]

The preacher needs to employ everyday imagery and concrete examples. Life is very specific, rooted in detailed experiences. For instance, in real life people do not have "car wrecks." Rather, a middle-aged man driving a blue Taurus runs a red light and crashes into a young coed's Honda Accord. Life experiences are concrete, and details can greatly enhance the telling of contemporary stories. Instead of just stating that something was wonderful, the preacher should describe it as such and let the readers (listeners) feel for themselves how wonderful it was.

2. Although couched within the familiar world of stories and everyday life, sermons on parables must ultimately produce shock among hearers. As Sallie McFague observes, "The parable does not teach a spectator a lesson; rather it invites and *surprises* a participant into an experience. This is its power, its power then and now to be revelatory, not once

upon a time, but every time a person becomes caught up in it and *by it.*"[33]

The shock might come in a clarification of the extravagance of God's grace, such as the parable of the servant who owed ten thousand talents (Matthew 18:21-35). Eugene Lowry surmises that this amount would have equaled 125 thousand years of earnings for this man.[34] Or consider the disgusting display of affection for a wayward son who finally returns home (Luke 15:1-32). This is especially shocking when you realize that Jesus is speaking to Pharisees about how tax collectors and sinners will be received into the kingdom, while the Pharisees will be out on the porch clucking their tongues, refusing to come inside (see vv. 1-2). Parables are shocking when heard correctly, and sermons based on parables must be shocking as well.

3. The preacher needs to focus on characters, both in the parable and in any contemporary stories that are used. People are fascinated by other people. Unfortunately, the characters in the Bible are generally thought of as lifeless, unreal beings who exist only on paper to teach lessons. Parabolic characters are almost universally regarded as fictional, but for a parable to be rightly heard, listeners must be able to identify with the characters, both in the biblical story and in any contemporary stories that are used.

Wayne Stacy brings both characters vividly alive in a sermon on the widow and the judge (Luke 18:1-8).

> "Get up! Get up!" The judge's wife carped at her erstwhile sleeping husband. "She's back again!"
>
> "Who?" the judge mumbled, barely moving his mouth.
>
> "That *widow*; I don't know her name; just some dead man's wife."
>
> "Her again? What's she want *now*? That woman will raise the dead with all that racket! Ah, I guess I'd better see what she wants, as if I didn't know. If I don't, none of us will get any sleep around here tonight, that's for sure!"

> She was a widow—we don't know her name; you usu-
> ally didn't in that culture. . . .
> It never ceases to amaze me. You ask a widow when she
> bought her home.
> "Oh, I don't know, I guess it was in '57. Yeah, yeah, it
> was in '57. Or was it '58?"
> But you ask her how long it's been since her husband
> died: "It'll be *exactly* 8 years and 7 months tomorrow."[35]

One aspect of the preacher's strategy is to determine which characters listeners ought to identify with and at what point in the sermon. The sermon event needs to be open-ended. Eduard Riegert confesses how he struggled with this issue in his own preaching of the parables: "As spoken by Jesus they had a certain lilt and suggestiveness about them; as spoken by me they were almost without fail sombre and heavyhanded. Jesus seemed to leave his hearers in an open-ended situation; I was tying up every loose string and nailing down everything that moved."[36] Most preachers have a hard time leaving things unsaid. We tend to think of ourselves as "answer" people. Parables, however, are more question oriented than answer oriented. This does not mean the sermon will end in a cloud of fog, but it does suggest the need for a sermon to "tease the hearers into active thought," as Dodd's definition points out.

For example, a sermon on the prodigal son and the older brother might conclude with the preacher noting, "We are not told if the brother ever came in or not. The parable simply ends with the father and his oldest son on the porch." The preacher might close with some contemporary story, such as a minister's daughter who gave birth to a child out of wed-lock and then brought the baby home to the shock of all the neighbors. The sermon could conclude:

> The minister and his wife came out to greet her as she
> arrived. All the neighbors expected a confrontation.
> After all, she had brought disgrace on the family name.

Were they ever shocked when the parents came running out to the car making a big fuss about their new
grandbaby! As they were going into the house, the
father leaned back out the door and shouted, "Aren't
you coming over? We're having a welcome home party.
Are you coming?"

Sermonic Movement

Of the many techniques that parables employ, two of them
directly affect the strategic movement a sermon might use
when preaching from the parables—end stress and repetition. Together, these two techniques relate to the different
plot structures used in parables.

Eugene Lowry's book *How to Preach a Parable* is most
helpful in this regard. His work is not so much about how to
preach parables as it is about how to preach sermons that
function like the parables of Jesus, whether the text is a
parable or some other kind of narrative. Lowry offers several
different shapes that parabolic sermons might take.[37] Along
with his first book, *The Homiletical Plot*, it offers a great deal
of help for preaching parables.[38]

As an example of how a sermon might learn from the plot
structure of a parable, let us consider the parable of the
prodigal son. The entire fifteenth chapter of Luke can serve
as text. The chapter begins with the religious leaders grum-
bling about Jesus' eating with sinners. The chapter ends with
the story of a father welcoming back a wayward son and
explaining that fact to the son who never left. The point is
obvious enough. Sinners are being welcomed into the kingdom. Whether or not the Pharisees come in is up to them.

How does the text get us from the beginning to that
ending? Three parables are used, not just one. In fact, there
is a specific strategy in how these parables are strung together. The first story is about a shepherd who loses one of
his hundred sheep. When he finds it, he has a party to
celebrate. The second story is about a woman who loses one

of her ten coins. When she finds it, she has a party to celebrate. The third story is about a father who loses one of his
two sons. When he finds him, he has a party to celebrate.

That plot seems simple enough, but consider what is
happening. The first two parables invite agreement. When
something that has been lost is found later, a celebration is in
order. That is true whether the thing found is a sheep or a
coin. The question that remained for the Pharisees was
whether that was also true for rebellious people and ultimately for the sinners who were getting into the kingdom.

A sermon on this passage could begin by setting the context, noting how the religious leaders were concerned with
Jesus' associates and noting how good Christians today are
concerned with that as well. "There are some kinds of places
we just shouldn't go, and there are some kinds of people we
just shouldn't associate with. What did Jesus have to say
about this?"

The preacher could point out that Jesus told a series of
stories. Following a brief retelling of the first parable, the
preacher might draw a brief modern parallel—perhaps telling a story of a parent and a child searching the neighborhood for their lost dog and then finding it. Following a
retelling of the second parable, the preacher might tell of a
couple on vacation losing their wallet and finding it later
with everything intact. The listeners would now be in a
position to hear a retelling of the third parable and perhaps
the story of that minister's family welcoming home their
daughter and new grandbaby.

A sermon like this is sensitive to both the mood and the
movement of the text, though mood is the one truly essential
component. As an example of responsible form-sensitive
preaching on a parable, we will now consider a sermon by
Eugene Lowry, who teaches preaching at the Saint Paul
School of Theology.[39]

"Down the Up Staircase"

by Eugene L. Lowry

Matthew 18:22-34

(Please read this sermon aloud.)
The man owed a whole lot of money. Surely he wasn't surprised when he was summoned to the inner chambers of the king. He left his abode, went across the territory until he reached the palace, climbed the flight of stairs, and went through the double doors. If you were listening closely, you noticed that Jesus did not mention the stairs. That was an inadvertent omission. He meant to say it.

There had to be a flight of stairs. You never go to the seat of power without climbing a flight of stairs. I was raised in western Kansas where there are no hills. Back in the old days when they built a county courthouse, they'd bring in the bulldozers and create a hill so they could build a flight of stairs. Today they'd be more sensitive. They'd put a ramp. It's still uphill all the way.

This man climbed a flight of stairs, went through the double doors, was ushered into the inner chamber of the king, and stood there waiting until the king made his appearance. The man bowed dutifully. Just then an aide carries out a huge ledger and opens it to the page where this man's name appears on the upper right hand corner.

[The sermon begins with a playful retelling of the parable. A contemporary experience from the preacher's past helps to illustrate the power the king held. Notice also the switch from past tense to present. We are there.]

The king looks at the bottom line on the ledger sheet, and says, "Servant, it says here you owe me a lot of money."

"Yes, Sir."

"You owe me ten thousand talents."

"Yes, Sir."

"I want my money."

"Yes, Sir."

"I want my money now."

"Oh, yes, Sir. Uh, no, Sir. I mean, I don't have ten thousand talents."

[The dialogue helps bring the text to life. It also helps point out the tragedy of the servant's unwillingness to forgive others in a later scene.]

The king turns to the aides who brought in the book, and they begin a discussion about selling this man, his wife and children into slavery, and disposing of their personal property to recoup what little they can of the huge debt. When the king turns around, he finds the servant down on the carpet on his knees.

The servant looks up at the king and says, "Sir, have mercy on me. Have mercy, and I will pay you everything. Give me a little time." You know what the king did. He did better than just give him a little time. He reached into that ledger book, took hold of the page, and ripped it out. He ripped it into shreds, turned to the servant on his knees, and said, "I forgive you the debt. You are now free and clear. Go in peace."

Can you imagine the viscera of that servant? Such utter ecstasy! I think the tears just dried up, and when he got up, he never touched the carpet again. He must have floated in the air. He didn't have to open the double doors. He simply slipped through, and didn't touch a single step on the way down. The man is off to freedom.

We might hope so, but that's not the way the story goes. He apparently touched every step on the way down, and when he gets to the bottom, he finds another servant who owes him a hundred denarii—twenty bucks. (That's three months wages for the average man in the days of Jesus— eighty dollars a year.) What's twenty bucks in contrast to ten thousand talents, which turns out to be ten million dollars in U.S. currency?

This man who has just been forgiven a debt of ten million dollars is grabbing a man by the throat for twenty bucks. He says, "Pay what you owe."

[Lowry turns to his listeners as he elaborates on the joy of forgiveness. Then he begins to discuss what it means not to forgive. In his explanation he translates the amounts in the parable into dollars. Throughout the remainder of the sermon he will use U.S. currency amounts. In doing so, listeners can better relate to the story.]

Notice that Jesus has the fellow servant get on his knees pleading with him as the first man had done before the king. He's saying, "Give me a little time. Have mercy, and I'll pay it all back." That turkey refused. He didn't give him more time. He didn't give him anything. He summoned a police officer and said, "This man owes me money. He's not paying me back. Take him to jail." The crowd gathered at the bottom of the stairs didn't like what they saw and heard. They went to the king and said, "You wouldn't believe what happened at the bottom of the stairs." The king said, "Well, the two of us need another conversation."

The king summons the servant back into his presence away from his abode across the territory, up the flight of stairs through the double doors, into the inner chamber.

The king comes in. The servant bows dutifully, and the king asks, "Weren't you here just a little while ago?"

"Yes, Sir."

"If I remember correctly, I had the ledger book open to the page on which your name appears, and the bottom line of that page said you owed me ten million dollars. Is that right?"

"Yes, Sir."

"Well, if I remember correctly, I told you I wanted my money now."

"Yes, Sir."

"You got down on your knees and begged for mercy. Do you remember what I did? I ripped the ledger sheet out of the book and told you to go in peace. Now, what's this I hear about what you did when you left this place? By the time you got to the bottom of the stairs, you seized a man who owed you twenty bucks, after I'd forgiven you ten million. Did you seize someone for twenty bucks and then throw him in jail? Is that right?"

"Ummmm, that is correct, Sir."

"Well," said the king, "I have news for you. You know that jail cell where your buddy sits?"

"Yes, Sir."

"Well, that happens to be a suite for two. Now, you go join your buddy in that cell. You stay there until you pay me ten million dollars." As far as we know he's still there.

[The retelling of this scene in vivid detail helps the listeners fully grasp the character of this unforgiving servant. Repetition of dialogue also helps stress Lowry's point.]

I'm glad you get the humor to that. He got what he had coming to him. That's what I would want to have happen. But the truth is, in terms of its humor, we've only touched the tip of the iceberg because we really haven't had the punch line yet. I told you it was ten million dollars, and I presume ten million dollars is a significant sum for most of us here. But what I didn't say was the sheer fact that nobody could owe ten million dollars in the days of Jesus. Jesus is telling a joke here.

I'm told that the entire annual revenue into the Roman coffers all over the globe was approximately 850 thousand dollars. With 850 thousand dollars you could pay all the judges, all the road builders, all the armies of the Roman empire, all the dancers, all the teachers, all the everybodies and still have plenty left over for rubies and emeralds and the nicer things of life. Even Herod the Great could not owe ten million dollars.

Why would Jesus say that somebody owed that much? Let's just figure it out. Herod the Great couldn't owe that so when Jesus collects this crowd of people around him and starts telling this tale and says, "There was this servant who owed ten million . . ." Do you get it? This servant owed ten million dollars. They choked with laughter; they got the joke.

In the middle of the tale Jesus has the servant on his knees begging for a little time. Do you know how much time he needs? At eighty dollars a year average annual wage without interest (if you have to pay interest, you'd really be in difficulty) to pay back ten million dollars would take 125 thousand years. The way Jesus put it was he owed ten million. He was in over his head.

[Lowry directly addresses the parable as a literary form. His discussion is simple, but listeners begin to understand Jesus' use of hyperbole.]

Even with the humor of this story, I've always been troubled by it because the hero to the tale is the king. The king forgives the servant and ten minutes later takes it back. That's not what I've been told about forgiveness. I've been told that if you forgive somebody, that's it. You can't say to me this morning, "I forgive you," and this afternoon catch me in the hallway of the Hyatt and say, "I've changed my mind." What's this deal about a king who forgave ten million dollars and then took the forgiveness back?

Now this isn't a story about a king who forgave and then took it back. This is a parable, not an allegory. Give Jesus a little poetic license. This is really the story about a servant who was offered the forgiveness of ten million dollars and did not receive it. He didn't let himself off the hook. I'll tell you why I know that. I know that because what happened at the bottom of the stairs simply could not have happened had he really received the forgiveness. It would have been utterly impossible had he really been forgiven and received it. He wouldn't even notice if the guy presented himself and said, "Hey, I owe you twenty bucks." He'd say, "What twenty bucks?"

[Again, Lowry directly addresses the interpretation of this parable. The sermon not only does something, it teaches listeners as well. Next he will use a contemporary story to illustrate the concept of forgiveness.]

Imagine that you've filled out the super-duper sweepstakes a couple of months ago, not expecting to hear anything in return, and now it's Sunday, and you're at the church. In Sunday school they have a special offering, and somebody nudges you, and says, "I forgot my money. Would you lend me a couple of bucks. I'll drop by later today and pay it back." You give him a couple of bucks.

Now it's Monday morning, and he didn't bring the two bucks back. About 8 o'clock on Monday morning you get a phone call from New York City, and at the other end of the line is this exuberant voice saying, "Congratulations, I'm pleased to announce that you've just won the super-duper sweepstakes. You have just won one million dollars." Imagine what you're feeling. Think how your eyes are just circling in both directions. You're so ecstatic that the only thing that keeps you tied to earth is the phone cord. Now, is it possible for you to remember as you hang up the phone, *This person who borrowed two bucks from me yesterday failed to bring it by?* Are you going to call him on the phone and say, "Don't forget you owe me two bucks." No! It's impossible.

The man in the parable never let himself off the hook. Why wouldn't he receive the gracious forgiveness that was offered? I'll tell you why. Because he went to the same Sunday school class I went to. Do you remember the text and the lesson? It says, "Never take anything from anybody. Everyone's got to pull his own weight."

Do you remember the lesson that said that anybody can become anything they're inclined to be if they work hard enough at it? Just go out there and go for it. It's the American way. I was taught in Sunday school that it is wrong to take candy from a stranger and that it is even worse to take it from a friend. Right? Because then you are in debt to a friend. Never be in debt to a friend. Oh, we learned that lesson very well, and so did he. He couldn't take a gift like that. We have learned the lesson so well that we can't even take a compliment any more. If I say to someone, "What a lovely dress you have on this morning," what does she say back? "These old rags?" Isn't that what we say?

Imagine it's your birthday. The doorbell rings. You go to the door and look through the screen. There's your dearest friend with a package in hand. What is it that you do not do? You do not look at the package. It's embarrassing—particularly on your birthday.

Pretty soon your friend holds the package so high you can't see him without seeing the package, and you say a dumb thing. You say, "Oh, is that for me?"

"No, I was just carrying it through the neighborhood. Of course it's for you. It's your birthday."

With great reluctance and embarrassment, you receive the package and stare at it for a while. Pretty soon you look up and say, "Should I open it?"

"No, just put in on the mantle and stare at it for all I care."

Of course you open it. You take out the present and say, "Oh, it is so lovely." Then you say the first decent thing you've said throughout the conversation when you say, "Thank you." But what else do you say at the same time? "You shouldn't have done it." Of course, they shouldn't have done it. If they should do it, it would not be a gift. It would be a payment for services rendered. That's the meaning of gifts.

[Lowry uses a contemporary vignette to show listeners how grace is hard to accept. The story is lighthearted, yet biting.]

You know the servant who was summoned across the territory and up the flight of stairs? That could have been you or me. In fact, perhaps it is. Let's just try it out. Let's head across the territory and up that flight of stairs and see. Having been summoned, we go up the flight of stairs and through the double doors, ushered into the inner chamber of the king by an aide. We wait there for the king to arrive. The king comes out with this huge ledger book, plops it on the table, opens it up to find the page where your name or mine is at the top right hand corner.

The king looks at the bottom line and says, "It says here you owe me a whole lot of money. In fact, is this figure right? It says a million/zillion that you're indebted. Is that correct?"

And every last one of us in this room this morning must answer, "That is correct, Sir. Indeed, I am heavily in debt. Even 125 thousand years of effort would not suffice to repay the debt."

Do you know what that king does? He takes that sheet (your name or mine) and rips it out of the book. He rips it to shreds, looks down at us, and says, "I forgive you the debt. You are now free and clear. Go in peace."

Do you know what that means to those of us who can receive the forgiveness? For those of us who can let ourselves off the hook, do you know what that means? It means a lot of things, but I'll tell you the first thing it means. It means nobody's going to have to remind us how to behave. Nobody's going to have to tell us how to act. Nobody's going to have to tell us what to do when we get to the bottom of the stairs.

[The sermon ends with a direct address to the listeners, though the actual application and the closing words will leave the results up to those who have truly heard.]

Exercises

Answer the following ten questions for the parable in each passage: Matthew 13:31-32; Mark 12:1-12; Luke 18:9-14.

1. What metaphorical aspects of the parable stand out in your initial reading? How does the metaphor affect you? What is its function?

2. What kinds of vivid imagery does the parable employ?

3. What techniques does the parable employ that affect mood?

4. What musical instruments might best accompany the text? What colors and/or textures describe the text's mood? What adjectives and adverbs best describe the passage?

5. What concrete contemporary images and/or stories might help congregations to relate to the parable's punch?

6. What kinds of details in your contemporary story could help bring it alive?

7. What techniques does the parable employ that might affect the movement of the sermon?

8. How could a sermon on this parable be open-ended enough to respect the freedom of the listeners?

9. What is the text saying? What is the text doing?

10. How could a sermon say and do the same?

Sermon Resources

Ronald J. Allen, "When You Can't Tell the Wheat from the Weeds" [Matthew 13:24-30, 36-43], in *Biblical Preaching Journal* (summer 1990): 12-14. Good blend of doing and saying what the text is doing and saying. Open-endedness perhaps its biggest strength. Wrestles with real life issues. Synopsis of exegesis also included.

American Bible Society, "A Father and Two Sons" [Luke 15:11-32], a multimedia translation on videocassette, 1994. Although not a sermon in the traditional sense of the term, it vividly re-presents the story of the prodigal in a modern context. Contemporary sound track as well.

Martin B. Copenhaver, "Building Barns, Postponing Life"
[Luke 12:16-21], in *Best Sermons 3*, ed. James W. Cox (Harper
and Row, 1990), pp. 255-60. Employs a wonderfully imaginative interview with the widow of the farmer in the parable.
Creative narrative approach combined with some direct
teaching.

Richard A. Jensen, "The Lonely Lady of Blairstown Park"
[Luke 15:11-24], in *Telling the Story* (Augsburg, 1980), pp.
162-68. Modern retelling of the parable of the prodigal but
without obvious overkill. Engaging and surprising. Does
very little, however, with the biblical materials.

Eugene L. Lowry, "Down the Up Staircase" [Matthew
18:22-34], in the *Preaching Today* tape series. Complete sermon
included with this chapter.

R. Wayne Stacy, "Living with the Limits" [Luke 18:1-8], in
Pulpit Digest (July/August 1993): 35-40. Masterfully weaves
together contemporary stories, creative retelling of the biblical story, and direct treatment of the interpretation and application of it all. Helpful exegetical endnotes also included.

Jerry Welborn, "Hidden Treasure" [Matthew 13:44], in
Preaching (July/August 1986): 32-35. Uses vivid details to tell
a contemporary story. Not a modern version of the parable.
Offers subtle insights into Jesus' parable. Does very little
with the biblical text, at least directly.

CHAPTER 5

Aphorisms:
The Proverbial Sayings of Jesus

William Beardslee put it mildly when he noted that "the proverbs in the Synoptic Gospels have not attracted the attention lavished on another wisdom form—the parable."[1] To put it another way, some passages have all the fun. In contrast to parables, the aphorisms of Jesus have been treated like a homiletical Cinderella, neglected and ignored. While the parables of Jesus (and other mainstays, like traditional Pauline texts) have been living it up at the royal ball, aphorisms have been left all alone at home.

It is ironic that aphorisms are so overlooked, since they, along with parables, constitute "the characteristic forms in the discourse material" within the Gospels.[2] Both are a form of wisdom literature that shows us, indirectly, how to live. John Dominic Crossan estimates that more than 130 aphorisms are recorded in the Gospels.[3] Their very numbers should provide impetus for preaching these sayings.

Alyce McKenzie argues that people's lives are saturated with proverbs, even if "consistently ignored by the preacher." These sayings appear on "billboards, T-shirts, coffee mugs, cartoons, magazine ads, bumper stickers, and posters."[4] Tex Sample believes that even in our highly technological and postliterate culture approximately half of the people in the United States still operate "out of a *traditional orality,* by which I mean a people who can read and write—though some cannot—but whose appropriation and engagement with life is oral."[5] Beardslee calls this the "fragmentariness of our existence."[6]

Proverbs continue to play an important role in contemporary society. Today's younger generation acknowledges a new form of communication—the "MTV style of commercial." It consists of dreamlike sequences in which one scene quickly follows another, with as many as twenty different images within the same fifteen-second commercial. It has caught on with several sponsors. This technique, known as phantasmagoria, fits today's fast-paced culture. Against this barrage of images, a well-worded one-liner reaches out and grabs the audience. These ads have arguably become a substitute for the proverbs of previous generations. Younger generations are more apt to know Madison Avenue's jingles than Ben Franklin's homespun sayings. In the fragmentary times we live in, it seems only natural to investigate Jesus' aphorisms—fragmentary sayings that stick with us easily.

What Is the Text Saying?

Aphorisms constitute the briefest of Jesus' sayings (though they are often found in groups).[7] They represent the proverbial sayings of Jesus—the relatively short, catchy phrases and sentences found on almost every page in the Gospels. Being related to proverbs, aphorisms demand a unique approach to interpretation, since wisdom literature differs so markedly from other literary forms.[8]

Along with typical issues of interpretation, aphorisms require special attention in areas such as grammatical form, type of parallelism employed, and context.[9] In the Gospels aphorisms appear in one of three forms: statement, question, or imperative, though some passages appear to combine these forms (Luke 12:6-7). James Bailey and Lyle Vander Broek list examples of each kind.

1. Announcement: A disciple is not above the teacher, nor a slave above the master; it is enough for the disciple to be like the teacher, and the slave like the master (Matthew 10:24-25).

2. Question: For what will it profit them to gain the whole world and forfeit their life? Indeed, what can they give in return for their life? (Mark 8:36-37).

3. Imperative: Strive to enter through the narrow door; for many, I tell you, will try to enter and will not be able (Luke 13:24).[10]

Each of these grammatical forms must be interpreted differently, since, as we shall see later, each functions differently.

Another variable in the interpretation of aphorisms is the type of parallelism. Sometimes the first line of one of Jesus' aphorisms is repeated (and frequently enhanced) in the second line, only using different wording. This is known as synonymous parallelism. An example of this is found in Matthew 10:27 where Jesus says, "What I say to you in the dark, tell in the light; and what you hear whispered, proclaim from the housetops."

Antithetical parallelism uses the second line of a saying to contrast the first. Matthew 7:17, for instance, reads, "In the same way, every good tree bears good fruit; but the bad tree bears bad fruit."

Recognition of parallelism is essential to interpretation. Parallelism affects what a text says and how it says it, though not all of Jesus' aphorisms use parallelism (the so-called Golden Rule being one exception [Matthew 7:12]).

Interpreting aphorisms also involves an awareness of the context in which a given aphorism occurs. Context is always crucial in the interpretive task but uniquely so in the case of aphorisms, due to their apparent portability within the Gospels themselves. For example, most people are familiar with

Jesus' line about salt losing its saltiness. Overlooking the lack of scientific evidence to support the claim, let us consider for a moment the issue of context. Matthew places that saying early on in Jesus' ministry in his Sermon on the Mount following a series of blessings (Matthew 5:13). Luke has Jesus speak it late in his ministry as a word of warning to those followers who might have been simply tagging along (Luke 14:34). Interpreters once tried to harmonize such so-called discrepancies, but now, illumined with insights from literary and redaction criticism, scholars have focused attention on the Evangelists and their various purposes.[11] The issue of context is crucial to understanding what a text is saying. Of course, texts not only say things, they do things.

What Is the Text Doing?

Analyzing the rhetorical strategy of an aphorism involves (1) the structure of the aphorism and (2) its deceptive simplicity. These issues relate directly to how aphorisms function and therefore have implications for how sermons can communicate this form more effectively.

The grammatical form and the type of parallelism employed relate directly to how aphorisms communicate. The grammatical form of an aphorism relates to more than just meaning; grammar affects the way an aphorism communicates, whether by statement, question, imperative, or some combination thereof. Bailey and Vander Broek describe the uniqueness of each form as follows: "A statement invites hearers to accept as true what Jesus asserts, a question seeks to engage hearers directly in pondering his saying, and an imperative challenges them to envision and act in line with the rhetorical force of his words."[12] Note the verbs in the various phrases: *"invites* hearers to accept," *"seeks to engage* hearers in pondering," and *"challenges* them to envision and act in line." Each grammatical form employs a different rhetorical strategy.

Generally speaking, proverbial forms tell us less how to live (prescriptive proverbs) than how things are (descriptive proverbs).[13] This is certainly true with aphorisms found in the form of a statement, which is the most popular form of the three. When Jesus announces that "prophets are not without honor, except in their hometown" (Mark 6:4), he does not point an accusing finger at his listeners. He does not warn them. He simply describes how things are. Aphorisms in the form of a statement are basically nonthreatening observations, at least on the surface. Whether or not they get applied is up to the listener-reader.

Not all aphorisms are that soft-spoken, however. Some are stated in the imperative. Beardslee contends that even imperative aphorisms generally have a "weakened force." He notes that when Jesus says, "Do not throw your pearls before swine," this is practically equivalent to a conditional, "If you throw your pearls before swine."[14] It is true that some imperatives convey a softer mood than others.[15] The imperative sentence, "Melissa, tie your shoe before you get hurt," is a command but obviously not meant in any harsh way. Imperative aphorisms, therefore, must be handled carefully, with the context and the motivation being considered carefully.

Between these two extremes is the question form, which is more engaging than the statement and less confrontational than the imperative. Questions tease hearers into pondering the meaning of the aphorism for themselves.

Besides grammatical form, parallelism (when used) also has implications for how aphorisms work. Synonymous parallelism invites listeners to hear again what has already been stated, to feel the impact reiterated. Consider again Matthew 10:27: "What I tell you in the darkness, speak in the light; and what you hear whispered in your ear, proclaim upon the housetops." Bailey and Vander Broek observe:

The second line verbally reinforces the first one, providing the hearers yet another opportunity to understand. Indeed, the second line actually furthers the message of the saying because "hearing in the ear" is more secretive than "saying" and "proclaiming upon the housetop" is more public than "telling in the light."[16]

Antithetical parallelism, however, creates tension between the first statement(s) and the last. Consider Luke 9:58, for example: "Foxes have holes, and birds of the air have nests; but the Son of Man has nowhere to lay his head." The first two lines make up a unit of synonymous parallelism, but the third line stands in sharp contrast. Again, Bailey and Vander Broek note:

> The interplay of these three lines created a rhetorical punch for first-century hearers. In Palestine, people probably did not readily observe the dens of foxes or bird nests. If, as the saying claims, even foxes and birds have "homes," then how extremely unsettled and risky was Jesus' existence as an itinerant preacher. The context implies the same risk for those who follow Jesus.[17]

The second broad area of concern related to how aphorisms work is their deceptive simplicity. Like parables, aphorisms use "homely and mundane" imagery.[18] Aphorisms do not concern themselves with philosophical concepts of abstraction but with birds that have nests, with men watching their hair fall out, with fruit trees, with one buddy trying to help another get something out of his eye, and with weather patterns.

The aphorisms of Jesus employ incredibly normal, everyday sorts of images, but this simplicity masks a profound depth of communication. Aphorisms not only communicate wisdom (how to live) but also require a type of wisdom (discernment) from listeners if they are to receive the full impact of the text.[19] These proverbial sayings "tease hearers into active thought,"[20] encouraging listeners to wrestle with the meaning of the passage the way you might wrestle with a poem, reading it over and over again until it begins to interpret you. Aphorisms have the ability at one and the same time to "make contact with the understanding already present in the everyday world" and to "jolt the hearer into new insight."[21]

The single most important literary device that delivers this jolt is hyperbole. "Exaggeration jolts the hearers into a new perception."[22] For example, in Matthew 5:29 Jesus says, "If your right eye causes you to sin, tear it out and throw it away." As Bailey and Vander Broek note, "The willingness to entertain a literal fulfillment brings home the meaning"[23]—lustful gazes are even more serious than maiming one's body.

Besides hyperbole, some aphorisms employ the rabbinic technique of arguing from lesser to greater. For example, Jesus asks, "If you then, who are evil, know how to give good gifts to your children, how much more will your Father in heaven give good things to those who ask him" (Matthew 7:11). It is the "how much more" aspect of the argument that unlocks how the text functions.

One final feature related to the deceptive simplicity of aphorisms is their implied use of story. Paul Ricoeur writes, "Without being a narrative, the proverb implies a story."[24] McKenzie refers to the proverb as the "cousin" of narrative.[25] Long posits the theory that proverbs cause listeners to reflect back on their own experiences of how the proverb has been true in the past. If his theory is valid, and it seems logical enough, aphorisms cause listeners to recall their own stories that parallel the saying at hand. This too has implications for preaching, which brings us to the third question of sermon composition.

How Can the Sermon Say and Do the Same?

How can the rhetorical strategies within the text influence the rhetorical strategies within the sermon? In other words, how can the sermon impact congregations today in the same way that the original oral text impacted its earliest listeners? In the case of aphorisms that means attention to context.

Any sermon that strives to be faithful to the text must pay attention to context. This is especially important when dealing with aphorisms. Traditional expository sermons have been long on explanation of issues such as context, but short on meaningful encounter with the text. Form-sensitive sermons place a heavy premium on encounter, but not at the expense of explanation. Context is one feature of an aphorism that needs to be explained by the preacher. A brief explanation conveyed in a crisp, relevant manner greatly enhances the overall message.

A preacher dealing with Jesus' aphoristic saying about salt might simply note, "Luke wants us to focus on the demands of discipleship, not the blessings. That's why Luke places this proverb here. Luke's story is not about missionary responsibilities, being the 'salt of the earth' in a corrupt world; rather, it is about how hard it is to be a follower of Christ" (Luke 14:34-35; cf. Matthew 5:13). The preacher might decide to explain the context in more detail, but at least this much must be said. It is important to remember that form-sensitive sermons not only *do* what the text is doing, but they also *say* what the text is saying. The chief means by which a sermon does the former is attention to mood and movement.

Sermonic Mood

Aphorisms appear in the New Testament in one of three forms (or a combination thereof), each of which has its own textual mood. The mood of the sermon largely depends on the grammatical form of the text. Aphorisms in the form of a statement (the most popular form) imply the need for sermons that are less hortatory and demanding. This form "invites hearers to accept as true what Jesus asserts."[26] The mood of the sermon, therefore, must be inviting, not demanding.

Jesus' statement about disciples' not being above their teacher is a truth presented in the form of an observation. The text does not allow for the preacher to rant, "If you want to be a follower of Christ, you had better look at his example. He is the master. You are the disciple, and you should be clear about who is in charge." Descriptive literature does not lend itself to preachers who favor pointing long, bony fingers at the congregation. The application of the sermon based on a statement must be more indirect than direct, bearing in mind that there is a difference between an indirect application and no application at all. Indirect application is subtle, not absent.[27] It is more like reading a short poem that you must wrestle with, reading it again and again. For instance, the preacher might simply reflect, "Every time I begin to look for ways to make a name for myself, to get ahead, I hear the voice of Jesus softly speaking, 'A disciple is not above the teacher.' Then I know that 'it is enough to be like the teacher.'" In this case, the preacher employs personal reflection rather than the language of command.

The imperative form of aphorism, however, can be a very direct form of address, although there are varying degrees of confrontation. The mood of the sermon needs to correspond to the degree of confrontation conveyed in the text. An inductive strategy is not out of the question. The sermon could be very direct and prophetic in dealing with the text, building up to that directness near the end.

Kenneth Gibble's sermon entitled "Mr. Witmer's Gift" is a good example of directness cloaked in the subtleties of story.[28] He begins with the innocent and funny story of Mr. Witmer, who was Gibble's high school principal. Mr. Witmer read verses from the Bible to the students every day over the loudspeaker. One of those passages just so happens to be the sermon's text, Matthew 7:1-5, a passage about not judging others. The sermon begins innocently enough, but when it

ends, Gibble's listeners are wrestling with their own judg-
mentalism. The sermon closes like this:

> Soon I was back to laughing at jokes about him, listening
> to and passing on nasty stories about him, fearing him,
> even hating him. But not as much as before, and always
> with a distinct twinge of conscience. Without knowing
> it, I had received a gift from Mr. Witmer: a lesson about
> judging.

Inductive sermon flow is a technique that Scripture uses
frequently. However, it need not be limited to passages that
are inductively structured themselves.[29] It is a powerful
preaching tool.

But even when the text and the sermon are forthright, it is
important to remember that prophetic confrontation does
not necessarily require a sermon that is condemning and
harsh. As one of my New Testament professors used to ask,
"If the Gospel is the greatest love story ever told, why do so
many preach it with a clenched fist?"

The question form of aphorism lies between the two extremes of statement and command. Questions seek "to engage hearers directly in pondering" Jesus' sayings.[30] The
preacher needs to engage the congregation directly, but in
such a way that the listeners are left to reflect on the implications of the text for themselves. Preaching on aphorisms in
the form of questions and statements is risky business, since
for the most part these forms depend on the discernment of
the listeners. The preacher may be interested in driving home
the point that gaining the whole world may entail forfeiting
one's life, but the text does not drive that home, at least not
directly. A different rhetorical strategy is at work in the
question form of aphorism. When Jesus asks what profit
people will gain if they forfeit their lives (Mark 8:36-37), he
is teasing hearers into active thought.

The preacher can do the same, perhaps using stories that
make this truth evident and using the text itself as a refrain

throughout the sermon: "For what will it profit them to gain the whole world . . ." In these cases the preacher must trust that God's word will not return void, although sermons often do.

The everyday imagery used in aphorisms also has implications for the mood of the sermon. Aphoristic imagery in the Scriptures is down-to-earth imagery. The sermon should be as well. The stories, images, and language within a sermon on aphorisms ought to be simple, though never trite. In a sermon on Jesus' advice to consider the lilies, Robert John Versteeg tells of Thomas Jefferson's going to see a monkey for the sheer frivolity of it, and on the very same day buying the paper on which he would pen the Declaration of Independence.[31] The story is lighthearted and fun, yet the point of comparison that Versteeg makes becomes a powerful metaphor for understanding Jesus' words about the lilies.

One reason for the neglect of proverbial literature in the pulpit, I suspect, is its simplicity. The sermon based on an aphorism must be more than the gospel according to Ben Franklin. Ultimately, the preacher must avoid two extremes: overly simplistic platitudes on the one hand and overly abstract material on the other. Like proverbs themselves, sermons preached from aphorisms should be full of life.

Proverbs come from life. For instance, I remember my grandfather's coming to live with us one summer when I was a little boy. Every day we would eat hot dogs together, and one day I asked him to teach me how to cook hot dogs. (This was before microwave ovens.) As I sat waiting impatiently for the water to boil, he quipped, "A watched pot never boils." He had to explain that line to me at the time, but I have not forgotten it. Proverbs are like that—they come from life experiences and they stick with you. Sermons based on aphorisms ought above all to be memorable and lifelike.

Preaching on aphorisms could benefit greatly from what Thomas Long calls "synecdoche-style illustrations," in which the story fleshes out how vague concepts might actually look.[32] In what ways do people "cast pearls before swine" today? How would it look if we really followed Jesus to become fishers of people? Long suggests a question: Specifically how does this call of Jesus come to the people who make up the congregation—the single parent, the woman who has cancer, the child beginning school this year?[33] Jesus' aphorisms are simple, to be sure, but they are not simplistic.

One of the engaging aspects of Jesus' simple imagery is his use of hyperbole. The preacher wishing to use exaggeration and irony needs to be careful, since some congregations are more open than others to exaggeration as a literary device. Still, hyperbole can have a tremendous impact on the sermon's mood.

Sermonic Movement

There is one issue above all others that determines how the sermon is structured—the type of parallelism within the text. Form-sensitive sermons do not have to follow the form of the text, but when the preacher decides to follow it, the parallelism of an aphorism is a helpful source of guidance.

Synonymous parallelism, in which the second line rephrases and enhances the meaning of the first line, implies that the textual flow can be regenerated within the sermon flow. One story (remember, proverbial literature implies a narrative) could be told, followed by another that reiterates the first. The cumulative effect of this could be very powerful within the sermon event. In between these stories the text itself could be repeated throughout the sermon as what Long calls an "interpretive refrain." He notes that "narratives, vignettes, story-like threads that the proverb tugs from the fabric of everyday life would be told, each thread punctuated by the proverb itself."[34] This phantasmagoric effect allows the sermon to move along rapidly, producing a fast-paced kind of sermonic movement akin to what David Buttrick has proposed.[35]

This same kind of fast-paced movement can also be applied to antithetical parallelism as well, though the overall movement is radically different. Consider the example of Luke 9:58 referred to earlier: "Foxes have holes, and birds of the air have nests; but the Son of Man has nowhere to lay his head." The first part of the text invites the hearer to agree with these nonthreatening observations on life, but the last line shifts the focus into a direct confrontation concerning the risks of following Jesus. This textual movement can be regenerated by means of inductive movement within the sermon, inviting hearers in the pews to agree at first, only to be confronted with the demands of the gospel near the end. Every text must be considered separately, of course, so for that reason, let us consider as illustrative a sermon by William H. Willimon, minister to Duke University.[36]

"A Second Look"

by William H. Willimon

Matthew 5:27-48

Some of you remember the uproar that President Jimmy Carter caused when he admitted to *Playboy* that he had committed "adultery in his heart."

Big deal. Show me a man who has never once "looked at a woman lustfully" and thereby committed, in Jesus' words, "adultery with her in his heart," and I will show you a candidate for a new heart. Though Matthew does not say so, I bet the same could be said for the looks and hearts of women.

I remember, as a student in Junior High, my righteous resolution to go through the day without thinking any impure thoughts about the opposite sex (perhaps in a youthful attempt to be faithful to Matthew 5:28). The resolution lasted no longer than my first fifteen minutes on the school bus.

[Everyday imagery is used right from the beginning in this sermon. The message will not be some ethereal lecture, but a reflection on life as we know it.]

Therein I learned the *impracticality* of Jesus' Sermon on the Mount. As you can see, I did not obey and pluck out the eye that caused me to sin. Rather, I took Junior High psychology, wherein I discovered all sorts of psychological reasons why it is utterly unrealistic to expect a normal fourteen-year-old male to be free of lustful eyes, heart, hand or whatever vital organ.

[The aphorisms in this text are imperatives, strong words of Jesus directly addressed to his listeners. Yet the preacher works up

to that directness. He begins by playfully questioning the wisdom of Jesus and the radical claims of Christianity. Directness will come later.]

And, in a way, that's what I did with the rest of the Sermon on the Mount. Did you? I found my psychological explanations for lust; my civil justifications for swearing an oath; the ability to return the blow to the stomach before he again slaps my cheek; and quite easily to say No to "him who would borrow from me." Even No to impecunious relatives and in-laws. This we have come to call "growing up," or "being realistic" about the Sermon on the Mount.

Not that I was always so. I remember the evening we had been visiting in New York when we were students. We had spent the day visiting anything that was free, walking the streets, eating our lunch out of a paper bag to save money. In Grand Central Station, on our way home, a young man came up to me and told me that his wallet had been stolen, that the last train to Albany was leaving, and that he needed ten dollars for a ticket. He would pay me back, he said, as he worked in Albany for IBM.

Perhaps remembering Jesus' words to "Give to him who begs from you, and do not refuse him who would borrow from you," I gave him the ten dollars, the only money I had. That night, when we got off the train, our car wouldn't start. Because I had no money, not even for a telephone call, we had a long, cold walk back to our apartment from the station in New Haven. I was miserable. Of course, the money was never paid back. There was no one by that name with IBM or anybody else in Albany.

I felt like a fool.

[Again the preacher employs everyday imagery. Every person listening to the sermon has had a similar experience.]

Yet at least I was "sadder but wiser." To this day, when approached by panhandlers, beggars, and even relatives, I see that man's face on their face and I think twice. If I had been able to see that liar for who he really was that night in Grand Central, I would still have my ten dollars.

You have heard it said by Jesus not to resist the one who is evil, but I say to you that you had better look out for number one. Give them an inch, they will take a mile. Don't feel bad about your innate self-interest. If you didn't look out for you, who would? Look twice before turning the other cheek, going the second mile, giving to him who asks.

[The mood of the sermon is enhanced here by means of hyperbole and satire. The preacher plays with the text using inductive doubt and exaggeration, then follows up with more of the same.]

Look twice, because your perspective makes all the difference. Occasionally one meets people who are naive, unrealistic, immature in their outlook, approaching the world with trusting smile and open hand, easy targets for the con-man, the sleazy operator, the opportunist. Someday they will grow up and be "mature"—which means hardened, calculating, shrewd, cautious, self-possessed. They will look at life like us.

How you look at it makes a difference.

Jesus, in His Sermon on the Mount, in saying "You have heard it said of old . . . but I say to you," is pushing a peculiar perspective, a different way of looking at things. And His instructions about what to do when struck, when begged, when ordered, when victimized, appear to call for a kind of "second naivete." It's as if He wants us to revert, to go back to what we have, with much heartache, outgrown.

[The preacher addresses the issue of context. This hard saying of Jesus occurs in the Sermon on the Mount and calls for a new approach to religion. This concept is directly addressed by the preacher.]

A lawyer friend of mine said to me, "You know, it's a little sad, but whenever I am doing business with someone, I start out on the assumption that this person is lying. I've learned the hard way that they usually are. Then, if by chance they are not lying—not misrepresenting the produce, not fudging on the facts—I'm pleasantly surprised."

He had learned, the hard way, to look at people that way.

Jesus urges us to look at people another way. "Everyone who looks at a woman [or a man] lustfully has already committed adultery with her in his heart."

Lust is here not defined as a normal, psychologically healthy urge, but as looking at someone as a *thing*, a thing to be used rather than as a person to be loved. The trouble begins before the act, in the *look*.

[The preacher makes a direct explanation and an application. The sermon must say what the text is saying.]

Perhaps it's that look which is behind Jesus' disagreements with divorce. In that day, when a man could send his wife away by merely giving her a certificate of divorce, Jesus condemns a practice which treats a wife as little more than a piece of property.

Someone strikes you on the cheek, some Roman soldier comes up and commands you to take his pack—how do you look at that person? Is it even a person that you see? As you mutter under your breath, and in quiet, seething resentment dodge the blow, clench your fist and pray for the day when you will be able—like Karate Kid, or the Equalizer—to return the injury, what do you see?

Someone said of Martin Luther King and his non-violence, "King tended to bring out the best in people. King dealt with people on the assumption that even a white segregationist had good somewhere within."

And sometimes that is the case: when we dare to treat people in an open, loving way, they become more open and loving.

But not always. Let's be as honest as Jesus. Martin Luther King treated Bull Connors in an open and loving way and Connors beat his head with a club.

No, the Sermon on the Mount is not a list of tactics for

bringing out the best in people. The Sermon on the Mount says that, even if this way does not produce good results, *this is God's way.*

[Although earlier in the sermon Willimon playfully questioned the teachings of Jesus, at this point he is very forthright and direct. Inductive movement has brought us to a point of direct encounter.]

Did you notice? I almost claimed that if you turn the other cheek, go the second mile, return good for evil, things will go better for you. But you're not that dumb. Nor was Jesus. He doesn't say to turn the other cheek because it works. Jesus says, *deal with evil the way God deals with evil.*

God's rain falls upon the just and the unjust and God's sun shines upon the heads of the evil and the good. God's love is uncalculating, non-discriminating, for the persecuted Jew and for the Roman soldier, there for the one who strikes and the one who is struck. God is, Jesus says elsewhere, "Kind to the ungrateful and the selfish" (Luke 6:35).

You have heard it said, an eye for an eye, this is the *lex talionis,* the law of retribution. But Jesus urges us *to live as if our lives were not determined by those who do wrong.* When the other seeks to harm or victimize, the disciple seeks to restore and heal. Others may victimize you, but you don't have to play the victim.

Disciples live not in response to, nor in reaction against, others' conduct. Neither our friends nor our enemies dictate our ethics. Jesus' way of looking at people is to be our way of looking at people. We are called to be *faithful* rather than merely effective.

[Again, the preacher is very direct. This is what the sermon is all about. An illustration of the concept follows.]

I shall never forget the student whom I heard describe his own attempt to live the Sermon on the Mount. His senior year of college, he felt called by God to spread the Gospel. But how? Should he go to seminary? Should he be a missionary?

Waiting for guidance, he decided to work for a year or so

as a bus driver in Chicago. "Some place for witness," he muttered to himself as he drove his route through inner city streets, "some place to serve Jesus."

On the route, a group of high school boys—no, I mean, young hoods—got on his bus every afternoon for a ride downtown. They would get on, stroll past the fare box, never put in a dime, slouching on the back of the bus, daring him to make them pay. Each day, at the same bus stop, they got on the bus, talked loud, intimidated the other passengers, didn't pay. Finally, one afternoon he met them at the bus door and said as courteously as he could, "Look guys, you've got to pay. Everybody else pays. It's not fair. If you don't pay, you can't ride."

And those four hoods dragged him off that bus and kicked and punched him until he was unconscious, leaving him half dead, bleeding on the sidewalk. So much for Matthew 5:27-48.

The police caught his assailants the next day, easily identified by the terrified passengers on the bus. A month later, he was called to testify at their trial for assault and battery.

He went to court, still bandaged from the beating, but hurting even more because he had failed to live out his Christian faith, failed to convert or convince anybody. At the trial, their lawyers pled for them. They were all high school seniors. A conviction would keep them from graduating, be a mark on their records for life. The judge was unmoved.

After the four were found guilty, the judge, preparing to sentence them, asked the bandaged driver, "What would make you happy? What would make you feel better? You're the one who suffered from these worthless thugs."

He looked at them, he saw thugs. Then he said, "The thing which would make me happy would be to serve their sentence for them, to go to jail on their behalf so that they could go back and finish school and do better."

The judge laughed. "What? That's ridiculous! Absurd! Impractical! *Nobody* has ever done that."

"Oh, yes He did," he said softly. "Oh, yes, *He* did."

[The direct commands of the text do not mean the sermon must be a verbal scolding of those listening. The sermon ends on the positive note of what God did in Christ, not in abstraction. The sermon fleshes out what it means to live up to Christ's demands.]

Exercises

Answer the following eight questions in regard to the New Testament aphorism in each passage: Matthew 7:13-14; Luke 11:27-28; Luke 12:6-7.

1. What does the context say about the aphorism? Does the aphorism occur elsewhere in the Gospels?

2. In what grammatical form does the aphorism occur? What kind of textual mood does that suggest?

3. What kind of textual movement is present? If parallelism is used, what type? What does that say about the mood and movement within the text?

4. Does the passage employ hyperbole? What other devices does the text use, such as argument from lesser to greater? What types of everyday imagery are used?

5. What musical instruments might best accompany the text? Are there mood swings present? Do any colors and/or textures help to describe the text's mood(s)? What adjectives and adverbs best describe the passage?

6. What is the text saying?

7. What is the text doing?

8. How could a sermon say and do the same?

Sermon Resources

Kenneth L. Gibble, "Mr. Witmer's Gift" [Matthew 7:1-5], in *Once Upon a Wonder: Imaginings from the Gospels* (Upper

Room, 1992), pp. 82-85. Short on exposition, but does what the text is doing. Marvelous creativity and engaging story.

Alyce M. McKenzie, "Finders Weepers" [Matthew 16:25], in *Preaching Proverbs* (Westminster/John Knox, 1996), pp. 128-34. An example of what McKenzie calls "dueling proverbs," the sermon employs inductive tension.

Alyce M. McKenzie, "Keep Your Hand on the Plow" [Luke 9:62; Hebrews 10:23], in *Preaching Proverbs* (Westminster/John Knox, 1996), pp. 143-49. A sample sermon that moves through both texts and lots of historical and contemporary stories.

Robert John Versteeg, "Consider the Monkeys" [Matthew 6:26-28], in *Best Sermons 4*, ed. James W. Cox (Harper and Row, 1991), pp. 253-57. Strong in both biblical and contemporary material. A simple sermon, but not simplistic. Inspiring.

William H. Willimon, "A Second Look" [Matthew 5:27-48], in *Preaching* (March/April 1988): 23-25. Complete sermon included in this chapter.

CHAPTER 6

Pronouncement Stories: Jesus' Character and Identity

Few presidential administrations are remembered more fondly by the American people than that of John F. Kennedy. The Kennedy administration is remembered for the Cuban missile crisis, the space race, even the assassination. Kennedy's words are also remembered, for instance, the famous line that he uttered in Germany, *"Ich bin ein Berliner."* Another example is a line that he delivered in his inauguration address, "Ask not what your country can do for you; ask what you can do for your country."[1] These are pronouncement stories.

Then there is the legacy of Martin Luther King Jr. His role in the American civil rights struggle is renowned—the marches in the South and on the Capitol. It was on the steps of the Capitol that he proclaimed, "I have a dream my four little children will one day live in a nation where they will not be judged by the color of their skin but by the content of their character. I have a dream today!" Later, on the night before his assassination, he said:

> And he's [God has] allowed me to go up to the mountain. And I've looked over. And I've seen the promised land. I may not get there with you. But I want you to know tonight, that we, as a people, will get to the

promised land. And I'm happy, tonight. I'm not worried about anything. I'm not fearing any man. Mine eyes have seen the glory of the coming of the Lord.[2]

These are pronouncement stories.

At the 1936 Olympics in Berlin, Germany, a black athlete from America named Jesse Owens stunned the world, winning four gold medals in a single day. He also stunned a certain spectator—Adolf Hitler, who had boasted of the superiority of the Aryan race. Hitler walked out of the stadium in protest. This too is a pronouncement story.

Broadly speaking, a pronouncement story is a brief story about someone or some event that culminates in a striking saying and/or action. In modern American culture these stories help us learn about famous people and their accomplishments. American children learn about honesty and integrity, for example, in the story of George Washington and the cherry tree. When asked by his father if he cut it down, the young Washington admitted his misdeed so as not to lie.

In ancient Roman culture pronouncement stories had a similar function. These stories were told "about and in honor of a famous man or simply as a means of preserving a humorous saying or incident concerning him."[3] In New Testament studies we discover pronouncement stories with similar characteristics. In such studies a pronouncement story has been described as "a brief story about Jesus that culminates in a short, striking saying (and possibly an action)."[4] These stories play a prominent role in the Gospels and Acts, but especially in the Synoptics, where we will focus our attention. (For further discussion on stories in the Fourth Gospel, see chapter 8, "Johannine Discourse: The Lengthy Speeches of Jesus.") These stories from the life of Jesus are wonderful preaching texts, but they require a keen understanding of their literary form, what they say, and how they work.

What Is the Text Saying?

Throughout the years a variety of terms have been applied to pronouncement stories,[5] each one denoting a unique emphasis in the history of form research. Some scholars emphasized the saying to the neglect of the story, and vice versa.[6] Recent studies, however, have tended to view this form more holistically, considering the importance of both the story and the saying.[7]

A pronouncement story, then, can be defined as "a brief narrative in which the climactic (and often final) element is a pronouncement which is presented as a particular person's response to something said or observed on a particular occasion of the past."[8] Scholars now note that a pronouncement story is the combination of a well-crafted saying and a well-told story.[9] Several different types of these stories have been identified.

Correction stories are those in which a position held by someone is corrected by Jesus' pronouncement. An example would be the request of James and John to receive positions of power in Jesus' coming kingdom, which resulted in Jesus' teaching on being a servant (Mark 10:32-45).

In *commendation stories* Jesus commends a position held by others. Simon Peter's being blessed by Jesus for correctly identifying him as "the Messiah, the Son of the living God" is a classic example (Matthew 16:16). In *objection stories* the pronouncement occurs in response to an objection by others. One example would be the religious leaders' questioning Jesus' association with tax collectors and sinners, and his reply about those who are sick being in need of a physician (Mark 2:15-17).

Quest stories portray someone seeking something from Jesus. Luke's story of the rich ruler seeking eternal life is one example, although it is an example of an unsuccessful quest (Luke 18:18-30). *Inquiry stories* involve someone seeking understanding, such as the disciples asking Jesus to teach them to pray (Luke 11:1-4), or someone testing the authority of the one making the pronouncement, such as whether to pay taxes to Rome (Mark 12:13-17).

Many *hybrid stories* have also been identified—stories that combine, for instance, both commendation and correction. When the mothers bring their children to Jesus and are forbidden by the disciples, Jesus corrects his disciples and commends the children (Mark 10:13-16).[10]

A recent study has proposed another type (or subtype) of pronouncement passage, *passion stories*, which occur during Jesus' suffering and death. Each passion story must be treated separately in order to determine what kind of pronouncement story is used in it.[11]

Familiarity with pronouncement stories is essential for a preacher, especially since there are approximately one hundred such stories in the New Testament.[12] Fortunately, newer commentary series are including discussions of forms such as pronouncement stories,[13] which enable preachers to consider how the form is functioning within the text. Rhetorical strategies that are at work must be analyzed.

What Is the Text Doing?

Two hallmarks characterize pronouncement stories: (1) they call for some kind of attitudinal shift in the readers[14] and (2) they reveal the character of Jesus, especially when he is challenged by others.[15] It is either Jesus' character or his authority that empowers him to call for change in matters such as "value commitments, emotional attachments, orientations of the will, and evaluative thought."[16] Jesus made pronouncements that challenged or commended certain attitudes and behaviors. A generation later the Gospel writers used them to say something about the character of Jesus as well. The former purpose, however, remained the primary one: pronouncement stories are intended to challenge the way we live our lives.

This challenge is stated variously in the different types of pronouncement stories, although there are two elements common to all of the types. First, the rhetorical strategy of both story and saying is crucial.[17] "A pronouncement story is a story with narrative tension and movement, not just a saying with a narrative setting which can be ignored."[18] The story appeals to the imagination, while the well-crafted saying closes with an appeal to reason. As such, pronouncement stories are holistic, touching not only imagination and reason but also, indirectly, the will.[19] Robert Tannehill compares the goal of the Gospel writer in shaping these stories to a playwright who intentionally shapes a story to influence an audience.[20] This shaping by the Evangelists would help to explain some of the differences that occur in the same story in the various Gospel accounts. As a part of this shaping, details within the story itself are usually included only to the extent that they move readers toward the saying. Even the characters are only briefly sketched out. The emphasis within the story is on the issue the characters stand for.[21]

Second, the saying represents what the Evangelist wants the readers to embrace. To that end, the plot of the story allows us to come to grips with the inadequacy of our own positions and the superiority of Jesus' teaching. The climactic position of the saying also insures that everything in the story points toward it, and that the saying makes the final impression on the hearers-readers.[22]

The various types of pronouncement stories point to a variety of ways that these stories seek to bring about change. Let us look briefly at the various types and their respective strategies. In *correction stories* the tension between Jesus and someone else may actually come as a surprise, since the story itself is not presented as a challenge. It is not until Jesus responds that the tension becomes fully evident. At that point the reader is faced with deciding between Jesus' view and some other one.[23] Initially the other position may seem innocent or even commendable.[24] The final saying does not introduce complex arguments as to why the initial opinion is wrong. A brief, well-worded saying is given to provoke thought and to effect action as well.[25]

Commendation stories, like correction stories, involve the initial presentation of some viewpoint, only in this case, Jesus' saying affirms the position. Thus the responder and the one commended are seen in a positive light.[26] Frequently Jesus' commendation is contrasted with the negative judgments of a third party. For example, when the woman anointed Jesus' feet with costly perfume, Jesus commended her action while condemning the disciples' attitude (Mark 14:3-9).[27]

In *objection stories* conflict is central. An objection is voiced at the very beginning of the story. Jesus is put on the spot, making the response even more impressive as it reveals the divine perspective.[28] Frequently the climactic saying is framed as a question, such as, "Is it lawful to do good or to do harm on the sabbath, to save life or to kill?" (Mark 3:4). Rhetorical questions such as this one actually make statements and call for a decision on the part of the hearer.[29]

Quest stories focus our attention on someone who is searching for something. The success or failure of that search is a significant part of these stories, and what the person seeks frequently represents society's needs on the whole.[30] "Jesus remains the figure of authority in the story and he must certify the success of a quest."[31] The overwhelming majority of Synoptic quest stories end in success, with a few exceptions (for instance, the rich ruler and those who wanted to bury their dead before following Jesus [Luke 9:57-62]). In most cases the seeker appears unworthy, but finds success in the end. Whatever obstacles appear to be insurmountable are usually the ones that the Evangelist wishes to emphasize.[32] The story of Zacchaeus (Luke 19:1-9) is one example, with riches being the obstacle.

Inquiry stories sometimes serve to express Jesus' teaching on a certain subject, such as the instructions on prayer in Luke 11. These stories can also involve a testing of Jesus, such as Jesus' view on divorce (Mark 10:2-9). Tension in these stories is frequently heightened through lengthening the story and through several exchanges of dialogue.[33]

Hybrid stories are capable of many rhetorical strategies, depending on the forms that the story combines. The form of the story itself may be misleading. For example, "the fact that Jesus is asked a question does not immediately tell us that the story is an inquiry, for Jesus may respond by correcting an assumption behind the question (a correction story)."[34] The key interpretive element and rhetorical strategy often lie with the identification. Are the readers to be identified with the children who are commended or with the disciples who are rebuked (Mark 10:13-16)?[35]

Passion stories, like the other types of pronouncement stories, serve to convey teachings about Jesus' identity. They inform us about the last days of Jesus' earthly ministry, but their social function relates to "remembrance and re-presentation."[36] These stories serve a vital role in determining how the Christian community will remember Jesus. It is crucial, however, in determining the function of a passion story, to treat each story individually. Some pronouncement stories invite suspense, while others are straightforward. The rhetorical strategy of an individual text can help the preacher determine not only what to say but how to say it and, ultimately, how to preach it.

How Can the Sermon Say and Do the Same?

Pronouncement stories are popular in society today. For that reason the preacher may not need to explain the form itself. If some explanation is necessary, examples like the ones about John F. Kennedy and Martin Luther King Jr. at the beginning of this chapter could be useful. Sermonic mood and movement, however, are of primary importance.

Sermonic Mood

As we already noted, a pronouncement story combines a well-crafted saying and a well-told story. The biblical story has everything to do with the mood of the sermon. An imaginative retelling of the pronouncement story with some elaboration will help unleash the power originally possessed by the text.[37] How stories do that is quite fascinating. The power of stories relates to how identification takes place, what one rhetorician refers to as "consubstantiation."[38] This term, as traditionally used by Lutherans in reference to the Lord's Supper, differs from the traditional Roman Catholic view of transubstantiation and also from the strictly symbolic view held by many Protestant traditions. Consubstantiation means that Christ is identified with the bread and the wine, but is not identical with them. In other words, the elements are more than just bread and wine (symbolism), but less than the actual body and blood of Jesus (transubstantiation). Instead, Christ is somehow present in the elements.

It is the same for stories and how they work. Obviously those listening to a story do not become the characters in the story, but neither are the characters just characters—mere symbols.[39] "Without being consciously aware of it, people hearing the story think and feel their way into the events of the narrative and its characters."[40] Why is it that people who grew up in rural America, who are not even Jewish, are moved by scenes from the Holocaust in *Schindler's List?* Why is it that dads decide to spend more time with their daughters after seeing *Father of the Bride?* Somehow the listeners are present in the story. It is the process of identification by means of consubstantiation. An imaginative retelling of the biblical story allows listeners to identify with the characters presented.

A device that is particularly helpful in retelling biblical

stories is anachronism, that is, telling the ancient story in modern terms. For instance, in a sermon about the rich man in Mark's Gospel (10:17-31), William Willimon writes:

> The rich young man did not expect to hear of his riches. He wanted to talk about social ethics, about the great social issues of our day. And he never would have engaged Jesus in theological debate had he not been sure that his own righteousness was impeccable. He obeyed the law. He voted Democratic in the last election, was a member of the Sierra Club and ate no non-union grapes. What can I do now to advance the cause of peace with justice? Write my congressperson? Join the NAACP?[41]

It is not just biblical stories, however, that have the power to affect us. All stories have that potential. According to Fred Craddock, one of the ways identification occurs in preaching is through analogy.[42] As Robert Tannehill notes, pronouncement stories were biting forms of communication for the original hearers of the gospel. But in our day Samaritans and tax collectors no longer arouse negative feelings. The preacher needs to relate the story to "different but analogous attitudes in the modern world."[43] For instance, in a sermon on the woman who anointed Jesus (Mark 14:1-10), Eugene Lowry emphasizes the celebration aspect of her act: it was totally unexpected and others who were present responded negatively to it. He offers a contemporary analogy:

> You know how it goes: You're clicking your heels in absolute glee for having accomplished what could not be done. What was it—the term paper in on time, the impossible sale, the meal ready for the unexpected guests—whatever! But unbelievably, it happened, it got done. Up comes your logical friend who has no use for such nonsense: "What do you mean, it was impossible? You did it didn't you? Obviously you simply miscalculated the thing."[44]

Preaching from a pronouncement story can be done by weaving together a retelling of the biblical story and some other analogous story (or stories). Lowry offers several structural options in his book *How to Preach a Parable*, which is really about how to preach sermons following the way that parables work.[45] The use of stories relates to the mood of a sermon, but a pronouncement story is made up of both a story and a saying. These two components together relate to the movement within the text.

Sermonic Movement

Pronouncement stories come in many different shapes, each having its own purpose. A correction story differs from a commendation story not only in purpose (which relates to the content of the sermon) but also in movement. Different strategies are at work in the various types of pronouncement stories. The one constant among all of them is an inductive structure.[46] Some position is put forth, which is either commended or corrected (or both), *but not until the end*. That is inductive movement. Sometimes a position is expressed that is met with disagreement in the beginning but is finally resolved in the end. This too is a type of inductive movement. Let us briefly consider how inductive sermon strategies might be employed with the various types of pronouncement stories.

In *correction stories* the initial position presented in the story frequently appears in a positive light, inviting us to identify with it. But then our world is turned upside down in the saying of Jesus. Beverly Roberts Gaventa, in a sermon about the woman's anointing Jesus in Mark 14 (which is both a correction story and a commendation story), uses satire and plays with the text, causing us to assume that Jesus will be on our side:

> Still, surely Jesus will correct her. Nudge her in the right direction. A sum of money such as this could be in-

vested, and the return on the investment given to local charities. Even if she did want to use it for Jesus, half of it could have been poured out and the *other* half used for the poor. A modest endowment fund could have produced an annual fund, to be distributed at Thanksgiving and Christmas![47]

Playing "devil's advocate" can help draw listeners in, only to be corrected by Jesus in the end. This same technique can be applied to *commendation stories*, since most of these are actually hybrids.

Objection stories are perfectly suited to inductive sermon development. Tension exists from the beginning. The Pharisees or some other characters have questioned Jesus—why he eats with tax collectors, for example (Mark 2:13-17). The preacher would do well to join in with their questioning: "Let's face it, there really are places that good Christians shouldn't go. What will people think if they see you associating with, you know, undesirables? Some standards must be upheld. Besides, aren't Christians called to be different? Let's face it, the Pharisees have a good point." Once identification takes place, the listeners are in a position to hear the words of Jesus.

Quest stories are about overcoming obstacles. A degree of suspense is built into these stories, which are perfectly suited for inductive preaching. The key once again is to side with the viewpoint of the character. The preacher might say something like, "Why would Jesus be so hard on this rich ruler? He didn't make Zacchaeus give all of his money away. What's wrong with keeping some of it?"

Inquiry stories are tools of teaching. The tension associated with other story types is not felt as sharply in these stories, but that does not rule out the possibility of induction. Inductive preaching means that the answer to the question is not revealed until the end of the sermon. Traditional deductive preaching does just the opposite; it tells the punch line before it tells the joke.

Mystery is built into some inquiry stories. In Mark 11 Jesus curses a fig tree for not bearing fruit, but it was not even time for trees to be producing. Why did Jesus curse the tree? That is the kind of question preachers can ask. The answer relates to something Jesus seeks to teach, and so the answer comes at the end.

Pronouncement stories offer the preacher any number of narrative and inductive possibilities. The sample sermon we will consider is by Thomas Long, who teaches preaching at Princeton Theological Seminary. The sermon just so happens to come from Mark's account of Jesus' cursing the fig tree.[48]

"Figs Out of Season"

by Thomas G. Long

Mark 11:11-25

Well, what do you think about the story of the fig tree?
Jesus and the disciples are on the way from Bethany to
Jerusalem when:

> *unfortunately*, Jesus becomes hungry.
> *fortunately*, there is nearby the path a fig tree—the
> kind that produces those fat, succulent, delicious
> figs in the middle of the summer.
> *unfortunately*, it is not the middle of the summer; it is
> early spring. The little fig tree is doing all it can—
> it has leaves, but no figs.

What do you expect? It wasn't the season for figs. Evi-
dently Jesus expected something more; without so much as
a word of explanation, he denounced the fig tree with a
withering curse. Within twenty-four hours the little fig tree
was *dead*.

*[Long immediately begins wrestling with the text. The tension
that any alert reader would feel is given voice by the preacher. The
recurring question, "What do you expect?" will help focus the
sermon.]*

As you can imagine, this story has produced a variety of
reactions in people, but in almost all of them there is at least
a measure of *shock*.

We seem to have caught Jesus, of all people, in an un-
Christlike deed.

No matter that he was hungry, Jesus, of all people, should
have known that a fig tree cannot produce figs out of season.

But no, he *kills* the tree. Albert Schweitzer wouldn't have done that. A member of the Sierra Club wouldn't have done that. Why does Jesus have to do that?

[Long continues to wrestle with the text. Instead of siding with Jesus immediately, he invites us to play devil's advocate with him. The tension continues to mount.]

It is some comfort to know that this story has perplexed New Testament scholars and commentators as well. Indeed, a good many of the commentators on Mark treat this story as if *it* were the man in the ditch in the parable of the Good Samaritan and *they* were the priest and the Levite: They pass by silently on the other side! Every now and then one of them pauses long enough to peer into the ditch and be shocked. One commentator, for example, observed: "This is one of the most perplexing stories in the Gospel. . . . What perplexes us is not so much the nature-miracle implied as the unworthy light it casts on the character of Jesus. With our knowledge of Jesus from other sources, we find it frankly incredible that he could have used his power to wither a fig tree because it did not yield figs two or three months before its natural time of fruitage. Let those who will, regard it as a 'miracle of judgement'; for ourselves we must ask Why . . . ?"[49]

[As if our own bewilderment with this text were not enough, we are told that even the scholars are baffled by it. The inductive tension grows.]

Why, indeed? Why would the writer of Mark, whose intention is to tell us "the beginning of the good news of Jesus Christ," give us a piece of bad news—a story that reflects unfavorably on the character of Jesus?

Matthew, who follows Mark, tones the story down.

Luke, who follows Mark, won't touch the story with a ten-foot pole. He leaves it out altogether.

One rather psychologically-minded interpreter has suggested that, in this case, maybe the "bad news" is really the "good news." It is difficult to be a follower of a flawless

master, and the passage stands as a comforting reminder that
even messiahs have their dark days and bad moods. So, the
next time we are surly to a waitress, obnoxious with our
families, or think withering thoughts about someone at
work, we can be comforted by the memory of that day when
Jesus got caught with his divinity down and cursed out a
little fig tree. Thank goodness it wasn't a disciple—or a
Samaritan town!

We would be tempted to leave it at that—one tiny fleck in
the otherwise stainless character of Jesus—were it not for the
fact that the writer of Mark practically slaps us in the face
with his insistence that this is no playful passage about a
peevish Jesus. For he moves immediately to tell us that Jesus
went on to Jerusalem, where he engaged in another act of
withering violence—throwing the money changers and the
buyers and sellers out of the Temple—saying: "Is it not
written, 'My house shall be called a house of prayer for all
the nations'? But you have made it a den of robbers."

*[A possible psychological explanation is offered and rejected, and
we are left wondering what this text is about. But its meaning will
become clear presently.]*

The next day they passed by the fig tree again, and Peter,
remembering, cried: "Look, Master! The fig tree you cursed
yesterday—it has withered!" Jesus does *not* grin sheepishly,
pat Peter on the back and say, "Yeah, I suppose I let things
get a little out of hand yesterday."

Instead, Jesus says, rather curiously: "Yes . . . have faith in
God. Whoever says to this mountain, 'Be cast into the sea,'
and does not doubt, . . . it will come to pass. . . . Whatever
you ask in prayer, believe that you will receive it, and you
will." Far from being a bad moment in the otherwise compassionate ministry of Jesus, this withering of the fig tree
comes to us as a word about faith, action, and prayer.

*[For the first time we become aware that this story is an inquiry
story, though Long does not actually refer to it as such. It is not*

necessary. The story is intended to convey a teaching about faith, action, and prayer.]

If we are called, then, to take this fig tree story seriously, the place at which we must begin to take it seriously is precisely at the point where it rubs us the wrong way—the *injustice* of Jesus' action. It is not fair for Jesus to expect a fig tree to produce fruit out of season. *What in the name of God do you expect?*

This turns out to be precisely the question Mark wants us to ask: *What in the name of God do you expect?*

[The thesis of the sermon comes clear for the first time. This is a passage about a God who shatters our everyday expectations. As in Mark's text, this teaching has not become clear until well into the story.]

It is the theme of the whole Gospel of Mark that

> into ordinary expectations—
> a new expectation was brewing.
> into ordinary history—
> a new and revolutionary history was bursting.
> into ordinary seasons—
> a new evergreen season was budding.

The very first words on Jesus' lips in Mark are: "The time is *now*, . . . the *kingdom* is at hand; repent, turn around, be revolutionized, believe in the gospel."

Mark gives us picture after picture of people whose lives had been out of season for years who, in the power of this kingdom comes in Jesus, blossomed with new life and hope:

The man in the graveyard, the village idiot—possessed by demons, crazy as hell, always had been, always would be.

What in the name of God do you expect?

> His life knitted together and made whole in Jesus.
> Bearing fruit out of season.
> *Jairus's daughter*—dead as a doornail. Hear the sounds of the wake? Weeping and wailing.

What in the name of God do you expect?

"Little girl, I say to you, arise." And immediately, she got up and walked! Bearing fruit out of season.

The Temple itself—so lousy with commercialism it looked like K-Mart at Christmas, but the bills have to be paid, the ceremonies must be observed.

What in the name of God do you expect?

Cleansed by the power of his word, "My house shall be a house of prayer for all the nations."
In the power of the kingdom come in Jesus nothing which is

redemptive
  just
    merciful
is *ever* out of season again!

[Several examples from Mark's Gospel are given to substantiate Long's claim. Contemporary applications will be made next.]

Weep then, not for the fig tree, but for all of us who don't know what season it is.

Weep for the church when it expects nothing but what the world expects—a world where justice, redemption, and mercy are never in season.

Weep for ourselves when we feel that our lives are so twisted that nothing can heal them, our enemies so hostile that we cannot love them, the poor so worthless that they are not worth our time, the world so corrupt it can never be renewed.

Weep for ourselves when we expect only more of the same—seasons come and seasons go.

But rejoice also! Rejoice in the power of the kingdom come in Jesus! Rejoice that in the power of the kingdom come in Jesus redemption, justice, and mercy are never out of season. Rejoice in the foolishness of the gospel which calls for mountains to be cast into the sea, which invites bold prayers for righteousness, which expects fruit when the world sees only a tree out of season!

[The contemporary application is very direct. We are confronted with our own complacency, having forgotten just what God can do.]

Sometime ago I found myself in a conversation with a man seated next to me on an airplane, a conversation that took a rather serious turn. He told me that he and his wife were the parents of a son, now in his thirties, who was confined to a nursing-care condition for a number of years because of an injury to his brain. "We had stopped loving him," said my companion. "It's a hard thing to admit, but we had stopped loving him. It's hard to love someone who never responds. We visited him often, but our feeling for him as a son had begun to die. Until one day we happened to visit our son and discovered a visitor, a stranger, in his room. He turned out to be the pastor of a nearby church whose custom it was to visit all the patients in the nursing home. When we arrived we found him talking to our son—*as if* our son could understand. Then he read Scripture to our son—*as if* our son could hear it. Finally he had prayer with our son—*as if* our son could know that he was praying. My first impulse was to say, 'You fool, don't you know about our son?' But then it dawned on me that, of course, he *did* know. He knew all along. He cared for our son *as if* our son were whole, because he saw him through the eyes of faith, and he saw him already healed. That pastor renewed in us the capacity to love our son."

[Along with the specific application, we are given a picture of what Mark is calling for. If the text were to be lived out, this is what it would look like.]

Rejoice! Rejoice that in the power of the kingdom come in Jesus even those broken in disease are never out of season in God's love.

Rejoice that in the power of the kingdom come in Jesus
nothing
redemptive
just
    or merciful is ever out of season!
[The sermon closes with an emphasis on the kingdom and the mercy of God. Direct teaching follows the revelation of the sermon's thesis.]

Exercises

Answer the following eight questions for the pronounce-ment story in each passage: Matthew 22:15-22; Mark 3:31-35; Luke 9:46-48.

1. What kind of pronouncement story is included in this passage: correction, commendation, objection, quest, in-quiry, hybrid, or passion?

2. Is Jesus' response in the form of an action, a saying, or both?

3. What is the mood of the story? Is there a mood swing in the story? What kind of musical instruments might convey the mood(s) of the text? What colors and/or textures does the text suggest?

4. What movements can be identified? Is there an induc-tive tension present within the story?

5. What contemporary stories come to mind?

6. What is the text saying?

7. What is the text doing?

8. How could a sermon say and do the same?

Sermon Resources

Beverly Roberts Gaventa, "The Discipleship of Extrava-gance" [Mark 14:3-9], in *Princeton Seminary Bulletin* 15 (1994): 52-55. Based on a hybrid pronouncement story. Combines a brief retelling along with an inductive use of satire. Contemporary stories also included. Both sides of the hybrid are treated.

Thomas G. Long, "Figs out of Season" [Mark 11:11-25], in *Preaching Biblically,* ed. Don M. Wardlaw (Westminster, 1983), pp. 94-100. Complete sermon included in this chapter.

Eugene L. Lowry, "Swept Upstream" [Mark 14:1-10], in *A New Hearing,* ed. Richard L. Eslinger (Abingdon, 1987), pp. 89-93. Begins with an extended retelling of the biblical story using anachronistic details. Playfully questions Jesus' response to the woman. Contemporary analogies help listeners identify with the issues of the text in their own day.

John P. Rossing, "Give 'Til It Helps" [Mark 10:17-31], in *Preaching* (May/June 1989): 29-31. Based on the quest story of the rich man in Mark's Gospel. Several different sources are employed: legends, biography, psychology, and finally the text. Develops inductively, but treatment of riches as an obstacle is the sermon's greatest strength.

William H. Willimon, "Love in Action" [Mark 10:17-31], in *Best Sermons 3,* ed. James W. Cox (Harper and Row, 1990), pp. 200-205. A blend of satire, inductive wrestling with the text, anachronisms, and several contemporary stories to proclaim the text. The kind of obstacle that riches present is treated directly.

CHAPTER 7

Miracle Stories: The Supernatural Identity of Jesus

Miracles. For some Christians, the word glares like a neon sign posted on a decrepit building along a deserted highway: The Tabernacle of Jesus and Modern Day Miracles, Inc. Many believers cringe at the thought of a preacher who goes on at length about the miracles God wants to perform in our midst. Perhaps images of Steve Martin in the movie *Leap of Faith* come to mind, images of an evangelist who performs so-called miracles by means of modern technology, duping the masses into giving him their money.

For others, the term "miracles" may bring to mind the age-old tension between liberal rationalizations ("Jesus didn't walk on the water, he merely appeared to walk on the water.") and fundamentalist affirmations ("If the Bible says he walked on the water, that's good enough for me.")

I suspect that for most preachers reading this book the most pressing issue is not whether the miracles recorded in the New Testament actually happened, but how to apply the teaching about them to our situation today.

For instance, the text says that Jesus calmed the storm. Good. Fine and dandy. But have we nothing more substantial to proclaim than the allegorical line, "Jesus still calms our storms and our struggles today"? Indeed there is much more that we can say and that we should say. Outside of the apocalyptic passages, miracle stories are quite likely the most abused passages in the New Testament. Preachers simply do not know what to make of them. Let us look at these stories in terms of the three questions of sermon preparation.

What Is the Text Saying?

"The broadest definition of miracle story includes any narrative that contains a description of a miraculous event."[1] Note the different terms—miracle story and miraculous event. According to Hans Betz, the distinction is crucial. He writes, "The miracle story is neither the miracle itself nor talk about the miracle but a narrative with the special assignment of serving as a kind of language envelope for the transmission and communication of the 'unspeakable' miracle event."[2] Simply put, miracle stories are not so much about the miracles themselves as about the stories the Evangelists tell us around and through the miracles.[3]

Frequently a "gap" occurs at the precise moment in which the miracle occurs. Somehow Jesus multiplies the bread and the fish, though we are not told how. Exactly how the miracle happens remains a mystery. What the miracle says in the context of the story is the central concern.[4]

Early twentieth-century writers focused almost exclusively on scientific claims that could corroborate or repudiate the Gospel accounts. Such an approach clearly misses the purpose of New Testament miracle stories. Jesus was not attempting to validate his divinity by means of the miraculous. The Gospels make it clear that others were equally capable of performing miracles (Matthew 7:15-23; 12:27; 24:24; Luke 11:19). Outside of the New Testament, Josephus notes several miracle workers in his historical writings.[5] In the newer literary-critical approach, the question is not whether the miracles actually happened (which apparently even Rudolf Bultmann accepted[6]) or whether they should be interpreted symbolically, but what "theological lesson" they impart. "This message," writes Jarl Fossum, "is what we are to understand from them."[7] Before we look at the various types of miracle stories and how to interpret them, we should say something about the various terms used in the New Testament for miracles. According to N. T. Wright, "the Greek New Testament doesn't actually have a word that means 'miracle'; when things happened which seemed to give normal ideas of reality some sort of jolt, the gospel writers used words like 'signs', 'powerful acts', or 'paradoxes'."[8] Other terms, such as "mighty work," "wonder," "portent," "strange thing," and "sign," are also employed in various translations.[9]

John uses the term "sign" in his Gospel, a usage that some scholars have made more of than others.[10] W. Nicol contends that John's signs, even more so than the miracle stories in the Synoptic Gospels, point to Jesus' unlimited power. Nicol points out that in the first three Gospels people seek out Jesus, declare their faith in him, and then receive a miracle —the Roman centurion, for example (Matthew 8:5-13; Luke 7:1-10). In John, however, if the account refers to the same event, Jesus takes the initiative, and the man believes after having seen the miracle (John 4:46-54). Nicol contends that John's signs are the most marvelous events in the New Testament. "One man has been dead for four days, another paralyzed for thirty-eight years, and another blind from birth." The signs in John's Gospel point toward Jesus.[11] For our purposes we will consider John's signs along with the Synoptic miracles, all the while recognizing not only John's unique emphases but also the unique emphases in the various types of miracle stories in the Synoptics and the unique emphases within any given miracle story itself.

James Bailey and Lyle Vander Broek identify six different types of miracle stories, each with its unique theological lessons: exorcism, controversy story containing a miracle, petition story, provision story, rescue story, and epiphany.[12] Fossum notes that miracle stories in themselves are "ambiguous," that is, they have to be interpreted.[13] The text merely says that Jesus fed five thousand. What that meant for the original readers and what it means for us today must be determined. Otherwise the text remains good history, but not good news.

The plot of miracle stories is somewhat predictable: the situation or need is described, Jesus becomes aware and acts accordingly, and the consequences are then described.[14] The preacher, however, needs to look beyond the surface plot to elements such as the interaction among characters (although the characters in miracle stories are rarely highlighted[15]) and the dramatic stress within the story.[16] If the miracle story is common to the Synoptics, it is crucial that attempts to harmonize the accounts be avoided, although comparison/contrast studies can be helpful in isolating unique emphases within the various accounts. For instance, in Matthew's version of the healing of the centurion's servant (8:5-13), the power of faith to effect healing is highlighted. In Luke's story (7:1-10), however, it is the worthiness of a non-Jew to receive the benefits of Jesus' power that is central.[17] After examining the role of the miracle in the Gospel plot, the preacher needs to note how the story "functioned in creating meaning for the earliest Christians."[18]

What Is the Text Doing?

Even as there are numerous words for miracles, Harold Remus notes a wide variety of terms that are used to describe people's reactions to these miracles—"amazed," "astonished," "fear," "awe," and "wonder."[19] From a literary-critical standpoint, the Gospel writers use these terms to describe how the crowds or disciples reacted, but they do not necessarily prescribe how readers were to react.[20] In fact, the terms for reaction used in the New Testament almost always implied an ignorance on the part of those observing the miracles. The people did not understand. It is the task of the preacher, therefore, to understand not only what the miracle story intended to say but also how it said it. To do this, let us consider the six types of miracle stories and their function.

The central characteristic of an *exorcism story* is conflict. These stories dramatize Jesus' struggles with and victory over the powers of evil that control people.[21] "Exorcisms have to be seen in the context of a cosmic conflict," writes Gerd Theissen. "The possessed person is the theatre of a conflict between supernatural, extra-human forces."[22] The central focus of these stories, therefore, is less on the characters, though Jesus obviously cared for them, and more on the struggle between good and evil.[23]

While possessed persons are presented as powerless victims, the possessing powers are clearly portrayed as violently evil. Meanwhile, Jesus is portrayed as being confidently in control.[24] Interestingly, demonic possession in the New Testament is always presented in the context of sickness, not immoral behavior. The possessed are helpless, not evil.[25] In exorcism stories Jesus confronts evil powers, not evil people.

The central feature in a *controversy story* is less the miracle and more the issues that the miracle raises, such as keeping the sabbath. In Luke 13:10-17, for instance, Jesus heals a woman who was bent over double. The controversy that ensues is about the sabbath, not her healing. In controversy stories the sequence of miracle and argument is immaterial. Even the person who is healed plays a minor role, though liberation theology has challenged us to consider these minor characters as well. The focus is on establishing who is in authority. Typically, Jesus is pitted against the religious establishment. "Each seeks to expose the other party as false before God and thereby to take from them the power to determine right conduct in this case."[26]

Beneath the surface of the story is a debate on the divine perspective on how people ought to live.[27] "The 'ethics' of the story in each case is negative, purgative, in a social sense revolutionary, breaking down the restrictions erected in God's name to maintain order and privilege."[28] In the story in Luke 13 the Pharisees do not really care whether the woman is healed or not. The issue at stake is the law of Moses, and the miracle serves to set the scene for debate on a controversial issue.

Unlike exorcism stories and controversy stories, the victims in *petition stories* play a major role. These persons are presented as helpless victims who nevertheless actively seek Jesus' help.[29]

The central conflict, however, is not their helpless state, but a variety of obstacles that stand in their way to wholeness. The blind man named Bartimaeus cries out to Jesus, while those around him try to keep him quiet. The woman with a hemorrhage attempts merely to touch Jesus' garment, but she has to fight her way through the crowds to do so. The most complicated obstacles, however, are the ones Jesus himself puts in front of petitioners. Jesus often asks, "Do you believe that I am able to do this?" He then adds, "According to your faith let it be done to you" (Matthew 9:27-31).

Antoinette Clark Wire maintains that overcoming obstacles is the key to understanding how these stories function, although they are not lessons in assertiveness training. These stories are not meant to teach lessons about faith, but to celebrate the faith of one who has overcome. Petition stories challenge hearers "to break out of a closed world and to demand, struggle and realize miracle in human life."[30]

Provision stories highlight people who are helpless, as do petition stories. The helpless masses in provision stories, however, have lost all hope. Their vision is so limited that they do not even seek help. It never even occurs to them that this person they are following might be able to feed all of them. Jesus takes the initiative in meeting their needs, most of which are as basic as food to eat.[31] Frequently preachers allegorize these stories because they have no other idea what to do with them. They cannot imagine the story's being about the provision of physical needs, since everyone they know is reasonably well off. These stories, however, are about the deep-seated longings within people. The "longing" that these stories express must be taken seriously.[32]

Finding enough food to live on is one of humanity's most basic needs, and provision stories portray Jesus as unexpectedly providing more than enough. These material goods are signs of grace, what Theissen calls "gifts."[33] He adds, "No type of miracle story derives more from imagination than these; none has so much lightness, so much of the quality of a wish or an unaffected fairy tale."[34]

The tension in *rescue stories* is associated with overcoming hostile forces. These stories are similar to exorcisms in that Jesus rebukes the hostile force, but the force in rescue stories is natural, not evil. Jesus rebukes the waves, not demons.[35] These stories remind us that victory can be had "over dull, 'mindless', purely physical violence."[36] The storms do not represent the storms of life, at least not in the sense of traffic jams and overdue bills, but actual waves and actual wind. The key to understanding these stories is to appreciate them in the context of Near Eastern mythology and the power of chaos that the seas represented. This rebuke of nature itself identifies Jesus as the Lord of creation, literally.[37]

In the broadest sense, every miracle story is an epiphany story, or an appearance story in which Jesus makes himself known. Technically, however, an *epiphany story* is one in which Jesus makes an extraordinary and unexpected appearance.

These stories typically involve "extraordinary visual and auditory phenomena, the terrified reaction of human beings, the word of revelation," and the miraculous disappearance.[38]

Jesus' postresurrection appearances to his disciples behind closed doors is one example. Epiphany stories frequently have a teaching function. Jesus' appearance to the two disciples on the road to Emmaus, for instance, is an obvious example of Luke's emphasis on the Lord's Supper as communal meal. It is in the breaking of bread that they recognize their Lord.[39]

In summary, conflict is the one constant in all of the miracle stories. Evil must be overcome. Oppressive authorities must be dealt with. The elements of nature and society wear people down. Jesus, however, breaks through "in the struggle against oppressive restrictions on human life."[40] The telling and retelling of these stories leads us to the task of preaching them.

How Can the Sermon Say and Do the Same?

Miracle stories are not part of our culture. Even the occasional stories of Virgin Mary statues bringing healing are met with a great deal of skepticism and cynicism in our day. Scenes from *The Exorcist* come to mind for a good number of listeners when they encounter these New Testament stories of exorcism. The preacher needs to overcome these misconceptions.

For instance, in a sermon on the exorcism of the Gerasene demoniac (Mark 5:1-20), Kenneth Gibble begins, "The story of Mark's Gospel about the maniac in the graveyard is an odd one. It sounds strange to our twentieth-century ears to hear about demons and demon possession. Our first inclination is to dismiss the idea of demons as the superstition of a bygone era before people knew anything about mental illness."[41] Gibble goes on to say that the story may still have truths to speak, which we should not ignore out of our modern-day arrogance.

The preacher needs to clarify the role of miracle stories in the New Testament, showing that they are not intended to be proofs of Jesus' divinity or displays of his power. Instead, the preacher needs to point to the literary-critical aspects of these stories. Such a teaching might be as brief and simple as Leander Keck's explanation of the feeding of the multitudes (Mark 6:30-44):

> We have labeled it the story of the multiplication of the loaves and fishes, and tourist guides in the Holy Land will take you to the ruins of a church built on the exact place where it happened. But Mark is not as interested in the miraculous as we are; in fact he doesn't tell us what happened to the bread and fish. He does tell us what happened to people.[42]

Or the teaching might be as extended and intricate as Michael Hough's contextualization of Jesus' coming to the disciples on the water (Matthew 14:22-33):

> The sea, especially a storm at sea, conjured up for the Hebrew people visions of this original state of terror and chaos [as described in Genesis 1]. They were just not a seafaring nation, and the savage storms that rushed down upon the Sea of Galilee and the Mediterranean seemed to attack the very order of nature itself. They felt powerless. Tossed around by forces that they could neither predict nor control. This was the state of things before the intervention of God.[43]

In a sermon on the healing of blind Bartimaeus (Mark 10:46-52), Wayne Stacy explains Mark's arrangement of his materials in chapters 8-11:

> Mark carefully has Jesus tell his disciples on three different occasions that He would be delivered up into the hands of the pagans by the chief priests, and the scribes, and the elders, and that He would be tortured and finally put to death. And there's Peter, raising his hand, interrupting Jesus: "Uh, Lord, that's a nice speech, but I think you've dropped a page somewhere. That's not how it goes! The Messiah is a 'winner', not a 'loser'!" And Jesus says:

"Get behind me, Satan! You're not thinking like God thinks; that's the way people think! In God's Kingdom, Messiahs carry crosses, and so also do His followers!"

Three times He tells them; three times they don't get it! Portraying the disciples as being blind to the truth, both about the Christ and about themselves, Mark carefully frames this section on discipleship with two stories about blind men whom Jesus has to heal so they can see things clearly, which is, of course, a parable of what He is trying to do with the disciples too![44]

For most listeners the historical aspect of the text is uppermost in their minds. These literary-critical emphases may be entirely new, and some explanation will probably be necessary. Once the preacher has determined how to address these issues, the mood and the movement of the sermon will need to be considered.

Sermonic Mood

The initial mood of the miracle stories is conflict. People find themselves in the grip of demon possession, facing starvation without any provisions or battling against strong winds at sea. Modern churchgoers experience these same feelings of hopelessness and helplessness, only in different ways. Feelings are common experiences, and the sermon needs to help listeners get in touch with these feelings.

If the sermon is to move beyond approaching the text propositionally (merely teaching its lessons), these feelings of hopelessness must be re-presented and experienced. As Wire notes, miracle stories are affirmative statements, not questions or commands. These stories are truly good news, the kind of news that must be experienced.[45]

The American Bible Society has sought to re-present that experience in a video on the healing of the Gerasene demoniac in Mark 5. This multimedia presentation, entitled "Out of the Tombs," is something of an MTV approach to the Bible.

Its appeal is primarily to the younger generation, but its power can be felt by anyone. The video comes with a discussion guide, and it can be used in any number of settings. The guide helps teach the text, but the video helps viewers experience the text. It is must viewing for any preacher wishing to understand how stories *do* something to us as well as *say* something to us.

In Kenneth Gibble's sermon on this same text, he seeks to remind us of the evil in all of us that may need to be exorcised:

> And there is one other thing we may hope for: that God, in divine mercy, will help each of us stop projecting onto others our own evil, will deliver us from the unclean spirits that threaten to possess us—our greed, our hatred of self and others, our despair, our denial of God's love and power. Our hope is in the Lord, who waits to forgive our sin, to break the chains that bind us, to embrace us with the arms of a loving father, a tender-hearted mother.[46]

Delivering us from the evil in our society and communities might be an even better application. Walter Wink reminds us that the demoniac was his society's deviant, but that deviants tell us something about society. Wink offers an example in the story of Major Claude Eatherly. Eatherly was the navigator on Enola Gay, the plane that dropped the atom bomb on Hiroshima. He was a national hero who helped to end World War II. But that's not how his story goes, not finally. The guilt he experienced became overwhelming. Nearly twenty years later he began to commit a series of petty crimes, apparently for the sole purpose of getting arrested and having us as a nation face up to what he *and* we had done in 1945. But no one paid attention. The so-called experts testified that he should be put away in a mental institution on the grounds of "lunacy." And so he was put away, just like the man among the tombs. Sometimes our demons are corporate.[47]

Random acts of violence also cause us to reflect on evil

today. Anyone who boards an airplane must give some thought to terrorism. Re-creating feelings of hopelessness among listeners is not very hard to do.

An even bigger challenge is presented by the mood swing that takes place within miracle stories. The initial mood is conflict, but Jesus overcomes in the end. The sermon needs to end on a note of realistic optimism—optimism because of Jesus' power over evil, but realistic optimism because of the eschatological nature of ultimate victory. The final victory is not yet realized. Of course, the different types of miracle stories require different moods. In *petition stories* listeners should be encouraged to pursue after righteousness and wholeness.

Sermons from *provision stories* must capture the fairy-talelike quality of Jesus' providing against all odds.[48] There is a wonderful scene near the end of the movie *A Little Princess* in which food has been "miraculously" provided and the servant girl says, "Oh, my Lord." Never have truer words been spoken. The sermon must end by showing how God has provided our needs. Prior to that ending, however, the sermon must capture the overwhelming sense of inadequacy that all of us have felt. Wayne Stacy, in a sermon on Matthew's account of the feeding of the five thousand entitled "So Little . . . So Much," identifies our inadequacies poignantly:

> Last week, U.N. troops in Sarajevo entered a hospital which had been vacated by the doctors and nurses in anticipation of the advance of the Serbian troops and found there 200 children, babies and toddlers, hungry, dirty, frightened, alone. Oh, they hadn't been alone the whole time! There was evidence that Serbian troops had indeed been there. You see, they had blown open the safe in the hospital and with the cash they found there purchased Vodka and had had a party. The U.N. troops found empty Vodka bottles lying everywhere while children wandered the halls helpless and frightened.

[Did] anybody watch that and not feel just a little impo-
tent, overwhelmed, outgunned? Caught in the crossfire
between massive needs and personal inadequacy, we
ask: "What am I doing here?" So much to do . . . so little
with which to do it, we feel overwhelmed.[49]

The sermon that is based on a *rescue story* needs to address
natural disasters, not human acts. Today we have all sorts of
technological devices that enable us to subdue nature's powers. We predict and measure earthquakes. We track hurri-
canes in order to alert the residents of coastal areas. These
attempts testify to our desire to control nature. But if you
have ever been the victim of a natural disaster, you know the
feeling of hopelessness that it causes. The sermon must initially arouse those same feelings, and then go on to evoke
the sense of security that comes from knowing Jesus' power
over nature.

Having identified the mood(s) of a miracle story, the
preacher then needs to consider the movement of the text to
determine its possible influence on the sermon's structure.

Sermonic Movement

Although a great deal of variety exists in the structures and
plot developments of the various miracle stories, they all
share one thing in common: they are stories. The preacher
needs to take advantage of the narrative possibilities af-
forded in dealing with these texts.

Retelling a miracle story will go a long way toward helping listeners experience the power of the text. Such a retelling
may be sketchy or it may be detailed. Preaching from Mark's
account of Jesus' rescuing the disciples at sea (Mark 4:35-41),
Jim Scarborough begins to retell the story in his own words:

I can see the disciples now, rowing toward the shore as
if there were no tomorrow and, at the same time, bailing
water out of the boat just as fast as they could. Certainly
they did not want to rouse the teacher, because they

knew how tired he was. They probably also felt the need to handle the situation by themselves. I mean, after all, they *were* grown men, several of whom had been fishermen on this very same sea that now threatened to swallow them up. But, finally, having exhausted their own resources and ingenuity, their fear overcame them, and they awoke Jesus.[50]

Contemporary stories can also be powerful. William Hethcock blends a retelling of Bartimaeus's healing with contemporary material. After noting the spiritual blindness of the crowd that tried to silence the blind beggar and the sight that Bartimaeus found, the preacher then adds:

> Hurricane Joan has ripped through Central America with winds of up to 125 miles per hour. Mudslides have engulfed wooden huts, people have died in their homes, and tens of thousands of homes have been destroyed. Whole villages in Nicaragua have been destroyed. The death toll has yet to be calculated. The pain of the disaster and the rebuilding will continue years after we finish reading about it here. When we are healed of our blindness, things like that can't be easily dismissed. When our blindness is healed, we see things we don't want to see.[51]

Eugene Lowry discusses in detail four different strategies for dealing with narratives, from simply retelling the biblical story to more elaborate patterns that weave together the biblical story and a contemporary story (or stories).[52] As an example of responsible preaching from a miracle story we will look at a sermon by Eugene Lowry, who teaches preaching at Saint Paul School of Theology.[53] The sermon is reproduced here in its original poetic format.

"Cries from the Graveyard: A Sermon"

by Eugene L. Lowry

Mark 5:1-19

(Please read this sermon aloud.)
It was an ordinary little gentile village by the lake's edge . . .
    indistinguishable from a dozen other little gentile
    villages, perhaps . . .
        except for at least one thing.

If you were to spend the night there, it's quite possible you
would lose some sleep.

    You would be awakened in the middle of the night with
    some awful cries and moans from some undisclosed
    source . . .
    cries that sounded half human, half like a wild animal.

Were you to inquire the next morning someone would tell
you about that crazy man in town.

*[Lowry begins with a brief retelling, setting the scene. Interestingly
enough, he includes his hearers in the story.]*

    He was beside himself,
        not in control of his faculties.

        In fact, folks said that he had unclean spirits.
        He had a demon.

They had tried to chain him up,
    but he was not only wild, but very strong . . .
        and would simply break the bonds . . .
        and continue to moan, and shriek and cry.

The town and the crazy man had developed a kind of
uneasy truce—that is, he would stay out there in the
graveyard among the tombs . . .

   and they would stay in town.

He wasn't fit to be among the living . . .
and so he lived among the dead.

That's the way it was.

Before we become too critical of the way they handled their
   social problems, we need to remember,
      after all, he was crazy.

Every now and then they could get a glimpse of him and
his bruises.

   Sometimes he was bleeding from having pushed himself
   against the edges of the rocks.

      Remember, in those days they didn't have any
         psychiatrists to help out.
            They didn't have any mental health societies.
            They didn't even have any United Way.
      So, we ought not to criticize too much.

*[Lowry continues to retell the biblical story, and then he begins to
address our contemporary aversions to the story.]*

Into this scene comes Jesus.

Now, we wonder how it was that the man knew it was
Jesus.

   Had he perhaps been closer into town than they had
      thought, and had overheard some conversations
      about the coming of Jesus?
         We don't even know that the community knew
         that Jesus was coming.

All we know was that this little boat appeared,
   and Jesus and a couple friends came in toward the shore.

As Jesus was getting out of the boat,
    this crazy man ran out,
        and he fell down in front of Jesus.

The text says he worshipped Jesus . . .
    looked up into his eyes and said:
        "What do you have to do with me?"
            "Jesus, son of the most high God, Do not
            torment me!"

Do you feel that ambivalence?

He is attracted to Jesus, and yet repulsed at the same time.

He wants desperately to be whole, to be sane—
    and also he wants not to have anybody tamper with the
    way things are.
                    You may call that crazy.

                        I call it familiar.

I remember one time when I had this horrible cold.

I was sick . . . and couldn't seem to get better with home
remedies,
    so I called my doctor.
        He wasn't the Great Physician, you understand, but he
        was pretty good . . .
            and patients knew the worship order quite well.

I mean, you walk into the office and the receptionist says:
    "Please be seated." That's the call to worship.

Then you wait for 45 minutes . . .
call them moments of meditation.

Then you go in and you get the word.

    On the way out you present your tithes and offerings.
        It's an act of worship.

Well, I went to my doctor. He gave me the word all right.
    He said: "You can't fight off any infection;

you don't eat anything but sugar.
Don't you know those bugs like sugar just
as much as you do? I'm taking you off all those
cookies and all those soft drinks you live on."
You know what I said to him?
I said: "Do not torment me!"

I wanted to get well, of course, but, but . . . well you know.

[Again, after resuming his retelling of the text, Lowry offers a contemporary analogy. He will return to this analogy later.]

Jesus asked: "What's your name?"

The man's answer is classic.

He said: "My name is Legion."

A legion? Why, a legion is a Roman army group
numbering 6,000 soldiers.

"My name is Legion." Get it?

To paraphrase: "I feel like 6,000 soldiers inside me . . .
sometimes they all march left,
sometimes right . . .
sometimes in all different directions.
I'm pulled one way, then another.
There's an army inside me, and I think I'm losing the war."

Crazy? . . .

Really familiar.

And we cry out. Cry out for unity, for integrity, for
wholeness.
We all would like to be one.

[Lowry continues to weave our stories into the biblical story. Listeners begin to identify the evil in themselves that needs attention.]

Well, Jesus gets to visiting with the demons.
I never quite understood this part of the story.

The text says they got to conversing . . .
and some of us may just begin wondering how
strange for folks in the days of Jesus to believe
in demons.

In case we presume to be "above" this sort of notion,
perhaps we ought to be reminded that we all talk about
having viruses.
Viruses?
What's a virus, anyway? Does anybody know?
Is it animal, mineral, vegetable?
Have you seen one lately?

What we mean when we speak of viruses, is that
something has hold of us—quite beyond our control.

Perhaps someday, another group of people will
look back on our era and exclaim with disbelief:
"You know what?
They believed in viruses."

Yes, we do. Well, they believed in demons—
which is to say, the man was out of his mind.
One might say: "possessed."
Well, yes they did.

*[Lowry now returns to the analogy employed earlier. He indicates
how demon possession in the New Testament differs from our
misconceptions.]*

About the time it becomes clear that because of Jesus, the
demons are going to take leave of the man,
the poor fellow yells out:

"Don't send them too far . . . don't send them too far!"

There's that ambivalence, again.

The demons seemed to like the idea of moving on to the pigs
close by, who presently are minding their own business.

They attach themselves to the pigs, some 2,000 pigs . . .

which figures out to be three demons per pig.

And the pigs get frightened with all those
demons, and go rushing down the steep
embankment into the sea, and are
all drowned.

The text says that word reached town very shortly of what
had happened.

I have a hunch that it reached town immediately.

I don't understand anything about pigs, you understand,
except that we have a little place in the country.
We call it a ranch.
The farmer next to us calls it a plot.

The farmer's house is about a quarter of a mile away,
and right next to his house is the feed lot for
his pigs.

Every now and then one of his pigs gets hurt
or upset or something.
I don't know exactly what goes on over there,
but I have learned the meaning of the phrase about
"squealing like a pig."
I bet folks can hear his pigs in the
next county.

Can you imagine what 2,000 squealing pigs sounded like
as they rushed down into the sea?

*[In order to help listeners identify with the sheer violence of the
exorcism, Lowry once again suspends the biblical story to offer an
analogy.]*

Well, I don't think they had to send a messenger
into town.

That would have been rather redundant,
don't you think?

Everybody in town came right out to find the cause of the
commotion.
     And there they found the demoniac.

          Sitting there,
                    clothed and in his right mind.

                    Think of that.

     Standing beside him was Jesus.

Can you imagine how excited they must have been?

     How utterly delighted?

          How joyful to discover this man who had been such a
          problem to them for so long was now whole?

          He was well again—thank God.

No they didn't.

Turning to Jesus, whose powerful presence caused this
miracle,
     they said:
          "Would you please leave our neighborhood?"

          It does have a familiar ring down through the
          centuries, doesn't it?

     You would think they would have given him the key to
     the city.
          Instead they suggest a bus ticket out of town.

               "Get out."

But, why?

     Why this kind of response, anyway?

          Is it because they had grown all too comfortable with

handling their social problems a particular way, and didn't
want the routine altered?
  "We've always done it this way."

Or, was it that they didn't trust the healing?
  "Just wait until tonight. He looks just fine all
    dressed up now—but wait 'til you hear him
    in the middle of the night!"

Well, these possible reasons do have a ring of plausibility
to them.

  But, they won't do . . .
    too small for the reaction to Jesus.

The reason the folks told Jesus to leave is simple.

  Very simple.

  You see, *they owned the pigs.*

That's right. They owned the pigs—some 2,000 of them
now drowned in the lake.

  And a bit of biblical research will back it up.
    The town's people owned the pigs and hired the
    herdsmen.
      It was the herdsmen who went in to report
      on the status of the flock—
        and reported to the owners what had happened.

I suppose we should have suspected it all along.

  Nothing too strange here.

  Any time healing takes place,
    somebody is going to pay a price—
      one way or another.

  Any time any person or group gets a freedom they never
  had before, somebody else loses some pigs.

    One person's freedom generally means somebody

else's loss of privilege.

Yes, we do like people "in their place."

You can't understand South Africa without understanding
the principle here.
One needs only to find out who owns the pigs.

Do we find our country's official policy toward Central
America strange and confused?
Well, who owns the pigs there, anyway?

On the other hand, it is amazing how
compassionate and just our foreign policy is
toward deprived, hungry and powerless people the
world over—

that is, when somebody else's pigs are at stake.

*[A series of social justice issues are cited, helping listeners to
identify today's evils.]*

Just outside Jackson, Missouri, and right on the banks of
the Mississippi, there is a park called the Trail of Tears
State Park.
Lovely place.

In the middle of the park is a monument with this
inscription:
"Here lies Princess Otaka, daughter of Chief
Bushyhead. One of several hundred Cherokee
Indians who died in the winter crossing of the
Mississippi River in the hard winter of 1838,
in the forced march from Georgia to Tennessee
and the Carolinas to the territory now known as
Oklahoma."

When I read that inscription a number of years ago, I drew
a blank.

I had never been told of the Trail of Tears when I studied
American history in school.

I did not know then how it was that thousands of
Cherokee Indians were forced to leave land white
folks wanted.

I did not know then that the Cherokee Nation—
with its code of law and constitution—
was known as one of the most respected civilized
states in the world.

I did not know then that their Chief of State had been all
over the world visiting with other heads of state.

I did not know then that when their Chief corresponded
with the President of the United States—
pleading for justice and protection—
that his letters utilizing English as a second
language exhibited a better command of the English
language than those written by the President.

I did not know then that they won their case for protection
in the Supreme Court of the United States—
a victory mocked by President Andrew Jackson
with the words:
"Well, let them enforce it."

I did not then know these things.

All I knew about the Cherokee Nation, was that on
several trips during my childhood,
I had been driven through reservations in
Oklahoma,

and saw people . . .
mute . . .
detached . . .
sitting with a distant
look in their eyes.

It was like a graveyard . . . it *was* a graveyard . . . of
smashed hopes, stolen dreams and broken promises.

They had met their match, all right . . . that once proud
Cherokee Nation.

> They had run up against some white folks who owned
> all the pigs.

And now upon reflection I can't help but wonder . . .
Did we chain them up on the reservation because they had
a demon . . .

> or did they get the demon because we tied them up
> on the reservation?

*[A lengthy example from history is cited, one that poignantly
describes the evil inherent within us as a nation, not just as
individuals. The searching question at the end of the story directly
confronts his listeners.]*

Whenever Jesus comes to any town,
the first folks to meet him are not the members of the
welcoming team from the Chamber of Commerce.

The first folks to meet Jesus will come running from out
of the tombs . . .
the ones called crazy . . .
the ones tied in chains, one way or another.

Certainly, they are not the only ones in town who need the
transforming power of Jesus.

> Somehow, they are the quickest to know their need.

When Jesus left that village, the man asked to go with him,
but Jesus said

> "No, go back to your friends."

> Back to your "friends"?
> What friends?

> He didn't have any friends—
> except the *new* kind which can be
> bonded among former "chain-*ers*" and

"chain-*ees*,"

both freed by Jesus' visit.

"Go back to your friends,

and tell the world what the Lord has done."

Yes, indeed, tell the world.

But, sometimes it is hard for me to tell the world,

because my ears are still being bombarded . . .

ringing with cries from the night . . .
and from squeals in the day.

And I know . . .

I know . . . I have some deciding to do.

[Lowry returns to the biblical story and having concluded it, once again appeals to his listeners and how they will act in regard to evil.]

Exercises

Answer the following eight questions for the miracle story in each passage: Matthew 9:2-8; Mark 6:45-52; John 2:1-11.

1. What type of miracle story does this passage relate: exorcism, controversy, petition, provision, rescue, or epiphany?

2. What sort of mood does the miracle story suggest? What musical instruments might best accompany the text? What colors and/or textures does the text suggest?

3. What is the text saying? What lesson does the miracle story convey?

4. What facets of this miracle story need to be explained?

5. What is the text doing? What is the central conflict within the story? How does Jesus prevail over the tension?

6. How could the conflict be re-presented in contemporary terms? How could Jesus' victory be re-presented?

7. Is elaborate detail needed in retelling the story, or would a sketchy approach suffice? How would the familiarity of the story affect your decision?

8. How could the sermon say and do what the text is saying and doing? What contemporary stories and/or materials could be used in preaching this passage?

Sermon Resources

American Bible Society, "Out of the Tombs" [Mark 5:1-20], a multimedia translation on videocassette, 1991. Although this is not a sermon in the more traditional sense of the word, it vividly re-presents the healing of the Gerasene demoniac so that the power of the story is felt.

William Sloane Coffin, "Sail On, O Ship of State" [Matthew 14:22-33], in Donald K. McKim, *The Bible in Theology and Preaching* (Abingdon, 1994), pp. 48-51. Based on a rescue story, this article addresses the literal aspects of creation over which Jesus reigns. Very prophetic.

Penelope Duckworth, "Who Touched Me?" [Mark 5:22-24, 35b-43], in *Pulpit Digest* (May/June 1992): 39-41. This treatment of a petition story clearly identifies the need for listeners to seek a miracle.

John R. Fry, "Blindness" [Mark 10:46-52], in *A Chorus of Witnesses*, ed. Thomas G. Long and Cornelius Plantinga Jr. (Eerdmans, 1994), pp. 139-45. This sermon begins by addressing the tension modern listeners perceive with respect to the ancient miracle story, then proceeds to retell the story in vivid detail. Preached to an inner-city congregation in Chicago, it ends with a frank discussion of the civil rights movement.

Kenneth L. Gibble, "Graveyard Maniac" [Mark 5:1-20], in *Pulpit Digest* (September/October 1990): 35-39. Openly addresses the strangeness of exorcism stories for modern persons, then blends together a sketchy retelling and elaborate discussion of contemporary implications of the text. Also identifies by name some of the evils of our day.

William Hethcock, "That We May Receive Our Sight" [Mark 10:46-52], in *Best Sermons 3*, ed. James W. Cox (Harper and Row, 1990), pp. 98-102. Of particular interest is the literary critical treatment of the story, along with the contemporary examples that it provides (see p. 101).

Michael Hough, "For Those Who Trust in God" [Matthew 14:22-33], in *Best Sermons 5*, ed. James W. Cox (HarperCollins, 1992), pp. 86-92. Does a good job of explaining the ancient mindset in respect to rescue stories. Literary critical teaching of the story also discussed.

Leander E. Keck, "Limited Resources, Unlimited Possibilities" [Mark 6:30-44], in Eugene L. Lowry, *How to Preach a Parable* (Abingdon, 1989), pp. 80-87. Blends implications of the story for ancient and modern times. Running commentary by Lowry in the pages that follow (pp. 88-103).

Eugene L. Lowry, "Cries from the Graveyard: A Sermon" [Mark 5:1-19], in *Daemonic Imagination*, ed. Robert Detweiler and William G. Doty (Scholars Press, 1990), pp. 27-39. Complete sermon included in this chapter.

Jim Scarborough, "What to Do When the Boat Is Sinking" [Mark 4:35-41], in *Pulpit Digest* (July/August 1992): 35-38.

Although some allegorical comparisons are drawn between the storm in the passage and the storms of our lives, it does a good job of retelling the miracle story and teaching its theological lessons.

Chapter 8

Johannine Discourse: The Lengthy Speeches of Jesus

Preachers who are familiar with the lectionary will recall that it consists of a three-year cycle (A, B, and C). The Gospel readings in year A are taken primarily from Matthew, those in year B from Mark, and those in year C from Luke. Preachers not familiar with the lectionary will probably be quick to ask, "What happened to John?"

Although John's Gospel does not have its own year in the lectionary, a substantial number of readings from John are included throughout the year, especially during Lent. Of course, this could be read in two different ways. So could John's Gospel. The Fourth Gospel is certainly the most enigmatic of the Gospel accounts. It is simultaneously familiar and puzzling. Familiar in that even in this postmodern world lots of people can quote John 3:16. Most years that verse shows up on posters behind home plate in the World Series. Puzzling in that the Gospel's authorship remains a mystery. John's Gospel includes many familiar scenes: the wedding at Cana, Nicodemus's visit with Jesus, Jesus' visit with the Samaritan woman, and the raising of Lazarus. Yet this Gospel differs remarkably from the other three accounts of Jesus' life and ministry.[1] Add to these considerations the sometimes overwhelming length of Johannine texts, and it is no wonder that many preachers prefer the Synoptics.[2] The story of the man born blind in John 9 occupies forty-one verses. Just reading such a lengthy text can offer a real challenge in a worship service.

These lengthy segments typically consist of a speech by Jesus. To further complicate matters, the connection between the speech and the story context is not always clear.[3] For instance, in John 14:22-23 we read, "Judas (not Iscariot) said to him, 'Lord, how is it that you will reveal yourself to us, and not to the world?' Jesus answered him, 'Those who love me will keep my word . . .'" I stop with those words because Jesus' response occupies the next fifty-two verses, uninterrupted. We are tempted to think that perhaps Judas was sorry he asked, but only because Johannine discourse is so foreign to us. Before we think about how to preach from this form, we must first understand it better. What is it, and how does it work?

What Is the Text Saying?

Simply put, Johannine discourse consists of lengthy monologues by Jesus, which often arise out of dialogue with another person. The fifty-two-verse monologue in John 14 is one example. Jesus' conversation with Nicodemus is another. The conversation begins with a discussion of Jesus as having come from God, moves to a misunderstanding about second birth, and finally has Nicodemus ask, "How can these things be?" The format then switches from dialogue to monologue without warning. Nicodemus never gets in another word. The narrative does not even mention him again until chapter 7, and then in a different context.[4] Thus a dialogue in John 3 ends in a monologue.

Johannine discourse occurs in different forms. Besides dialogue leading to monologue, there is *pure monologue,* like the one in John 5:19-47 in which Jesus discusses his authority and those who witness to his identity. The monologue fits logically enough within the context, but to whom is Jesus speaking? Apparently the healing just prior to this "serves primarily to launch a revelation discourse."[5] Other forms include *monologue framed by dialogue* (John 16:16-30); *dramatic dialogue* (like the one with the Samaritan woman in John 4); and about eight short *controversy dialogues* (for example, John 7:14-24).[6]

So whereas the narrative sections in the Synoptic Gospels are composed of several smaller vignettes, the narratives in John serve mainly as a "framework" for series of discourses.[7] The Evangelist masterfully intertwines story and theological reflection, sometimes blurring the lines altogether. As a result, a reading of the Fourth Gospel cannot be rushed.[8]

One of the chief reasons for reading the Fourth Gospel slowly and thoughtfully is its poetic nature, which relates directly to the devices that the Evangelist employs. (Recall that form-sensitive preaching pays attention to form and literary devices.) Johannine scholars Rudolf Schnackenburg and Raymond Brown note the Gospel's poetic traits. In keeping with the poetry of the first-century world, Johannine poetry uses some parallelism, but even more significantly, rhythm. Theories of accentual beats have been proposed over the years.[9]

In addition to its use of poetic devices, John's Gospel is poetic the way a Flannery O'Connor short story or *The Brothers Karamazov* is.[10] Even the prose sections say more than initially meets the eye. Alan Culpepper, in his seminal work on the literary nature of John's Gospel, notes its artistry and challenges the notion of the Gospel as pure history. We do not read the Fourth Gospel to discover what happened sequentially in the life of Jesus. The Fourth Gospel (as well as the Synoptics) is not a biography of Jesus. Rather, it tells stories about Jesus. It was written to specific communities facing specific issues. Culpepper describes John's Gospel as a "literary creation of the evangelist," which challenges readers with a new way of looking at their world, through the eyes of the Evangelist and ultimately, through the eyes of Jesus.[11] The writer of John's Gospel is a poet-theologian, not a historian.

John's Gospel is extremely hard to follow chronologically and geographically, but the stories are strung together masterfully. For instance, the Evangelist strategically places the story of the Samaritan woman after the Nicodemus account. "Nicodemus" is a distinguished name. The Samaritan's name is not even supplied. He is Jewish. She is Samaritan. He is male. She is female. He is a ruler. She is fetching water. He is a Pharisee. She has been abandoned in five relationships.[12] He is honored. She is shamed. Yet it is the woman that Jesus seeks out. Jesus starts the conversation. In chapter 3 Jesus welcomes Nicodemus. In chapter 4 Jesus decides to visit with this woman. What a wonderfully poetic way of telling the stories!

The writer employs a variety of techniques in telling the stories, including literary devices such as symbols (for example, light, water, and bread[13]); signs (for example, turning water into wine and healing a blind man[14]); riddles (or figures of speech[15]); irony; and double entendres (or meanings). Irony and double entendre have been the focus of recent Johannine scholarship, and we will consider them in some detail.

John's Gospel displays numerous misunderstandings that occur on the part of those who speak with Jesus, usually through a brilliant use of irony and/or double meaning. Culpepper notes a fairly consistent threefold pattern: (1) Jesus says something that is ambiguous or metaphorical or that includes a double meaning; (2) the person in dialogue responds literally or with a question that demonstrates misunderstanding; (3) Jesus then explains himself.[16]

The use of double meanings in Jesus' speech is harder for modern readers to catch than the irony[17] because these wordplays typically occur in the Greek. The Nicodemus text is a classic example. Jesus speaks of the necessity of being "born from above," while Nicodemus interprets Jesus as referring to being "born again." One Greek term is used in both expressions, and it can be translated either way. Fortunately, the New Revised Standard Version has clarified this point in its translation. The Nicodemus text also plays with the words "Spirit" and "wind," which are identical in Greek.

Perhaps the best-known of the literary devices used in John's Gospel is irony. Paul Duke refers to Johannine irony as a kind of "fellowship" between the author and the reader. "Together they watch, wink, and smile, because together they share the perspective that blinded characters and perhaps less adept observers do not share."[18] For example, in John 4 we are given the story of Jesus' conversation with the Samaritan woman at the well. It becomes obvious to us as readers (or at least it is supposed to be obvious) that when Jesus talks of giving her living water, he is not referring to the potable liquid. The woman, however, does not seem to catch his drift. She respectfully points out, "Sir, you have no bucket, and the well is deep."

We chuckle because we are supposed to. Johannine irony is downright funny. The way it works, however, is highly sophisticated. It is "two-storied."[19] Jesus speaks on a higher plane than the persons with whom he dialogues. They do not get it, but we are supposed to if we are astute. These ironies are rarely explained and thus remain covert.[20] Why they remain hidden relates directly to *how* irony and the other rhetorical devices in John's Gospel work.

What Is the Text Doing?

Like the Synoptic parables, the symbols and ironies in the Fourth Gospel can conceal great truths, as well as reveal them.[21] Culpepper notes that the "most obvious function" of the recurrent misunderstandings in John help "to enforce a marked distinction between 'insiders' and 'outsiders.'"[22] The reader has to pay attention in order to catch the Evangelist's drift. Notice that the focus here is on the readers, not the original, historical context. Whatever misunderstandings happened during Jesus' ministry happened; they are history. John does not write to record history, but to make sure that his readers do not misunderstand.

Johannine scholars have speculated for some time that much of the Fourth Gospel may have originated as sermons in John's community.[23] Johannine discourse is not about a Jesus who gets carried away in conversation, rambling on while someone looks on confusedly. Regarding the Nicodemus story, for instance, scholars have often wondered where the "red letters" should end. Perhaps it is the Evangelist who begins preaching through Jesus' extended speech in John 3.

But while the "most obvious function" of Johannine misunderstandings is to distinguish insiders from outsiders, Culpepper believes that their "most significant function" is "to teach readers how to read the gospel." Readers who do not learn become like the Jews described in John's Gospel who did not comprehend the ministry or the identity of Jesus.[24] As astute readers, we begin to see the true meaning of Jesus' words and thus become insiders as we read, while those who rejected (past tense) and do reject (present tense) Jesus remain outsiders.[25]

The Evangelist does this by means of what literary critics call "implicit commentary." It is "commentary" in that its purpose is to help readers see what the characters apparently do not see. It is "implicit" in that it allows readers who are not paying close attention to miss it.[26]

The fact that these enigmatic features of the Fourth Gospel are intended for thoughtful readers does not mean, however, that reading John is solely a mental exercise intended only for intellectual giants. The major effect of Johannine imagery and vagueness is poetic. "It moves not just the mind with a new idea but evokes the response of the whole person through the evangelist's major weapon, language."[27] The poetry is "sensitive," conjuring up a "wealth of feelings and associations."[28] The major effect of Johannine poetry is touching our capacity for affective response.

So how do we preach such poetry? How do we compose sermons that do more than just talk about John's vagueness? Are there ways to produce the same impact on our listeners? These questions bring us to the third element of sermon composition.

How Can the Sermon Say and Do the Same?

In poetry, mood and movement are both crucial. The poetic nature of Johannine literature is no exception, though mood appears to be more important. Let us look at both of these areas.

Sermonic Mood

One obvious yet useful suggestion for capturing the poetic mood of a sermon in John's Gospel is to read the text well. Johannine texts are lengthy, and we may tend to hurry through them to avoid boring anyone, the preacher included. What a loss! For example, Johannine irony is comical, and this comedy can be released in the reading of the text. I once heard a former colleague of mine read the entire ninth chapter of John's Gospel so well I was not sure I needed to preach it afterward. She captured the mood, and the congregation actually laughed aloud at the irony.

As for the sermon itself, Fred Craddock has pointed out that one clear advantage to preaching from John is that we are preaching from a preacher's material. The Evangelist models for us what it means to tell the story of Jesus to another generation without getting in the way.[29] If the poetry is to remain poetry, the sermon and the preacher cannot get in the way either. Let me explain.

Frequently material from the Gospel of John is explained to assist the reader, but these asides are always brief and never interrupt the flow of the story. For instance, in Jesus' conversation with the Samaritan woman, the Evangelist sticks his head out through the curtain just for a moment: "The Samaritan woman said to him, 'How is it that you, a Jew, ask a drink of me, a woman of Samaria?' (Jews do not share things in common with Samaritans.)" The writer supplies us with an important piece of information, but not for the sake of information alone. The narrative asides are more about function than content.[30] They serve as guides to the readers.

Perhaps we can learn from John at this point. Preaching from the Johannine discourse passages frequently involves materials and ideas foreign to our listeners. We may need to explain certain items that characterize the text, but without interrupting the flow and the mood of the sermon. Richard Lischer, in a sermon on the man born blind in John 9, begins by briefly retelling the story. He interrupts the story momentarily to tell us something important about the passage: "In the Evangelist's story, the cure itself takes exactly two verses; the controversy surrounding the cure takes thirty-nine verses, and that, as Paul Harvey would say, is the rest of the story."[31]

Of course, the preacher might find it helpful to look for modern parallels and dwell for a few moments on such an analogy. Eugene Lowry, for instance, in a sermon on Nicodemus wants his listeners to catch the lack of communication present, even in the greetings exchanged between Jesus and Nicodemus:

And I must say I am a bit shocked at Jesus.
    Wouldn't you expect Jesus to respond to Nicodemus's compliment with at least a gracious "Well, thank-you"?
    I mean, the minister is greeted by a parishioner on a Sunday morning with, "Preacher, you must have been

inspired today, for nobody can preach the way you preached except God be with them."

I hope the preacher will respond, "Well, thank you so much," or, at least, "How long did it take to figure that out?"

I presume the preacher will not respond with, "Well it *is* almost two hundred miles from Des Moines to Kansas City"—which is the truth of course—but what does that have to do with the previous comment?[32]

Lowry's technique, for which he is well known, is what he calls "suspending the story."[33] He proposes that preachers use it when working through a text that brings us face-to-face with a problem. Perhaps the listeners catch the misunderstandings between Jesus and Nicodemus. Perhaps they do not. In either case, Lowry helps point out the initial misunderstanding in the text. Such suspension also allows the preacher to move from engagement with the text to engagement with the listeners, something the writer of John's Gospel does quite well also.[34]

Sometimes the preacher simply needs to explain double meanings that are not apparent in many of our English translations. When preaching from a Johannine passage that contains such double meanings, I have frequently interrupted the narrative with an explanation:

You can't really catch it in our English translations, but John loves wordplays. He likes puns. He's the kind of guy who would have enjoyed working through the daily crossword puzzle in the newspaper. In this case, he uses one word to mean two different things . . .

One final suggestion relates to the ambiguities of John's Gospel. Some have advised us to take our cues from the texts themselves. Since John's discourses are ironic and puzzling, our sermons should be too, in a sense.[35] This does not mean that our sermons should send our listeners home after church with no idea as to what the whole thing was about. The idea is to respect the mystery within the text itself, resisting an urge to explain it all away.[36] Even if John's Gospel was intended for insiders, should our sermons be also? (This idea clearly goes against contemporary "seeker" movements in worship and preaching where "outsiders" are supposed to feel like "insiders."[37])

Robert Kysar tells about an abstract painting of the crucifixion that hangs in his office. A first-time viewer typically cannot make it out, and so he has to explain how to see it. About halfway into his explanation the visitor typically blurts out, "Oh, yes, I see it now."[38] Kysar's story points out not only his role as guide but the burden placed on the viewer as well. The viewer must be interested enough to ask and to keep looking. In John's Gospel we must remain open to the truth,[39] to be sure, and yet true insight into Jesus' higher meanings comes only by grace, as "a gift to be granted" by God.[40]

Even the most avant-garde preachers would admit to feeling a bit squeamish about leaving some things unsaid in a given sermon. At least some of us like everything to be nailed down. The problem is that even when we do nail things down in sermons, the wind (or is it the Spirit?) has a way of blowing them around and disturbing our neat little pronouncements.

So how do we communicate the implicit stories of John to people living in our own day? Kysar points out that what the Evangelist says initially on one level also has a higher meaning. He goes on to suggest that we use stories from everyday life that can do the same, that is, bring together the physical and the spiritual dimensions of our existence. As an example, let me share a story that I have used.

In a sermon on John 3 in which I had earlier explained the wordplays of "from above"/"again" and "Spirit"/"wind," I closed with a story that I felt not only fit the sermon but also preserved some of the mystery:

I have some friends who used to live in Kansas City—
Eric and Felecia Douglass. She's a minister, one of my
former students, and he's a physician. They live in
North Carolina now. A couple of years ago he was diag-
nosed with cancer, a rare type that usually attacks people twice his age. They said he only had a short time to
live. He went into depression, even some fits of rage.
The medicine was partly to blame, but I suppose anybody could be expected to react like that. But lately he's
feeling pretty well.

Anyway, they called me a while back. Actually, she did.
She said they wanted to give us some money to help with
our kids' college funds. I was overwhelmed. What do you
say? She said, "Mike, you have to take this money." She
went on to tell me that it was Eric's idea. She said, "All of
a sudden, he's become very generous."

Don't misunderstand; this man has never been selfish.
In fact, he's a kind and gentle man. A good Christian. A
very bright and articulate person. But now, she said, he's
become incredibly generous. He volunteered to do eye
exams at the elementary school, and he decided to give
money to several different causes.

As I hung up the phone, it occurred to me that my doctor
friend, an anesthesiologist, who has also delivered his
share of babies, may have just been born himself, from
above . . . again.

It's hard to say what exactly happened to cause the
change. But I have visited their home in North Carolina. I
stayed in their guest room one December. I arrived late,
and we stayed up talking into the night. As I got into bed,
I remember being struck by the beauty of the scenery
outside. There was a full moon that lit up that guest room
and the night sky. I could see those tall Carolina pines
outside as well.

But I also remember, as I drifted off to sleep, listening to
the wind blow. Who knows where that wind will blow
next?

Sermonic Movement

Johannine discourse is a unique literary form and certainly one that is foreign to modern readers of the Gospel. Thus the structural movement of these discourses may need to be explained to our listeners. Most churchgoers probably have not noticed that the dialogues in John's Gospel end in monologue. Pointing that out to them will be a revelation, though not necessarily one of religious significance. These are the kinds of things that excite us preachers, but not our listeners.

It may nevertheless be helpful to point out how Jesus' speeches function in the text. Most of our listeners will have had the experience of conversing with someone who used the conversation to launch into a monologue that left the other person behind. We can explain, by way of contrast, that these discourses function differently, showing how the Evangelist is preaching through these stories.

In a sermon on John 9 entitled "The Tragicomedy of the Gospel," Michael Fuhrman not only explains that the text may be based on a seven-scene play, he even shapes his sermon around these seven scenes.[41] It is important not to allow attention that is given to movement to violate the mood of the text and sermon.

Another example of attention to movement is Cindy Witt's sermon, "A Marriage Made in Heaven."[42] She begins by showing how certain forms of speech in our day condition us to expect certain things. For instance, if we begin with the words, "Once upon a time," we expect some kind of fictional story. She then shows how Israelites in the ancient world were familiar with betrothal stories, tales of young men meeting young maidens at wells and eventually marrying. Isaac and Rebekah is one Old Testament example. Witt then comes to the Gospel reading for the day, John 4, and lets the listeners begin to see a Jesus who comes to offer love, even a form of courtship, to a rejected Samaritan woman.

As with the other literary forms, it is always helpful to

consider one example in detail. The following sermon is by Barbara Brown Taylor, rector of Grace-Calvary Church in Clarkesville, Georgia.[43]

"I Am Who I Am"

by Barbara Brown Taylor

John 8:25

The eighth chapter of John does not do much for me. I like stories, not speeches. I like a passage with a plot, with characters, with a beginning and an end. I like something you can get hold of—something with boats in it, or bread, or birds of the air. But the Bible does not always give me what I like, and what it has given me this time is a really mean-spirited debate between Jesus and the Pharisees in the temple at Jerusalem.

For two whole pages they call each other names and question each other's sanity and dispute each other's parentage. It is not pleasant, and it is not even very clear. Most of it sounds like a course in advanced metaphysics, but I decided to stick with it because I believe that God never wastes my time or yours either. Whether we like what we get or whether we do not, God has promised to be present to us in it, and that is as true in life as it is in Scripture.

[The preacher begins by openly discussing the strangeness of John's speeches, not only the form but even the content of this one. At the same time she anticipates the hidden riches that are surely present.]

Our tendency is to pick and choose—to reject the parts of life we do not like and keep shopping for some we do. When God's gifts come wrapped in shiny paper and curled ribbons, we say, "Thank you very much," but when they arrive on our doorsteps held together with newspaper and barbed wire, most of us take out our magic markers and write "Return to Sender" on the box. But there is another way open to us. We can accept what we have been assigned and work with it—taking it apart piece by piece, if necessary, in order to discover the God inside.

What we have been assigned today is one more episode in Jesus' long controversy with the Pharisees about who he is. From our safe distance, it is easy to simplify any story with Pharisees in it by making them the bad guys, but they are just doing their job. They are the defenders of the faith; they are the religious authorities in charge of keeping holy things holy, and they do not like Jesus' type—especially the way John's gospel presents him. In John's gospel, Jesus says "I" a lot—I, I, I— "I am the bread of life" (6:35), "I am the good shepherd" (10:11), "I am the true vine" (15:1), "I am the way, and the truth, and the life. No one comes to the Father, except through me" (14:6).

[Now the preacher begins to acknowledge the context as well as Jesus' unique language in the Fourth gospel. She also allows us to begin to see the point that the Pharisees are making. This will be essential when we later deal with our own understanding of who Jesus is.]

Those are fairly outrageous claims for anyone to make, but for a Hebrew they are really unthinkable. For a Hebrew there is only *one* good shepherd, *one* true vine, *one* bread of life, and that is almighty God. Who does Jesus think he is? That is what the Pharisees want to know. He passes himself off as a believer in God, but that is not how he sounds. He sounds like a rival, one of those dangerously attractive preachers who get carried away by their own charisma and get the message all confused with the messenger.

[The preacher's brief allusions to a contemporary analogy, tele-vangelists, may help us, the listeners, begin to think differently about the Pharisees and this bizarre conversation.]

"I am the light of the world." That is the last thing Jesus said, the remark that brought the Pharisees charging after him like bulls to a red flag. But when they challenge him, things get worse, not better. "You are from below," Jesus tells them. "I am from above; you are of this world, I am not of this world . . . you will die in your sins unless you believe that I am he."

[Although the preacher does not point it out here in any detail, she has recognized the two levels of John.]

"Unless you believe that I am he." That is the way it reads in English, but in Greek there is no "he" on the end: "Unless you believe that I am." That is what Jesus really says, and it drives the Pharisees wild. They hear what he is up to; they hear the echo that he means them to hear. "I am," he says, and any Hebrew worth his salt remembers another voice that said, "I am who I am."

[Notice how the subtleties of Jesus' speech in John are pointed out to readers/listeners who would have missed it. We would have missed it, not because we are outsiders, but because we do not know Greek.]

It was the voice of almighty God, addressing Moses from the burning bush, making him the first being on earth to know the name of God. "Thus you shall say to the Israelites," God instructed him, "I AM has sent me to you" (Exod. 3:14). "I AM." The name of God. "You will die in your sins unless you believe that I am."

Can you see why the Pharisees get upset? Jesus is using God's name—*abusing* it, as far as they are concerned—but when they try to show him the error of his ways, he tells them *they* are the ones who are wrong, and if they do not believe he is who he says he is, then they will die in their sins. "Who are you?" they ask him, and you can almost hear the exasperation in their voices, but you can hear it in Jesus' reply as well: "Why do I speak to you at all?"

He does not answer the question. Did you notice that? "Who are you?" hangs in the air, and for many of us it hangs there still, *the* question of the faith, the one question we ought to know the answer to and the one question that continues to haunt many of us because we do *not* know the answer, not completely, not in any way that is easy to say. "Who are you?" That is the question. Who is Jesus, and who is he to us, and what does our answer to that question have to do with our eternal lives?

[Worth noting here is that the preacher (1) briefly explains how the text functions, with an unanswered question that nevertheless must be answered, and she (2) switches from engagement with the text to engagement with her listeners. The unanswered question not only has to be answered, but it has to be answered by us.]

I am not talking about proper names, by the way. We have plenty of those. He is the Messiah, the Lamb of God, the second person of the Trinity, the Savior of the world. But knowing someone's name is not the same thing as knowing that person. If you do not believe me, then try it on a three year old.

"Who is Jesus?" she asks, riding home from church with her Sunday school picture in her hand: a tall thin man in a blue robe, with sheep around his legs and a lamb in his arms.

"He is the son of God," you say, with great authority.

"I know that," she says, "but who *is* he?"

"The redeemer of the world?" you say. "The Lord, the giver of life."

"I thought that was God," she says.

"Jesus is God too," you say.

"Then how can he be the son of God?" she asks.

"That is a very good question," you say, and offer to buy her a frozen yogurt for being such a smart little girl, but you have not answered her question and it hangs there between you, the question you both want the answer to: "Jesus, who are you?"

[The point is driven home with a contemporary story, but there is more to it than that. The preacher tells a story about a little girl and about us in conversation. Comic relief helps ease some of the

tension the listeners feel, but not all of it. Hearers of the sermon are forced to wrestle with it.]

One afternoon when I was a sophomore in college I was sitting in my dormitory room minding my own business when someone knocked on the door. I opened it and found two young women clutching Bibles to their breasts. My heart sank. With my parents' help, I had avoided organized religion most of my life, and these two—with their gleaming eyes, their earnest faces, their most plaid skirts and sensible shoes—these were just the sort of people I had hoped to continue avoiding as long as I could. The Holy Spirit had sent them, they said. Could they come in? While I was thinking of a suitable reply, they did come in, and I was a goner. They sat down on my bed, opened their Bibles, and began to ask me questions.

"Are you saved?" one of them asked.

"Well," I said, "that depends on what you . . ."

"No," the other one said, writing something down on a pad of paper.

"Do you want to be saved?" the first one asked, and both of them gleamed at me while I thought how awful it would sound to say, "No."

"Sure," I said, and they leapt into action, pulling me down to sit beside them on the bed, one of them reading selected passages of Scripture while the other one drew an illustration of my predicament on her pad.

"Here you are," she said, drawing a stick figure on one side of a yawning chasm. "And here is God," she said, drawing another figure on the other side. "In between is sin and death," she said, filling the chasm with dark clouds from her pen.

"Now the question is, how are you and God going to get together?" she asked me.

"I don't have a clue," I said, and they both looked delighted. Then the one with the pen bent over her drawing and connected the two sides of the chasm with a bridge in the shape of a cross.

"That's how," she said. "Jesus laid down his life for you to cross over. Do you want to cross over?"

"Sure," I said, and the look in their eyes was like one of those old cash registers where you crank the handle and the little "Sale" sign pops up. They told me to kneel by my bed, where they knelt on either side of me and instructed me to repeat after them: "I accept Jesus Christ as my personal Lord and Savior and I ask him to come into my life. Amen." Then they got up, hugged me, gave me a schedule of campus Bible study, and left.

The whole thing took less than twenty minutes. It was quick, simple, direct. *They* did not have any questions about who Jesus was. You are here, God is there, Jesus is the bridge. Say these words and you are a Christian. Abracadabra. Amen. It is still hard for me to describe my frame of mind at the time. I was half-serious, half-amused. I cooperated as much out of curiosity as anything, and because I thought that going along with them would get them out of my room faster than arguing with them.

[The story poignantly describes a simplistic approach to the identity of Jesus, and yet it points to at least part of Jesus' true identity. At this point, however, listeners cannot begin to expect what the preacher will say next.]

I admired their courage, in a way, but nothing they said really affected me. Most of it was just embarrassing, the kind of simplistic faith I liked the least, but something happened to me that afternoon. After they left I went out for a walk and the world looked funny to me, different. People's faces looked different to me; I had never noticed so many details before. I stared at them like portraits in a gallery, and my own face burned for over an hour. Meanwhile, it was hard to walk. The ground was spongy under my feet. I felt weightless, and it was all I could do to keep myself from floating up and getting stuck in the trees.

Was it a conversion? All I know is that something happened, something that got my attention and has kept it through all the years that have passed since then. I may have been fooling around, but Jesus was not. My heart may have not been in it, but Jesus' was. I asked him to come in and he came in, although I no more have words for his presence in my life than I do for what keeps the stars in the sky or what makes the daffodils rise up out of their graves each spring. It just is. "Who are you?" "I am."

[In a wonderful turn of events, the preacher describes the mystery of her encounter with God. She does not try to nail it all down with the quasi-religious jargon of our day.]

That is the answer the Pharisees could not accept because they could not see through it. It was opaque for them, a claim that caused terrible problems for them no matter how they looked at it. Whether Jesus was speaking *for* God or *instead* of God, he was way, way out of line, claiming equality with a God who has no equals. The way they saw it, there was only one great I AM and Jesus was not it.

[Engagement with the listeners has now switched back to engagement with the text and the Pharisees. This time their inability to understand Jesus' higher, cryptic meaning is noted. In the section that follows the preacher will begin to explore another way of looking at Jesus' words.]

But there is another way to view his answer—not as opaque but transparent—the answer of someone who does not claim equality with God, but intimacy, whose being is so wrapped up in the being of God that when he says, "I am," there is no difference between the two. When you look at him, you see God. When you listen to him, you hear God. Not because he has taken God's place, but because he is the clear window God has glazed into flesh and blood—the porthole between this world and the next, the passageway between heaven and earth.

"When you have lifted up the Son of Man, then you will realize that I am he," he tells his critics. He is speaking, of course, about his own death. When that has come to pass, then they will be able to see through him. Then they will know what his "I am" means—that he claims nothing for himself, not even his own life; that he does nothing under his own authority. The only reason he *is* at all is to reveal the "I am" of his father and to bring others into intimate relationship with the Chief Being of the universe.

"Then you will realize," he said, but he was wrong. They lifted him up and still they did not realize who he was, just as we lift him up in the broken bread of communion and wonder ourselves. "Who are you?" That is the question that hangs in the air, drawing us deeper and deeper into the mystery. We realize who he is, but who is he, really? He has come into our lives and rearranged our worlds and made our faces burn with his brightness, but who is he and why can't we be more articulate about who he is?

[Once again the preacher acknowledges the puzzling nature of Jesus' words, the mystery of his identity, and puts it all back on us. The Christ whose presence we partake of in Communion remains a wonderful mystery.]

One reason, perhaps, is that the answer is not ours to give. "Who are you?" is a question addressed not to us, but to Jesus, and one that he does not, on this particular day, answer. He has answered before and he will answer again, but it is rarely the same answer. "I am the bread, the shepherd, the vine, the light; I am the way, the truth, the life." Which is it? All of the above? Or none of them? God, or son of God? My personal Lord and Savior, or the cosmic Christ?

We cannot nail him down. We tried once, but he got loose, and ever since then he has been the walking, talking presence of God in our midst, the living presence of God in our lives.

If we cannot say who he is in twenty-five words or less, it is because he is our window on the undefinable, unfathomable I AM, and we cannot sum him up any easier than we can sum up the one who sent him.

"Who are you?" That is the only question worth asking.

"I am." That is the only answer we need.

[The sermon ends with a healthy sense of mystery, but not in confusion. It assures listeners of the presence of the One who cannot be boxed in by our simple understandings.]

Exercises

Answer the following nine questions for the Johannine discourse in each passage: John 6:1-71; John 9:1-41; John 10:1-21.

1. What kind of discourse is this? Dialogue leading to monologue? Pure monologue? Monologue framed by dialogue? Controversy?

2. How does the discourse relate to the context? What idea(s) does the discourse seem to discuss? What might the passage have said to the Johannine community?

3. What poetic features can you identify? Symbols? Signs? Irony? Double meanings?

4. How does the poetry affect you? What is the mood of the text? What kind of musical instrument(s) might convey the mood(s)? What colors and/or textures does the text suggest?

5. What movements can be identified?

6. What insights do "insiders" observe that "outsiders" seem to be missing in the discourse?

7. What features in the text might need to be explained? How could such an explanation be included without interrupting the flow of the narrative? Identify contemporary parallels.

8. What puzzling features in the passage might best be left as mystery? How could that be done?

9. What is the text saying? What is the text doing? How could a sermon say and do the same?

Sermon Resources

C. Michael Fuhrman, "The Tragicomedy of the Gospel" [John 9:1-41], in *Best Sermons 4*, ed. James W. Cox (Harper-Collins, 1991), pp. 69-76. Suggests a seven-act scheme that might have existed in the ancient world and adapts it for the structure of the sermon. A good job of explaining the irony within the text.

Richard Lischer, "Acknowledgment" [John 9:1-41], in *Best Sermons 5*, ed. James W. Cox (HarperCollins, 1992), pp. 16-21. Masterfully blends a retelling of the story with comments about the story. Neither aspect is neglected. Also captures the scandalous nature of the irony and how it relates to today.

Eugene L. Lowry, "The Drink" [John 4:3-19], in *Best Sermons 2*, ed. James W. Cox (Harper and Row, 1989), pp. 237-46. Closely follows the textual plot, but with many asides from the contemporary world to keep the sermon flowing. The poetry in the text is captured in some ways through the poetic format in which the sermon is printed.

————, "Strangers in the Night" [John 3:1-9], in *Journeys toward Narrative Preaching*, ed. James Bradley Robinson (Pilgrim, 1990), pp. 78-84. Alternates the textual story with brief contemporary analogies. Openly addresses the repeated misunderstandings and ironies.

Barbara Brown Taylor, "I Am Who I Am" [John 8:25], in *The Preaching Life* (Cowley, 1993), pp. 100-106. Complete sermon included in this chapter.

William H. Willimon, "Lord of Life" [John 11:1-16, 17-44], in *The Intrusive Word* (Eerdmans, 1994), pp. 9-14. Blends a retelling of the story with Johannine symbolism to speak a powerful word for today.

Cindy Witt, "A Marriage Made in Heaven" [John 4:5-42], in *Best Sermons 2*, ed. James W. Cox (Harper and Row, 1989), pp. 125-31. Makes superb use of numerous form analogies to allow the congregation to hear the John 4 text in a new way. The scandal of Jesus' love as told in the Fourth Gospel comes shining through.

CHAPTER 9

Adventure Narratives: Stories of the Early Church

William Willimon begins his commentary on Acts with an interesting comparison between most church histories and Luke's account of the early church in the Scriptures:

> I have probably a dozen histories of local churches, most of them as scintillating to read as a telephone directory. All of them are affectionately written by some sincere local historian to insure that the contribution of dear Uncle Mortimer to the construction of the banisters on the front steps of the church will not be forgotten. Such church history is down-home hagiography, idealized remembrance with most of the messy, really interesting stuff lovingly censored. Fierce arguments over the purpose of the church—the trustees' debate over what to do with the 1948 Christmas offering, the person who stormed out in a huff in 1959 over the selection of a new pastor—are nowhere to be found, swept under the carpet. In their place we have lists of former pastors, past teachers of the Men's Bible Study Class, and fascinating data on the square footage of the new parsonage.[1]

Luke's account is much more honest than that. Bystanders

accuse believers of being drunk, a couple dies in church during the offering, a group meeting for prayer refuses to believe that Peter has been released from jail, a missionary team splits up due to petty disagreements. The list goes on and on.

In addition to being painfully honest, the book of Acts is adventurous, much more so than most church histories. From street riots to danger on the high seas, Acts has it all. No wonder it has captivated so many readers over the years. Preaching from Acts includes stories of "soiled saints" (the kind of people most listeners will be able to identify with) and engaging tales of adventure that will keep them interested. Let us now consider how to preach from these passages by asking the three preliminary questions of sermon preparation.

What Is the Text Saying?

Several aspects of interpretation demand attention when we interpret any passage of Scripture, literary form being just one. In the case of Acts, we must also examine the larger genre that consists of the various forms.

The title "Acts" was rather common in its day, with at least ten works by that name, other than Luke's version, in circulation. The term describes content more than genre.[2] Exactly what kind of literature Acts is has been widely debated over the years. In the ancient world there were three basic types of narrative: the history, the biography, and the novel. According to Mark Allan Powell, "The book of Acts is perhaps the only work surviving from antiquity to have been ascribed to all three."[3] David Aune views Acts as a variation of general history, though not in the pure sense of historiography, with which modern readers are familiar.[4] Charles Talbert contends that Luke-Acts, when taken as an inseparable unit, should be seen as an ancient kind of biography known as "succession narrative."[5] Richard Pervo views it as an adventure novel, written to entertain while instructing in subtle ways.[6]

Determining the genre of Acts depends in large measure on how it is viewed in relation to Luke's Gospel. In recent scholarship the unity of Luke and Acts (Luke-Acts) has been acknowledged almost without exception.[7] Most scholars and certainly most preachers have recognized Acts as the second volume from the pen of Luke. As such, scholars have tended to assume that Acts is also of the same genre as the Gospel. A recent work by Parsons and Pervo, however, has questioned that assumption.[8] They maintain that just because Luke wrote a two-volume work does not necessarily mean that each volume represents the same kind of literature.[9]

Part of the struggle to identify Acts literarily has focused on the tension between Luke's literary finesse and his attention to historical details.[10] It is almost universally acknowledged that the historical aspects of Acts are not meant to be taken as history in our modern sense of that word. As Ernst Haenchen notes concerning Luke's approach, "He writes not for a learned public which would keep track of all his references and critically compare them, but rather for a more or less nonliterary congregation which he wants to captivate and edify."[11]

There is less agreement about how large a role Luke's literary finesse actually played in writing Acts. Haenchen notes in his classic work on Acts that the author was traditionally viewed as historian and then theologian. What Haenchen thinks is needed is an examination of Luke as writer.[12]

Several critical methodologies have been used in recent years to carry out that examination. The one thing that is obvious even among those who disagree on the unity of Luke and Acts is that whatever Acts is, it is not a dull history book that simply records for us a series of events in the early church.[13] Acts is an edifying and entertaining book about the adventures and daring deeds of the early church.[14]

Having arrived at a general description of the broad genre of Acts, we must now consider the smaller constituent literary forms found within that genre. Aune lists several distinct forms at work in Acts: historical preface, travel narratives, letters, dramatic episodes, digressions, and speeches.[15] In recent years the speeches in Acts have received a significant amount of study, but they make up only 20 percent of the book.[16] I have chosen to focus on the travel narratives and the dramatic episodes of Acts, or what I am calling the adventure narratives.

Pervo lists thirty-three separate adventures in Acts, which he catalogs into six types: (1) sacred incarcerations; (2) persecution and martyrdom; (3) plot, conspiracy, and intrigue; (4) crowds, mobs, riots, and assemblies; (5) trials, legal actions, and punishment; and (6) shipwreck and travel.[17]

The single most significant aspect of interpreting these accounts is recognizing their purpose in light of their literary form. These accounts were not written as historical narratives describing one event after another, just in case generations to come might wonder what happened, any more than Luke's Gospel was written to teach about the landscape of ancient Palestine.[18]

A story line is at work in Acts. Jesus is leaving his followers to carry on without him. Persecution from without and problems from within will make the task arduous. Ultimately, the gospel must be preached to the Gentiles and the known world. A redirected Pharisee named Saul has been chosen to make that happen. Of course, all kinds of obstacles await his efforts.

Acts is not, however, merely entertaining. The dramatic episodes that Luke includes serve to make "programmatic statements." The Cornelius episode (Acts 10:1—11:18), for example, reveals that the Gentile mission is a part of God's plan. It does so dramatically (telling stories) rather than propositionally (using theological arguments).[19]

The book of Acts is anything but dull. It is an exciting story, and the adventure narratives are an important part of the plot. In order to understand them better, we must consider just how these narratives function.

What Is the Text Doing?

If the Acts account is the adventurous story of the early church rather than a chronological history in the modern sense of the word, we need to examine the various literary techniques and devices used to engender excitement and intrigue. In order to do so, we will consider the various types of adventure narratives separately, although we will combine some of Pervo's categories for the sake of convenience.

Incarcerations and trials "dot the pages of Acts. From beginning to end the danger of sudden seizure—on false charges— is a constant threat."[20] These arrest narratives capture the reader's attention. They build suspense by introducing great danger while evoking the reader's sympathy and inviting participation. No two jail accounts are the same in Acts. "Luke's several prison escapes are wonderfully varied through the addition of suspense, local color, trials, allusions to literature, crowd scenes, torture, martyrdom, threatened suicide, and speeches, no less than in the use of different plot structures."[21]

All of this attention to detail, variety, and suspense is relevant to the function of these incarceration narratives. As Pervo states, they demonstrate "the triumph of a new religion over all opposition."[22] In their quest to spread the good news, the messengers will be jailed unfairly. Nevertheless the gospel will go forth.

As church history demonstrates, tales of *persecution and martyrdom* almost always prove entertaining to Christians. This was true for well over a millennium after Acts was written. The reason is fairly obvious. Persecution allows Luke to vividly portray the struggle between good and evil. Ultimately, persecution is about vindication. Readers recognize unjust suffering, and in many cases they empathize with the sufferers. What they hope for is what Acts delivers—ultimate vindication. As Stephen is dying an unjust death, he sees "the heavens opened and the Son of Man standing at the right hand of God!" (Acts 7:56). The readers see it along with him. Justice will be served.

Conspiracies and crowds constitute another type of adventure narrative. Conspiracies help to thicken the plot, so to speak. They build suspense and enhance the drama. Conspiracies are devices of resistance to the messengers and the message of the gospel. How will the gospel move westward if the powers that be continue to threaten it? Conspiracies are masterminded by authorities. Luke's portrayal of the early church's overcoming these dastardly plots is a statement of the church's triumph over the ruling authorities.[23]

Crowds, on the other hand, serve as popular reactions to the gospel message. Sometimes they receive the apostles gladly. At other times they foster resentment and demonstrate rejection.[24]

In Acts 4 the reaction of the people is juxtaposed with that of the authorities. Among other things, the story of Acts is a story of the gospel's reception among people.[25]

Accounts of travel in antiquity took several forms: the march signifying military accomplishments, land travel that noted geography and ethnography, *sea travel* accounts, and sometimes a combination of these. Acts describes travel by land and sea, but not for the purpose of observing the lay of the land or its peoples. The sea-travel narratives in Acts are "well-organized and essential to the story."[26] Vernon Robbins notes that throughout Luke's Gospel and the first twelve chapters of Acts there is no mention of sea travel. In Luke's Gospel Jesus crosses the lake of Gennesaret, but not the sea. Not until Acts 13 does Luke mention sea travel, and not until Acts 15 does that sea travel become fully narrated adventure.[27]

The sea-travel accounts form the climax of Luke's writings, with each account being more significant and extended than the one before it. Luke devotes nine verses to Paul's stay in Thessalonica, seventeen to his stay in Corinth, and twenty to the treatment he received in Asia. Paul's voyage to Rome, however, occupies sixty verses. According to Pervo, shipwreck stories were "a staple of ancient adventure writings."[28] Paul's voyage to Rome is the most exciting adventure of all. As Robbins notes, "The detailed description of the maneuvering of the ship by the sailors, the sounding for fathoms, the casting of anchors, and the manning of ropes and sails ranks this account among the most exciting depictions of storms and shipwrecks in the sphere of Greek and Roman literature."[29]

The purpose that informs these sea-travel narratives is the furtherance of the gospel. Yet there is more at stake. The ancient world tended to see natural disasters as acts of divine retribution. Sea travel, many feared, involved the risk of God's becoming angry and allowing or causing the passengers to drown. Innocent passengers might get thrown overboard along with ritually polluted passengers (compare the story of Jonah in the Old Testament). Paul's survival thus proved his innocence. God was truly with him.[30]

Luke involves his readers in the adventure as well. Three of the sea-travel narratives have become known as the "we" passages, in which Luke writes in the first person ("When we had parted from them and set sail . . ." Acts 21:1). As Robbins notes, "This style contributes directly to the author's scheme of participation in history through narration of its dramatic episodes," though some scholars interpret the "we" passages differently.[31] Luke intends for us as readers to join in on the adventure. "The final voyage takes the gospel to ports and islands far away, and the adventure, danger, and fear bring 'Paul and us' to Rome with thanksgiving."[32] The many dramatic episodes included in Acts serve to "heighten the dramatic conflict just before a resolution, often exhibiting the structural unity of short stories (novellas)."[33] The adventure narratives in Acts all move from conflict to resolution, and they are anything but dull. Luke wants his readers to be involved, and we as preachers want our listeners to be involved as well.

How Can the Sermon Say and Do the Same?

Perhaps the biggest obstacle to preaching from the adventure narratives in Acts is not a general aversion to adventure stories, but an aversion to reading the Bible in that fashion. Children who attend Sunday school every week leave behind their comic books and mysteries to hear the adventurous tales in the Bible treated like dull history. There is a difference, of course, in that the biblical adventures are rooted in fact, not fiction. Still, the adventure narratives in Acts clearly parallel the adventure literature from ancient works of fact and fiction.

The preacher needs to explain what kind of history Acts is. Modern listeners tend to think of the narratives in Acts as history in the sense that newspaper reporters detailed the Watergate break-in or wrote accounts of the Oklahoma City bombing. Perhaps early in the sermon, the preacher needs to explain the genre and literary form(s) at work in Acts. The preacher might begin, "The text before us is a wonderful tale of adventure. This is not a history book loaded with names and dates that we must memorize. The text before us conjures up images of Indiana Jones. Will the Paul get to Rome? Will he live to preach again? This is an adventure."

Other listeners may have been exposed to more allegorical approaches to interpreting Acts, in which the preacher explains how the four anchors in Acts 27 stand for prayer,

Bible study, witnessing, and some other element obviously not meant by the text. Such allegorizing is certainly creative but hardly compares to the adventure of a jailbreak or a shipwreck.

Form-sensitive preaching from the adventure narratives in Acts necessitates some skillful teaching at the beginning of the sermon. The remainder of the message can focus on regenerating the impact of Luke's adventure stories.

Sermonic Mood

The sermon must convey excitement and adventure. For many preachers, if not most, this means recapturing the excitement for themselves, reading the Acts account as if for the first time, employing what Paul Ricoeur calls a "second naiveté."[34] Ricoeur suggests a three-phase hermeneutical movement: (1) recognizing the first naiveté, (2) arousing the critical consciousness, and (3) returning to the text in a second naiveté. In the first phase we take the text at face value without questioning its world-view, literary form, and so forth. In the case of Acts we might find ourselves interpreting a trial as just that, a trial and nothing more.

In the second phase we pull back from the text and begin to ask the critical questions. As Ronald Allen notes, "The important function of the critical consciousness is to destroy our sense of cozy familiarity with the text."[35] If our reading of Acts has lost its zing (or if it never had it in the first place), we are in desperate need of raising our critical consciousness.

The third phase means returning to the text for a naive yet informed reading. In the case of an adventure narrative in Acts we would now recognize some of the important theological truths behind a mob scene, for example, but we would also be able to enter into the narrative with a sense of adventure. Leonard Griffith, in his sermon on the story of Paul's shipwreck, describes that adventure in marvelous detail while inviting his listeners to participate:

You can almost smell the salt air of the Mediterranean Sea as you stand on the deck of the ship with the gathering gale howling in your ears. As the tempest reaches its fury, and the monstrous waves lash your body like a whip, you cling desperately to the rail to save yourself from being swept overboard. Blinded by the rain, drenched to the skin, numbed by the cold, you toss to and fro like a drunken man, certain that every lurch of the creaking timbers will plunge you to a watery grave. In terror you scream, as do the other passengers, but the sound of your voice is lost in the shrieking wind. This is the end, and you steel yourself to meet it as the shuddering ship grinds itself to splinters against a shoal.[36]

So one technique the preacher can employ is to retell the biblical adventure so that listeners are caught up in it. Another technique is to search for contemporary analogies. When we read a text of persecution or even martyrdom, like Stephen's, we immediately think of missionaries who have given their lives for the sake of the gospel. The preacher might describe the deaths of Jim Elliot and his comrades at the hands of the Auca Indians in Ecuador back in the 1950s as they tried to bear Christian witness among them.

The story of Elliot's martyrdom could easily regenerate excitement and adventure, but most churchgoers would not be able to relate. For one thing, most of our listeners will never serve as overseas missionaries in hostile environments. Besides, America is a country where "freedom of religion" is practiced. In our day Stephen would be allowed to preach on the steps of the Capitol if he wanted, much as Martin Luther King Jr. did in 1963. The latter example, however, reminds us that even tolerance runs thin when the message hits too close to home. The irony of it all is that while "freedom of religion" allows anyone to say anything, the gospel drowns in a sea of irrelevance among many voices.

Responsible preaching from Acts requires hermeneutical

savvy as well as attention to the mood of the adventure narratives. Once the issues have been clarified and the mood has been determined, the preacher must also consider the movement of the sermon.

Sermonic Movement

William Willimon writes that "preachers would usually do well to preach Acts as we preach Luke's gospel," that is, more like fiction than history.[37] Though novels and histories are unique literarily, they employ some similar techniques that relate directly to sermonic movement. Storytelling is one of those techniques. Luke wrote "history by telling stories."[38]

Contemporary trends in narrative preaching are well suited to preaching the adventure narratives in Acts. The preacher will probably want to retell the biblical story, as well as some contemporary stories. Those who attend church on Sunday are often the same people who went to the movies the night before. Today's listeners are apt to think of adventures in space rather than at sea. In Luke's day the sea was the frontier. In our day it is another Luke—Skywalker—and outer space is the frontier. The preacher could consider trends in contemporary culture that explore the frontiers of our world—outer space, the bottom of the ocean, or technological advances. By their very nature people are interested in the unknown. The stories of Acts, as well as contemporary stories of adventure, offer much appeal when properly told.

The other technique that Luke employs is inductive development, an essential aspect of good storytelling. Nobody would ever recommend a murder mystery to a good friend by saying, "Here, I think you'll enjoy this. By the way, the butler did it." Stories are inductive by their very nature. We do not know how they end until we come to the end.

The adventure narratives in Acts are no exception. Luke, the masterful storyteller, "likes nothing better than to slip up upon us from behind with the truth."[39] But we have read Acts before, and we know that Paul will make it to Rome. A few observations merit examination at this point. First, people have a remarkable ability to relive adventures that they are already familiar with. People bite their fingernails while watching a movie that they have rented twice before. Sports fans get nervous viewing a tape of a game that was played some time ago. Of course, not all those listening in church will have read the Acts accounts before, and certainly not in the sense of adventure. As Fred Craddock reminds us, a lot of the people who say, "Uh, oh, here we go again," have never really been there before.

Second, the outcome of the text may be known and yet run counter to how listeners feel it should have turned out. The preacher might retell the Stephen narrative, for instance, and then ask, "What about Stephen? Paul makes it to Rome, but Stephen doesn't. He doesn't even make it out of the courtroom, so to speak. What gives?" In this case listeners may know how it ends, but they can hardly like that ending. Inductive development allows listeners to become engaged in a narrative conversation with Luke, facilitated by the preacher. Near the end of the sermon it should become clear that justice will be accomplished eventually, even if it does not happen now.

Third, not all inductive strategies need to hinge on what happens in the text, but on the significance of what happens. There is a difference between knowing how the story ends and understanding what the story means. A brief retelling of the text and some contemporary stories followed by or interspersed with interpretive questions could greatly enhance the appeal of the sermon. "They keep arresting the preachers. Throughout the book of Acts the authorities keep arresting the preachers and the preachers keep getting out. What's the point, Luke?" Finally, near the end of the sermon:

> The last word in the book of Acts is "unhindered." Did you know that? "Unhindered." What a funny way to end a book full of hindrances. Or maybe that's Luke's

message. The struggle to live out the gospel and proclaim it in a world full of hindrances will *ultimately* give
way to one final word—"unhindered."

There are any number of variables that might enter in
when we preach from the adventure narratives of Acts,
especially since there are so many different types of narrative. For that reason, let us consider a sermon by William
Willimon, minister to Duke University, who has written a
good deal about Acts.[40]

"Freedom"

by William H. Willimon

Acts 16:16-40

"One thing that I like about living in New York," he said, "as opposed to where you live, is the freedom. Here there is freedom to live the life-style I choose—to eat where I want and to dress as I like. Freedom."

Then he closed the door behind us. He locked the latch, turned the dead bolt, inserted the chain, and switched on the electronic alarm, telling me, "Don't dare open the door without switching off the alarm or all hell will break loose and the cops may shoot you dead."

If there is one virtue on which we can all join hands this morning it is freedom. We Americans may disagree on taxes, national defense, policy in Central America, and whether the crust is better at Pizza Hut or Pizza Inn, but we all agree that freedom is good. Freedom of religion. Freedom of choice.

I have something called a "freedom phone." Most calls on this telephone sound as if they are being made in Moscow, but I don't mind. How wonderful to be free to receive calls while standing in the street in front of my house!

"And the truth shall make you free," was carved in big letters over the entrance to our high school. *Veritas vos liberabit*. I thought it was something that the principal thought up—a sign like No Smoking in the Boys' Rest Room. But no, it's in the Bible.

And while we sometimes played loose with the truth at my high school, my, how we clung to our freedom. Freedom—that blessed quest of adolescence! Freedom to have the car to go where I want and to do what I want. Freedom not to account for comings and goings to Mama and Daddy.

Freedom—the blessed treasure of academia. Here at Duke, "The Basset Affair" was a landmark case for academic freedom in this country—freedom to think, teach, and publish.

Freedom of the pulpit—freedom to speak as I feel led by God to speak.

Academic freedom? Free to rehash my yellowed old notes rather than to prepare for class. Freedom from accountability for the mediocrity of my lectures, that's what it too often means.

Freedom of the pulpit? Do I need it when preaching is mellifluous repetition of the sweet, conventional clichés of yesterday, sugarcoated with pop psychology to make them go down easier?

Freedom? Surrounded by our burglar alarms and medicine cabinets, our fears—heart attack, impotency, insanity, insolvency—this is freedom?

We Americans have built a society that has given an unprecedented measure of freedom to its citizens. I am given maximum space aggressively to pursue what I want, as long as I don't bump into you while you are getting yours. What we call culture is a vast supermarket of desire where citizens are treated as little more than self-interested consumers. I've got freedom of choice, but now what do I choose? We are free, but also terribly lonely, terribly driven. The nine-to-five job, monthly mortgage payments, overprogrammed kids, dog-eat-dog contest for grades at the university—this is our freedom.

You see, *there is freedom and then there is freedom.* And our problem, in this matter of freedom, is that *we may not even know what true freedom is.*

[Willimon begins with a series of specific examples whereby he deliberately juxtaposes competing images of freedom. Some are

funny. Some are not. Already, though, we have begun to think more
deeply about freedom.]

The book of Acts tells wonderful stories. Luke, master
artist, tells a story, then lets you make up your own mind.
Today's lesson from Acts tells some stories about people who
were in bondage and people who were free. Listen and tell
me who in this story is free.

[Before the text is read or the story is told, we are given some
clues as to what we will find, but only clues. Willimon tells us that
things are not always as they appear. The sermon will be an
inductive adventure into the text and its meaning for today.]

[Read Acts 16:16-34.]

Paul and Silas were going to church one day and were
accosted by a slave girl. Because this girl could tell people's
fortunes, her owners made lots of money hiring her out to
read palms and provide entertainment at business conven-
tions. She was possessed by a demon (mentally unbalanced,
we would say). She took to following Paul and Silas around,
shouting at them, saying things about them.

Here is a picture of enslavement. If you have suffered
through the torment of mental illness, if someone whom you
love is in the grip of schizophrenia or terrible depression, you
could tell us something about bondage. It is as if something
has you, something you can't shake, some dark, uncon-
trollable force which you are powerless to hold back.

Paul has enough of the young woman's raving and, in the
name of Christ, cures her. Thank God, she is free!

But no, she is not free, because she is a slave, someone who
is not a person but a piece of property, owned by someone
else. And some of you, back in your own roots and family
tree, had great-grandparents who were bought and sold. A
slave. Can there be a more vivid image of human bondage?

Luke says, "When her owners saw that their hope of gain
was gone, they seized Paul and Silas and dragged them into

the market place before the rulers." Let's hear it for the business community!

One day Jesus healed a mentally deranged man by casting his demons into some swine (Luke 8:33). For this act of charity, Jesus was promptly escorted out of town by the local Pork Dealers Association.

Later, at a place called Ephesus, Paul had a big revival and many were converted and it was all wonderful—except for the members of the Local 184 of the International Brotherhood of Artisans of Silver Shrines to Artemis. They didn't like it at all.

[A series of biblical stories and images are laid before us. Willimon wants us to begin sensing the tension and opposition the church faces when it does the right thing. These biblical images come alive with modern-day details thrown in.]

A student of mine at the divinity school led a crusade of his church to clean up his community. Good! Clean up the town, get out the dirty books and the beer joints, make it a better place for children and families. No, bad. How was he to know that one of his prominent church members owned the convenience store on the corner across from the high school?

My friend John Killinger, pastor of Lynchburg's First Presbyterian, will preach here next fall. In a sermon, John criticized Jerry Falwell. None of his church members attended Falwell's church and none of them agreed with his theology but, to John's chagrin, he learned on Monday morning how many of his church members had loaned Liberty Baptist money or had large accounts with Falwell enterprises.

[Following the biblical examples, we now hear of modern examples. Being the church has never been easy, and it is not easy today.]

Here is a young woman, chained her whole life to the hell of mental illness, and she is free. There ought to be rejoicing. But no, her owners are not free to do that. It was fine to give a dollar to the Mental Health Association drive last fall, but this is another matter. Religion has somehow gotten mixed up with economics here, and so her owners do what the vested ones always do when their interests are threatened.

Oh, we don't come right out and say that God is interfering with our business. We're not so dumb. No, we hire a public-relations firm that teaches us how to talk in front of a camera and how to answer reporters and put a good face on the corporation.

You have seen the ads: "Gee, Dad, I'm going to work for 'X' chemical company (you know the company, Dad—the one that made napalm back in Vietnam days) and I'm going to get to grow food to feed hungry people."

And the girl's owners say, "Judge, we're not against a little religion, as long as it is kept in its place. But these Jews are disturbing our city. They advocate customs which it is not lawful for us Romans to accept or practice."

No, we don't come right out and say that our financial self-interest is threatened; we say that our nation is threatened. "These missionaries are foreigners." Buy American!

Besides, these are Jews. And we all know what they are like. Money-grabbing, materialistic.

And if the nationalism and the anti-Semitism don't work, we'll throw in an appeal for old-time religion, saying, "They advocate customs that it is not lawful for us to practice." Nation, race, tradition—all stepping into line behind the dollar.

[Willimon's prophetic style becomes fully evident here. Direct application begins to indict us for our improper uses of freedom.

Then the crowd (democracy in action) falls into line behind the town's business leaders. They attack and beat Paul and Silas.

Paul and Silas are put into the back cell of the town prison, and the jailer locks them in the stocks. The liberators have become the imprisoned. Jesus has helped set a pitiful woman free, but two of Jesus' people get jailed in the process.

The one who came preaching, "You will know the truth, and the truth will make you free," well, you know where he ended up.

[Here the preacher employs inductive doubt. He plays with our commonsense understanding of right and wrong, and he shows what happens to others who practice their understanding of it.]

So Paul and Silas end up in prison, languishing there. No, that's not the way the story goes. The story says, "About midnight Paul and Silas were praying and singing hymns to God, and the prisoners were listening to them . . ." Wait, these men in chains, legs locked in the stocks, are singing, praying, having some kind of rally, there, in jail?

A few years ago, we were honored with a visit by Bishop Emilio de Carvalho, Methodist Bishop of Angola. What is it like to be the church in a Marxist country? we wanted to know. Is the new Marxist government supportive of the church? we asked.

"No," the bishop responded, "but we don't ask it to be supportive."

"Have there been tensions?" we asked.

"Yes," said the bishop. "Not long ago the government decreed that we should disband all women's organizations in the church.

"Oh, the women kept meeting. The government is not yet strong enough to do much about it."

"But what will you do when the government becomes stronger?"

"Well," he said, "we shall keep meeting. The government does what it needs to do. The church does what it needs to do. If we go to jail for being the church, we shall go to jail. Jail is a wonderful place for Christian evangelism. Our church made some of its most dramatic gains during the revolution when so many of us were in jail. In jail, you have everyone there, in one place. You have time to preach and teach. Sure, twenty of our Methodist pastors were killed during the revolution, but we came out of jail a much larger and stronger church."

And, as if seeing the drift of our questions, Bishop Carvalho said, "Don't worry about the church in Angola; God is doing fine by us. Frankly, I would find it much more difficult to be a pastor in Evanston, Illinois. Here, there is so much, so many things, it must be hard to be the church here."

[The complex differences between Luke's world and ours are clearly brought to light, but not in some technical discussion of hermeneutics. There are places even in our day similar to the first-century world of Acts, but America is not one of them. Willimon shows how hard it is to be the church in a "free" country.]

The earth heaves, the prison shakes, the doors fly open, and everyone's chains fall off. The jailer wakes, and when he sees that the doors are open, is horrified. Knowing what happens to jailers who permit their prisoners to escape, he draws his sword and prepares to do the honorable thing for disgraced jailers. (Just having the key to someone else's cell doesn't make you free. Iron bars do not make a prison.)

[Along with insights into the significance of the text, Willimon invites us to participate in the adventure for a moment—an earthquake and a near suicide.]

Paul shouts, "Don't do it! We're all here, just singing."

The jailer says, "But you were bound in chains; now you are free to escape."

Paul says, "No, we prisoners are free to stay and you, our jailer, are chained to your sword, but now you can be free to escape."

And the jailer asks, "What do I have to do to be saved? What do I have to do to be free?" And he was baptized.

What is freedom? By the end of Luke's story, everyone who at first appeared to be free—the girl's owners, the judges, the jailer—are shown to be slaves. And everyone who first appeared to be enslaved—the poor girl, Paul, and Silas—are free.

[Willimon employs very direct teaching here. He gives us the answer to his earlier question about who is free and who is not.]
Jesus does things like that to people.

Who pulls your strings?

Speaking at a conference on women in the church, someone rose and said, "The federal government has done more for the cause of women in this country than the church ever thought about. At last, because of government help, women are enabled to be on an equal level with men in the workplace."

And I had just heard, on the radio, that for the first time in history, the percentage of lung cancer among women who smoke is nearly as high as it is among men. The rate of hypertension, heart disease, and other stress-related diseases is climbing among women, and some feel that, in not too many years, the life span of the average American woman will have shrunk to that of the average American man.

You've come a long way, to get where you got to today?

There is freedom and then there is freedom.

Earlier, Jesus had said, "If you continue in my word, you are truly my disciples, and you will know the truth, and the truth will make you free" (John 8:31-31).

They stiffened their necks, held their heads high, and answered, "What is this 'will make you free' business? We are descendants of Abraham, and have never been in bondage to anyone. How is it that you say, 'You will be made free?'"

They lied. The ones who spoke so pridefully of their freedom spoke with the heel of Caesar upon their necks, slaves of Egypt, Assyria, Babylonia, and now Rome, anybody big enough to raise an army and blow through town. In truth, they were not free. Their boasts of freedom were but the rattling of their chains.

And Jesus said, "If the Son makes you free, you will be free" (John 8:36).

[Willimon returns to Jesus' teaching on freedom and the resis-
tance of the Jewish authorities to heed that teaching. It is left up to
the listeners to decide whether or not to receive that freedom today.
The sermon has led us to participate in an adventure, but not just
for the sake of adventure. We have emerged with rich insights that
challenge our ways of thinking and being in this world.]

Exercises

Answer the following six questions for the adventure
narrative in each passage: Acts 4:1-22; 23:12-35; 28:1-10.

1. Which type of adventure narrative does this passage
relate: incarceration, trial, persecution, martyrdom, conspiracy, crowd scene, or sea travel? What does that say about the
function of the passage?

2. What is the mood of the passage? What musical instruments might best accompany the text? What colors and/or
textures might describe the mood of the text? What adjectives
and adverbs best describe the passage?

3. What kind of narrative techniques and inductive movement does the text use? Is there any contemporary story that
the biblical story brings to mind?

4. What is the text saying?

5. What is the text doing?

6. How could a sermon say and do the same?

Sermon Resources

Ronald J. Allen, "Good News for Those Who Are Cut Off"
[Acts 8:26-40], in *Preaching* (January/February 1989): 34-37.
Wrestles with the text inductively. Is sometimes playful but
ultimately makes the point. Discusses Luke's literary finesse,
but not as a substitute for allowing listeners to enjoy the
adventure.

Leonard Griffith, "Christianity at Its Best" [Acts 27], in *Best*
Sermons 2, ed. James W. Cox (Harper and Row, 1989), pp.

215-25. One of the best descriptive sermons on the adventures of Acts. Describes the shipwreck in vivid detail and then begins to analyze the implications of the text for today. Unfortunately resorts to some allegorical interpretation and turns an inductive opening into a deductive sermon.

Jan M. Lochman, "Herod—Peter—James" [Acts 12:1-11, 21-24], in *Best Sermons 2*, ed. James W. Cox (Harper and Row, 1989), pp. 92-99. Begins by acknowledging the adventurous nature of the text. The story is briefly told and then considered from the perspective of the three main characters and what they can teach us.

Michael E. Williams, "What's a Nice Jewish Boy Doing in a Place Like This?" [Acts 10:34-43], in *Biblical Preaching Journal* (winter 1990): 3-6. Retells the story in vivid detail. Closes with a series of brief applications to contemporary situations. Includes a brief synopsis of exegetical resources.

William H. Willimon, "Easter Power" [Acts 14:8-18], in *Pulpit Digest* (March/April 1990): 39-42. Weaves together a retelling of the biblical story with anachronistic detail and contemporary images that resonate with today's listeners. Very prophetic.

William H. Willimon, "Freedom" [Acts 16:16-40], in *Preaching to Strangers*, by William H. Willimon and Stanley Hauerwas (Westminster/John Knox, 1992), pp. 17-25. Complete sermon included in this chapter. An interesting analysis by Hauerwas follows the sermon (pp. 25-28).

GENRE: EPISTLES

CHAPTER 10

Vice and Virtue Lists: Poetic Exhortations

Sweat, stomp, shout, and spit. These terms typically de-scribe the kind of preaching we associate with exhortation. Maybe we picture an outdoor revival in a tent with the preacher laying guilt trips on us, waving a big Bible in our faces and pointing an accusing finger. Or maybe it is a more refined setting in which the distinguished pastor courteously beats us over the head with a list of do's and don'ts. There are passages of serious warning in the New Testament, and those passages must be preached, but vice and virtue lists constitute a unique form of exhortation—poetic exhortation. As we shall see, this kind of exhortation requires a unique approach to preaching.

According to Abraham Malherbe, three broad types of exhortation existed in antiquity: protrepsis, diatribe, and parenesis. Protrepsis attempts to demonstrate the superiority of one way of living over another. It became a popular form of exhortation around the second century,[1] although Romans is somewhat protreptic in style.[2] Diatribe is a form of dialogue with an imaginary other for the purpose of moral instruction. Romans makes heavy use of diatribe, and James uses it to some degree.³ Parenesis is ethical exhortation generally characterized by verbs in the imperative mood, and it is the broad form that we will consider in this chapter.⁴

David Bradley defines parenesis as "exhortation to seek virtue and shun vice, and the giving of rules or directions for proper thought and action in daily living in a form which permits a wide applicability of the teachings."⁵ In other words, parenesis is advice on how to live as Christians. This form of exhortation tended to be consistent with traditional moral values in the larger Hellenistic world.⁶ Paul frequently assumes that his readers are acquainted with the material of his parenetic passages as evidenced by the phrase "as you know" (for example, 1 Thessalonians 1:5; 2:2; 3:4), and the negative phrasing, "Do you not know?" through which he implies that his readers do in fact know (for example, 1 Corinthians 5:6; 6:2, 15; 9:13). The kinds of exhortations found in parenetic passages are universally recognized as morally upright behavior. In the case of the New Testament, parenesis is concerned with the believer's relationship with the Christian community.⁷

Parenesis takes on many different forms in the New Testament: *proverbs* (Galatians 5:9); *household codes* (Colossians 3:18—4:1); *admonitions* (Romans 12:9-21); *topoi* (Romans 13:1-7); and *vice and virtue lists*.⁸ (Admonitions and topoi are discussed in chapter 11.) This chapter focuses on Paul's lists of vices and virtues.

What Is the Text Saying?

Vice and virtue lists contain three or more independent items whereby the author intends to make certain parenetic statements.⁹ In Ephesians 4:32 Paul lists three virtues by which the believer ought to live: "be kind to one another, tenderhearted, forgiving one another, as God in Christ has forgiven you." First Corinthians 6:9-10 is an example of a vice list in which Paul characterizes the kind of people who will not inherit the kingdom of God: "fornicators, idolaters, adulterers, male prostitutes, sodomites, thieves, the greedy, drunkards, revilers, robbers." These passages teach us how to live and how not to live, respectively.

In the ancient world these lists served primarily as the basis for a rational approach to life—how civilized people ought to live. In the New Testament the focus is more on God's standard for right living.[10] In the ancient world these lists tended to emphasize vices and virtues related to the individual, whereas the New Testament lists are more concerned with the individual in relation to the Christian community.[11]

The focus of this type of parenesis is not with bringing about a change within "the existing world order and structures," but rather with the ethical responsibilities of Christians in the present world order.[12] These lists, then, are primarily addressed to Christians and teach them how to live their lives in relation to each other and to the prevailing culture in which they find themselves.

The evidence suggests that these New Testament lists were "not constructed according to a set pattern drawn up from a uniform point of view" and that no catalogues were in circulation from which writers could borrow.[13] Still, vice and virtue lists were used commonly in the ancient world. Philo, for example, lists 147 vices in his work, "On the Sacrifices of Abel and Cain." The Church Fathers carried on the practice in their writings, the most famous list of vices being "The Seven Deadly Sins."[14]

The New Testament includes approximately twenty virtue lists[15] and twenty vice lists.[16] Scholarly opinion differs on the precise number of lists, depending in large measure on how a list is defined. From these lists, G. Mussies identifies sixty-one distinct virtues and twenty-two distinct vices. *Love* is the most frequently cited virtue, appearing in ten of the New Testament lists. *Longsuffering* is included in six lists.[17] Victor

Paul Furnish observes that Paul's virtues tend to cluster around three central themes: love, purity, and truthfulness.[18] This observation has important ramifications for interpreting these lists.

There are three issues that merit attention with regard to the interpretation of these lists: (1) the context in which they appear, (2) the importance of thematic unity, and (3) the arrangement of the items listed. Burton Scott Easton notes that many of the lists are not integral to the context and flow of thought. In 1 Corinthians 6:9-11, for instance, Paul lists the kinds of people who will not inherit the kingdom, but there appears to be no logical connection with the discussion of lawsuits in the preceding verses (vv. 1-8),[19] other than perhaps a play on words ("wrong" in v. 8 and "wrongdoers" in v. 9). Apparently the biblical writers felt free to introduce these lists either randomly in some cases or with a strong tie to the context in others (for example, Galatians 5:19-21).[20] Interpreting these lists requires determining whether the list in question is integral to the epistle's flow or is an aside on ethical behavior in general.

Easton also notes that one of the dangers with these lists is the fragmentary impression they might make on listeners. The items listed, though distinct, were intended to be heard as a unit, not so much as individual behaviors.[21] The preacher needs to determine not only the meaning of the individual terms but also, and more importantly, the meaning of the terms considered as a unit.

Sometimes the arrangement of the items in a list can provide a key to interpreting the passage. In Galatians 5, for example, the virtue list known as the fruit of the Spirit is arranged in groups of three with love serving as the chief of the virtues.[22] Several scholars have also detected a pattern of arrangement in the list in 1 Timothy 1:9-10 corresponding to the two tablets of the Ten Commandments.[23] Ordinarily, however, the arrangement of the items listed relates more to impact than to meaning. For that reason, let us now turn to a discussion of how these lists function.

What Is the Text Doing?

Vice and virtue lists in the New Testament exhibit three primary forms: (1) *polysyndectic lists*, which use connective particles such as "and," "nor," and "or" (1 Peter 2:1); (2) *asyndectic lists*, which lack connective particles (2 Corinthians 12:20); and (3) *amplified lists*, which expand on some or all of the items listed (Colossians 3:5).[24] The difference between lists with conjunctions and those without has nothing to do with meaning, but everything to do with impact.[25]

New Testament epistles were meant to be read, and in the ancient world that meant read aloud (Colossians 4:16). Silent reading did not exist.[26] As James Bailey and Lyle Vander Broek note, "The power of vice and virtue lists lies in repetition. Content is emphasized through the cadence established." Frequently the repetition is enhanced by means of consonance or euphony (that is, words that begin with the same letter or sound good together).[27]

In Romans 1:29-31 and 2 Timothy 3:2-4 there is no clear pattern of arrangement regarding content. There is, however, a very clear pattern "according to consonance in the initial sound of the word[s]."[28] This pattern is readily observable in the Greek. In the Timothy passage, for instance, the first two words and the last two words all begin with "ph" φ, nine consecutive words begin with "a" (alpha privative), and two words begin with "pr" πρ. A similar pattern is detectable in the Romans passage.

This technique served a dual purpose. On the one hand, the content instructed believers in how to live. On the other hand, the form helped listeners remember the material.

Since vice and virtue lists were a form of parenesis, or exhortation, the preacher might be tempted to conclude that all of the New Testament lists are in the imperative mood, the mood of command. That is not the case. Colossians 3:12 is clearly a command. Paul tells his listeners to clothe themselves with several virtues. The language is prescriptive. The vice lists in Romans 1 and 1 Corinthians 6:9-11, however, are descriptive. In the Corinthians list, for example, Paul does not command his readers. He simply makes the observation that certain persons/lifestyles will not inherit the kingdom. He does so to make the point that some of the Corinthians used to be such persons, but they no longer are, due to God's grace. This descriptive form of parenesis is a subtle form of exhortation. Paul's recounting of how God had delivered the Corinthians from their sinful ways would be not only a reminder of God's forgiveness but also a *subtle* reminder of how not to live.

Vice and virtue lists in the New Testament not only teach us how to live, but they do so in the various ways that we have just considered. How can the preacher do justice to these lists in preaching?

How Can the Sermon Say and Do the Same?

Vice and virtue lists have no real parallels in modern society. But there are forms that have similar functions. Criminal "rap" sheets and professional résumés remind us of qualities to avoid and to embrace. Having your name entered into a volume of *Who's Who* along with a list of accomplishments may be a contemporary version of a virtue list.[29] The preacher could look for ways to explain these ancient lists by means of comparisons with such modern forms.

Or the preacher may choose to be more intentional in addressing the use of vice and virtue lists in ancient times. This treatment can be brief, avoiding technical jargon. Robert P. Mills, in a sermon on the virtue list in Philippians 4:8-9 entitled "Wayside Sacraments," notes:

As he nears the end of his letter, Paul lists eight things for the Philippians to "think about." His list is more suggestive than comprehensive. And it doesn't include what we have come to think of as characteristically Christian attributes; love, joy, peace, patience, gentleness, self-control. Instead, it sounds almost as if Paul lifted his list straight out of a secular Greek textbook on ethics or philosophy.[30]

In addition, the preacher may address how these lists sometimes were used in a logical context and at other times were arbitrarily inserted. These brief explanations can prepare listeners for receiving the impact of the lists themselves. That impact can be achieved through attention to mood and movement.

Sermonic Mood

Although poetic in nature, vice and virtue lists constitute a form of exhortation in the New Testament. As we have noted, however, some of the passages are more descriptive than prescriptive. The ultimate purpose of both may be the same, but they differ radically in approach and mood. The preacher needs to identify whether the text is descriptive or prescriptive. Descriptive passages imply the need for less confrontational strategies within the sermon. Not all prophetic preaching is done at the top of the lungs. It is worth noting that the New Testament identifies three times as many virtues as vices. Paul obviously knew that the gospel was good news. Preaching these exhortations need not be uniformly negative.

The poetic nature of these lists is most clearly demonstrated in the oral nature of their euphony and consonance. These qualities are hidden from listeners who must rely on English translations and whose reading of biblical texts is generally silent. The oral nature of vice and virtue lists, however, is perfectly suited to the oral nature of preaching. Ancient narrations were full of animation and expression, including appropriate facial expressions and gestures.[31] An appropriate use of these techniques can enhance a modern-day presentation as well.

An oral reading of the English text can capture the poetic meter of the text. There is a big difference between reading a list that uses conjunctions and one that does not. For instance, read aloud the following two lists with a pause before reading the second list: "I fear that there may perhaps be quarreling, jealousy, anger, selfishness, slander, gossip, conceit, and disorder" (2 Corinthians 12:20). "Rid yourselves, therefore, of all malice, and all guile, insincerity, envy, and all slander" (1 Peter 2:1).

The meter of a biblical text ought to be reflected in the reading of that text and in the meter of the sermon. Thomas McComiskey's book *Reading Scripture in Public* is a helpful resource in this regard.[32]

Of course, the real poetry in these lists is in the original Greek. The preacher could simply say, "This passage has an artistic aspect hidden from our hearing, since the words Paul uses in Greek sound the same." A poetic reading of the Greek might be even more effective. I once heard Thomas Long do this with a list of Greek words, and the effect was quite powerful. The same kind of effect could be achieved with a poetic reading of English synonyms such as selfish, stingy, sinful, and scornful. Whatever method you choose should serve to bring out the poetic flavor of these lists.

Above all, the preacher must remember that these lists are poetry and must be handled poetically. Mussies notes that some writers (outside of the New Testament) even began to use the poetic device of personification in their teachings of vices and virtues, writing, for example, that death begat children such as jealousy and wrath.[33] The preacher can try using personification as well, though such a technique might seem corny.[34]

One of the hallmarks of poetry (contemporary or ancient)

is its refusal to look at life in the abstract. Poets speak of life in concrete imagery. If the biblical writer calls for perseverance, the preacher can paint a picture of what perseverance looks like in real life. These synecdochical illustrations (in which the concept is fleshed out in a narrative fashion) allow listeners to experience what love, peace, and joy might be like in everyday situations.[35]

For instance, Paul exhorts the Colossians to get rid of anger, wrath, and malice, among other things, and to show instead compassion, kindness, and humility (Colossians 3:8, 12). Instead of talking about the concept of anger and the need for compassion, the preacher can tell a story:

> In a motion picture called *The Mission* Robert DeNiro plays Mendoza, a ruthless mercenary who makes his living selling Indians on the slave market. One day he kills his brother in a fit of rage. Unable to live with the guilt, Mendoza goes to live in a monastery where he meets Father Gabriel. The priest suggests that Mendoza accompany him to a mission in the mountains where the Indians live. As penance Mendoza carries a huge sack of armor along the way. Near the end of the climb Mendoza struggles up a slippery hillside, still carrying the sack, when he comes face-to-face with one of the natives. The Indian man holds out a knife, and Mendoza assumes he will be killed. But the man uses the knife to cut the rope, and the sack of armor goes tumbling down the hillside. Not anger, wrath, and malice, but compassion, kindness, and humility. That's what Paul writes about.

A well-told story can help capture the mood of a passage in concrete terms. A story can also help in relation to a text's movement, as we shall see next.

Sermonic Movement

The poetic nature of vice and virtue lists means that items might be included for aesthetic reasons as much as for content. A list of similar-sounding words can be strung together to produce a memorable effect on the listeners. As Easton cautions, one of the dangers with these lists in the New Testament is treating them as individual items rather than as a unit of thought.[36]

In the Colossians example just cited, the preacher need not address every vice and every virtue in elaborate detail. What is crucial is to capture the central thrust of the passage. The Mendoza story helps flesh out the virtues Paul has in mind without elaborating on each of them separately. In other words, the structure of a list, more often than not, relates to mood, not movement.

Exceptions do exist, however. For instance, if the vice list in 1 Timothy 1:9-10 does reveal some pattern of arrangement similar to the two tablets of the Ten Commandments, the preacher might want to structure the sermon around that arrangement. Something similar might be done with the fruit of the Spirit in Galatians 5. Some group the virtues in three clusters with three virtues in each. The sermon could identify these three clusters and deal with them one at a time, perhaps even in the sense of traditional sermon points. What the preacher needs to avoid is a nine-point sermon on the fruit of the Spirit and focus instead on the overarching purpose.

In the final analysis the poetry of the text must be respected. These lists of exhortations have a poetic flavor to them that the preacher should not ignore. The sample sermon we will consider is a model in that regard. It is a baccalaureate sermon by the writer and preacher, Frederick Buechner, who is certainly one of the most poetic preachers of our time.[37]

"Be Holy"

by Frederick Buechner

Exodus 19:3-6; 1 Peter 2:1-2, 9

"Rich man, poor man, beggar man, thief, doctor, lawyer, merchant chief" or "Indian chief" sometimes, if that's how you happened to be feeling that day. That was how the rhyme went in my time anyway, and you used it when you were counting the cherry pits on your plate or the petals on a daisy or the buttons on your shirt or your blouse. The one you ended up counting was, of course, the one you ended up being. Rich, Poor. Standing on a street corner with a tin cup in your hand. Or maybe a career in organized crime. What in the world, what in heaven's name, were you going to be when you grew up? It was not just another question. It was the great question. Whether we remember to ask it or not, I strongly suspect that it may be the great question still. What are you going to be? What am I going to be? I'll turn fifty-eight this summer, and I've been in more or less the same trade for a long time, and I contemplate no immediate change, but I think of it still as a question that's wide open. For God's sake what do you suppose we're going to be, you and I? When we grow up.

[Buechner begins with the question all of us wrestled with as kids, What are you going to be? This would be most appropriate for a baccalaureate setting, especially since Buechner pulls it off in such distinguished fashion, using a nursery rhyme at that.]

Something in us rears back in indignation of course. At twenty-eight, fifty-eight, seventy-eight or whatever we are, surely we've got our growing up behind us. We've come many a long mile and thought many a long thought. We've taken on serious responsibilities, made mature decisions, weathered many a crisis. Surely the question is, rather, what are we now and how well are we doing at it. If not doctors, lawyers, merchant chiefs, we are whatever we are—computer analysts, businesswomen, schoolteachers, artists, ecologists, ministers even, or if the job isn't already in our pocket, it's well on its way to being. The letters of recommendation have all been written. The résumés have gone out. The interview on the whole went very well. We don't have to count cherry pits to find out what we're going to end up being, because for better or worse the die has already been cast. Now we simply get on with the game. That's what commencement is all about. That's what life is all about.

[*The sermon has now begun to address the present needs of the graduates gathered together on this important day in their lives. Next Buechner will go beyond the rhymes, back to the ancient texts. His descriptions are wonderfully poetic.*]

But then. Then maybe we have to listen—listen back farther than the rhymes of our childhood, thousands of years farther back than that. A thick cloud gathers on the mountain as the book of Exodus describes it. There are flickers of lightning, jagged and dangerous. A clap of thunder shakes the earth and sets the leaves of the trees trembling, sets even you and me trembling a little maybe, if we have our wits about us. Suddenly the great *shophar* sounds, the ram's horn—a long-drawn pulsing note louder than thunder, more dangerous than lightning—and out of the darkness, out of the mystery, out of some cavernous part of who we are, a voice calls: "Now therefore, if ye will obey my voice indeed, and keep my covenant, then ye shall be a peculiar treasure unto me above all people"—my *segullah*, my precious ones, my darlings—"and ye shall be unto me a kingdom of priests and a holy nation." Then, thousands of years later but still thousands of years ago, there is another voice to listen to. It is the voice of an old man dictating a letter. There is reason to believe that he may actually have been the one who up till all but the end was the best friend that Jesus had, Peter himself. "So put away all malice and all guile and insincerity and envy and all slander," he says. "Like newborn babies, long for the pure spiritual milk that by it you may grow up to salvation; for you have tasted the kindness of the Lord." And then he echoes the great cry out of the thunderclouds with a cry of his own. "You are a chosen race, a royal priesthood, a holy nation, God's own people," he says, "that you may declare the wonderful deeds of him who called you out of darkness into his marvelous light."

What are we going to be when we grow up? Not what are we going to *do*, what profession are we going to follow, what niche are we going to choose for ourselves. But what are we going to *be*—inside ourselves and among ourselves? That is the question that God answers with the Torah at Sinai. That is the question that the old saint answers in his letter from Rome. Holy. That is what we are going to be if God gets his way with us. It is wildly unreasonable because it makes a shambles of all our reasonable ambitions to be this or to be that. It's not really a human possibility at all because holiness is godliness and only God makes holiness possible. But being holy is what growing up in the full sense means, Peter suggests. No matter how old we are or how much we've achieved or dream of achieving, we are not truly grown up till this extraordinary thing happens. Holiness is what is to happen. Out of darkness we are called into "his marvelous light," Peter writes, who knew more about darkness than most of us if you stop to think about it, and had looked into the very face itself of light. We are called to have faces like that—to be filled with light so that we can be bearers of light. I've seen a few such faces in my day, and so have you, unless I miss my guess. Are we going to be rich, poor, beggars, thieves, or in the case of most of us a little of each? Who knows? In the long run who even cares? Only one thing is really worth caring about, and it is this: "Ye shall be unto me a kingdom of priests and a holy nation."

[Buechner's treatment of the New Testament text is equally poetic. He quickly clarifies the difference between being and doing. Rather than treating the individual vices in the negative, he emphasizes the positive—holiness.]

Israel herself was never much good at it, God knows. That is what most of the Old Testament is mostly about. Israel didn't want to be a holy nation. Israel wanted to be a nation like all the other nations, a nation like Egypt, like Syria. She wanted clout. She wanted security. She wanted a place in the sun. It was her own way she wanted, not God's way, and when the prophets got after her for it, she got rid of the prophets, and when God's demands seemed too exorbitant, God's promises too remote, she took up with all the other gods who still get our votes and our money and our nine-to-five energies, because they couldn't care less whether we're holy or not and promise absolutely everything we really want and absolutely nothing we really need.

[The poetic exhortations of the text lead Buechner to begin to involve us, but not in a condemning sort of way. A narrative about ancient Israel comes to be a reflection of our own lives.]

We can't very well blame Israel, because of course we are Israel. Who wants to be holy? The very word has fallen into disrepute—holier-than-thou, holy Joe, holy mess. And "saint" comes to mean plaster saint, somebody of such stifling moral perfection that we'd run screaming in the other direction if our paths ever crossed. We are such children, you and I, the way we do such terrible things with such wonderful words. We are such babes in the woods the way we keep getting hopelessly lost.

And yet we have our moments. Every once in a while, I think, we actually long to be what out of darkness and mystery we are called to be; when we hunger for holiness

even so, even if we'd never use the word. There come moments, I think, even in the midst of all our cynicism and
worldliness and childishness, maybe especially then, when
there's something about the saints of the earth that bowls us
over a little. I mean real saints. I mean saints as men and
women who are made not out of plaster and platitude and
moral perfection but out of human flesh in all its richness and
quirkiness for the simple reason that there's nothing else
around except human flesh to make saints out of. I mean
saints as human beings who have their rough edges and their
blind spots like everybody else but whose lives are transparent to something so extraordinary that every once in a while
it stops us dead in our tracks.

*[Buechner dispels in vivid detail any false notions of holiness
and describes for us what he has in mind.]*

I remember going to see the movie *Gandhi* when it first
came out, for instance. We were the usual kind of noisy,
restless Saturday night crowd as we sat there waiting for the
lights to dim with our popcorn and soda pop, girlfriends and
boyfriends, our legs draped over the backs of empty seats;
but by the time the movie came to a close with the flames of
Gandhi's funeral pyre filling the entire screen, there wasn't
a sound or a movement in that whole theater, and we filed
out of there—teenagers and senior citizens, blacks and
whites, swingers and squares—in as deep and telling a silence as I've ever been part of or has ever been part of me.

*[A synecdochical illustration is used now to picture what holi-
ness is like, not just in the life of some saintly figure from the past,
but in our lives as well.]*

"Like newborn babes, long for the pure spiritual milk that
by it you may grow up to salvation, for you have tasted of
the kindness of the Lord," Peter wrote. We had tasted it. In
the life of that little bandy-legged, bespectacled man with his
spinning wheel and his bare feet and whatever he had in the
way of selfless passion for peace, and passionate opposition

to every form of violence, we had all of us tasted something that at least for a few moments that Saturday night made every other kind of life seem empty, something that at least for the moment I think every last one of us longed for the way in a far country you yearn for home.

"Ye shall be unto me a kingdom of priests, a holy nation." Can a nation be holy? It's hard to imagine it. Some element of a nation maybe, some remnant or root. "A shoot coming forth from the stump of Jesse," as Isaiah put it, "that with righteousness shall judge the poor and decide with equity for the meek of the earth." The eighteenth-century men and women who founded this nation dreamed just such a high and holy dream for us too and gave their first settlements over here names to match. New Haven, New Hope, they called them—names that almost bring tears to your eyes if you listen to what they are saying, or once said. Providence. Concord. Salem, which is *shalom*, the peace that passeth all understanding. Dreams like that die hard, and please God there's still some echo of them in the air around us. But the way things have turned out, the meek of the earth are scared stiff at the power we have to blow the earth to smithereens a hundred times over and at our failure year after year after year to work out with our enemies a way of limiting that ghastly power. In this richest of nations, the poor go to bed hungry, if they're lucky enough to have a bed, because after the staggering amounts we spend to defend ourselves, there isn't enough left over to feed the ones we're defending, to help give them decent roofs over their heads, decent schools for their kids, decent care when they're sick and old.

The nation that once dreamed of being a new hope, a new haven, for the world, has become instead one of the two great bullies of the world who blunder and bluster their way toward unspeakable horror. Maybe that's the way it inevitably is with all nations. They're so huge and complex. By definition they're so exclusively concerned with their own self-interest conceived in the narrowest terms that they have no eye for *holiness*, of all things, no ears to have the great command to be saints, no heart to break at the thought of what this world could be—the friends we could be as nations, the common problems we could help each other solve, all the human anguish we could join together to heal.

[Following the lead of the text, Buechner does make some brief corporate application. He will, however, return to personal application.]

You and I are the eyes and ears. You and I are the heart. It's to us that Peter's letter is addressed. "So put away all guile and insincerity and envy and all slander," he says. No *shophar* sounds or has to sound. It's as quiet as the scratching of a pen, as familiar as the sight of our own faces in the mirror. We've always known what was wrong with us. The malice in us even at our most civilized: the way we focus on the worst in the people we know and then rejoice when the disasters overtake them that we believe they so richly deserve. Our insincerity: our phoniness, the masks we do our real business behind. The envy: the way other people's luck can sting like wasps. And all slander: all the ways we have of putting each other down, making such caricatures of each other that we treat each other like caricatures, even when we love each other. All this infantile nonsense and nastiness. Put it away! Peter says. Before nations can be holy, you must be holy. *Grow up* to salvation. For Christ's sake, grow up.

[Buechner openly addresses the familiar nature of these lists, only he does so in poetic style. He then speaks directly to concrete examples of these vices in our lives, though he quickly returns to the overall theme of holiness and growing up.]

People at my stage of the game—fifty-eight come July? For us isn't it a little too late? People at your stage of the game? For you isn't it a little too early? No, I don't think so. Never too late, never too early, to grow up, to be holy. We've already tasted it—tasted the kindness of the Lord, Peter says. That's such a haunting thought. I think you can see it in our eyes sometimes. Just the way you can see something more than animal in animals' eyes. I think you can sometimes see something more than human in human eyes, even yours and mine. I think we belong to holiness even when we can't believe it exists anywhere, let alone in ourselves. That's why everybody left that crowded shopping-mall movie theater in such unearthly silence. It's why it's hard not to be haunted by that famous photograph of the only things that Gandhi owned at his death: his glasses and his watch, his sandals, a bowl and spoon, a book of songs. What do any of us own to match such riches as that?

[The Gandhi photograph is a striking image in this sermon. It is a vivid portrait of what holiness can look like.]

Children that we are, even you and I, who have given up so little, know in our hearts not only that it's more blessed to give than to receive but that it's also more fun—the kind of holy fun that wells up like tears in the eyes of saints, the kind of blessed fun in which we lose ourselves and at the same time begin to find ourselves, to grow up into the selves we were created to become.

When Henry James, of all people, was saying good-bye once to his young nephew Billy, his brother William's son, he said something that the boy never forgot. And of all the labyrinthine and impenetrably subtle things that that most labyrinthine and impenetrable old romancer could have said, what he did say was this: "There are three things that are important in human life. The first is to be kind. The second is to be kind. The third is to be kind."

In the unlikely event that as the years go by anybody should ever happen to ask you what it was that the speaker said when he was telling you goodbye on this commencement day, I would be willing to settle for that. Be kind. That is what in his own labyrinthine way the speaker tried to say at least.

[Buechner summarizes what his message has been about, only he does not do so in any mundane fashion. He will go on to address the relation of kindness and holiness using poetic imagery.]
Be kind because though kindness isn't the same thing as holiness, kindness is next to holiness; because it's one of the doors that holiness enters the world through, enters us through—not just gently kind but sometimes fiercely kind.

Be kind enough to yourselves not just to play it safe with your lives for your own sakes but to spend at least part of your lives like drunken sailors for God's sakes, if you believe in God, for the world's sake, if you believe in the world, and thus to come alive truly.

Be kind enough to others to listen, beneath the words they speak, for that usually unspoken hunger for holiness which I believe is part of even the unlikeliest of us and, by cherishing which, you can help bring to birth both in them and in yourselves. Be kind to this nation of ours by remembering that New Haven, New Hope, Shalom, are the names not just of our oldest towns but of our holiest dreams, which most of the time are threatened by the madness of no enemy without as dangerously as they are threatened by our own madness.

"You have tasted the kindness of the Lord," Peter wrote in his letter, and ultimately that, of course, is the kindness, the holiness, the sainthood and sanity we are all of us called to. So that by God's grace we may "grow up to salvation" at last.

The sounds of the birds. The way the light falls through the trees. The sense we have of each other's presence. The feeling in the air that one way or another we are all of us here—you who are graduating and we your well-wishers—to give each other our love. This kind moment itself is a door that holiness enters through. May it enter you. May it enter me. To the world's saving. Amen.

[The sermon ends with a challenge to live authentic, holy lives. The challenge is not a scolding, however, but a high and holy challenge, a poetic challenge that inspires us to be different.]

Exercises

Answer the following seven questions for the list of vices and/or virtues in each passage: Galatians 5:19-23; Ephesians 4:31—5:21; 1 Peter 3:8.

1. What kind of list is this? Does it use conjunctions? Is the context crucial to understanding what the list is saying?

2. What is the common thread that connects the items listed?

3. What is the mood of the passage? What musical instruments might best accompany the text? What colors and/or textures might best describe the mood of the text? What adjectives and adverbs best describe it? How would you go about demonstrating the poetry of the Greek text?

4. What synecdochical illustrations or stories come to mind as you read the text?

5. What is the text saying?

6. What is the text doing?

7. How could a sermon say and do the same?

Sermon Resources

Frederick Buechner, "Be Holy" [Exodus 19:3-6; 1 Peter 2:1-2, 9], in *Best Sermons 2*, ed. James W. Cox (Harper and Row, 1989), pp. 199-206. Complete sermon included in this chapter.

Robert P. Mills, "Wayside Sacraments" [Philippians 4:8-9], in *Best Sermons 5*, ed. James W. Cox (Harper and Row, 1992), pp. 272-79. Takes its title from a line in a poem by Ralph Waldo Emerson. This sermon is very poetic, but treats virtues separately.

George E. Thompson, "Putting on New Clothes" [Colossians 3:1-11], in *Pulpit Digest* (March/April 1990): 65-70. Employs the clothing imagery of the text as a motif for a baptismal message. Vices and virtues treated as a unit, not individually.

CHAPTER 11

Admonitions and Topoi: Appeals for Moral Living

I appeal to you therefore, brothers and sisters, by the mercies of God, to present your bodies as a living sacrifice, holy and acceptable to God, which is your spiritual worship (Romans 12:1).

My brothers and sisters, do you with your acts of favoritism really believe in our glorious Lord Jesus Christ? For if a person with gold rings and in fine clothes comes into your assembly . . . (James 2:1-2).

Beloved, I urge you as aliens and exiles to abstain from the desires of the flesh that wage war against the soul (1 Peter 2:11).

These are examples of parenesis from the New Testament. The epistles of Paul, James, and Peter (as well as others) include heavy doses of parenesis, that is, exhortations for moral living.

Exhortations in the ancient world could take one of three forms: protrepsis, diatribe, and parenesis.[1] Parenesis was a broad form of ethical exhortation generally characterized by verbs in the imperative mood,[2] though parenesis in the New Testament tends to be less harsh than it was in other ancient writings.[3] Parenesis is distinguished by its use of precepts, that is, "principles by which one should live."[4] These precepts, or principles, tend to be consistent with traditional moral values in society at large, though the New Testament stresses that the motivation for such behavior is based on a relationship with the risen Christ.[5]

These hortatory passages constitute a large part of the New Testament epistles, especially those of Paul. "Exhortation plays a major role in all the letters of Paul and the Pauline school except Philemon."[6] Beyond Paul's concerns with preparations for the parousia, he was intensely concerned with believers living a virtuous life.[7] Almost half of 1 Thessalonians (including the thanksgiving sections) is parenetic in nature.[8] The pastoral epistles are so parenetic in content and style that even the prescript uses the language of command: "Paul, an apostle of Christ Jesus *by the command of God* our Savior and of Christ Jesus our hope" (1 Timothy 1:1).[9]

It is not just in Paul, however, that parenesis is used. Other epistles use it as well—1 Peter, 1-2 John, and even tractates such as Hebrews and James that assume epistolary forms.[10] Of course, parenesis incorporates several different forms in the New Testament, including *proverbs* (Galatians 5:9), *household codes* (Colossians 3:18–4:1), *vice and virtue lists* (see chapter 10), *admonitions*, and *topoi*.[11] In this chapter we will examine the latter two forms.

What Is the Text Saying?

"Topoi are extended paraenetical statements on particular themes or topics."[12] As such, a *topos* is a sharply defined form that is easily identifiable within the New Testament. In contrast, *admonitions* are brief exhortations generally strung together without any clearly discernible pattern. Topoi are largely restricted to Romans 13, 1 Thessalonians 4, and James 2, whereas admonitions are found scattered throughout the epistles of the New Testament, including Romans, 1 Thessalonians, and James. Together, these two forms constitute a dominant part of the epistles. Sometimes these parenetical

forms appear after the body of the letter (Romans), sometimes they precede it or actually frame the body of the letter
(1 Corinthians), and at other times they actually constitute
the body of the letter (1 Thessalonians).[13]

As for "topoi," David Bradley coined the term in an article
published in 1953 in which he defined a topos as the treatment of a topic in independent form.[14] Romans 13, for example, consists of four separate topoi: the subject of authority
(vv. 1-5), paying tribute (vv. 6-7), love (vv. 8-10), and the
eschatological hour (vv. 11-14). Bradley shows how each
topos is independent of the others, and how each could have
existed as an "independent teaching" before its inclusion in
Romans 13.[15] Three elements are essential in topoi: the injunction, the reason, and the discussion.[16]

Admonitions are less organized and less predictable. A
series of admonitions can be strung together to form a
lengthy section of exhortation, as in Romans 12:9-21. A brief
admonition can be included along with a different literary
form, such as Paul's admonitions in Philippians 2:1-4, which
are followed by the Christ hymn in verses 5-11.[17] Admonitions, unlike topoi, are relatively short, structurally diverse
forms of exhortation.[18]

The interpretation of these hortatory passages requires
some special attention. To begin with, it is crucial that the
interpreter be able to recognize a topos in the biblical materials. Passages of exhortation are not that hard to recognize
in themselves, but topoi are highly specialized forms. The
interpreter also needs to distinguish between independent
admonitions and other forms, such as household codes and
proverbs.

In addition, the interpreter needs to be sensitive to the
context of the passage. Some exhortations are directly connected to the immediate context, while others may seem to
have been inserted. Some address very specific problems

related to the epistle's overall purpose, while others are of a more general nature.[19]

The biggest challenge in interpreting topoi is determining the relevance of the teaching for today. It is crucial that the interpreter be able to distinguish between what was culturally determined and what still applies today.[20] Is Paul's injunction regarding the believer's relation to ancient Roman government meant to be applied to American believers living in a democracy in precisely the same manner (Romans 13)? What about malevolent dictatorships? Or what about Peter's injunctions about suffering (1 Peter 4)? How do they apply in a democracy? Paul instructs the Corinthians regarding the eating of meat (1 Corinthians 8). How many of our listeners are struggling with this issue? James speaks to believers of his day about wealthy unbelievers who were arrogant and uncaring (James 5). What does this mean for the church in North America, which is made up of relatively wealthy believers? The preacher must consider all these hermeneutical issues, among others. Good critical commentaries, journal articles, and works like *Literary Forms in the New Testament* by James Bailey and Lyle Vander Broek offer valuable assistance. Having determined what the text is saying, the preacher must next consider what the text is doing, that is, how it functions.

What Is the Text Doing?

Topoi generally follow a predictable structural pattern of injunction, reason, and discussion. The writer usually begins with a demand, gives the supporting reason for that demand, and then discusses the consequences.[21] A topos is a highly developed literary form. Admonitions, in contrast, are not nearly so rigid and predictable in form, often being strung together in a loosely organized fashion. Despite their structural differences, topoi and admonitions employ several similar techniques in order to challenge listeners. We will consider four of these techniques.

1. Although these parenetic forms are characterized by imperative verbs, they are not nearly so insensitive and uncharitable as the preacher might think. Greek imperatives can take on different moods, from permission to the harshest of commands.[22] Paul's use of parenesis, for example, combines "authoritative demands with diplomatic sensitivity."[23] In 1 Corinthians 4:14 he says, "I am not writing this to make you ashamed, but to admonish you as my beloved children." It is not just Paul who demonstrates this care. The same can be said for all of the New Testament writers. "The teachers, though sometimes harsh, are really friends who by frankness rather than flattery seek not to harm but to improve their charges."[24] For instance, 1 John 2:1 reads, "My little children, I am writing these things to you so that you may not sin." This verse is clearly an exhortation of the highest magnitude, but the next line adds, "But if anyone does sin, we have an advocate with the Father, Jesus Christ the righteous." Law is tempered with gospel.

Parenesis can challenge listeners-readers to live in a way never thought of before, or it can take the form of a reminder.[25] At other times the recipients of the instruction are complimented for what they are already doing, though such compliments appear rather backhanded. Consider Paul's words in 1 Thessalonians 4:1, "Finally, brothers and sisters, we ask and urge you in the Lord Jesus that, as you learned from us how you ought to live and to please God (as, in fact, you are doing), you should do so more and more." The parenthetical compliment is meant to encourage them in their moral living, just as Paul's injunction is meant to exhort them. Ultimately, the topoi and admonitions of the New Testament are expressions of care for the believers to whom the instructions are given. Some of the most challenging passages in the New Testament are written by Paul to churches that he toiled to help establish. He cared for these people and how they lived their lives in Christ.

2. The exhortations are concrete, not abstract. The biblical writers do not write about being "good, not bad." They spell out exactly what they have in mind. In 1 Thessalonians 4:3-5 Paul writes, "For this is the will of God, your sanctification: that you abstain from fornication; that each one of you know how to control your own body in holiness and honor, not with lustful passion, like the Gentiles who do not know God." Paul speaks of sanctification, but he does not leave it at the abstract level. He explains precisely what he means by that term.

In addition to using precise language, the writer frequently refers to himself as an example to be followed in order "to provide concreteness."[26] This practice was common in the writings of antiquity, and was not a mark of conceit. Rather, it provided role models for others to follow.

Concreteness was also provided through illustrations. In 2 Timothy 2:1-7 three illustrations are offered—the soldier, the athlete, and the farmer. Athletic metaphors and comparisons were quite common in the ancient world as a means of identifying the kind of commitment required for moral living.[27] These brief illustrations gave readers something more concrete to think about than simply being told to "be strong in the grace that is in Christ Jesus."

James goes a step beyond illustrations—brief illustrative metaphors—and tells stories:[28]

> For if a person with gold rings and in fine clothes comes into your assembly, and if a poor person in dirty clothes comes in, and if you take notice of the one wearing the fine clothes and say, "Have a seat here, please," while to the other one who is poor you say, "Stand there," or, "Sit at my feet . . ." (James 2:2-3)

These stories serve to project the exhortations into the concrete experiences of the listeners.

3. The topoi and admonitions in the New Testament are much more poetic than might be imagined. In fact, Martin Dibelius sees parenesis as the prose form of what was once poetry in the Old Testament wisdom literature.[29] Keeping in mind that the epistles in the New Testament were read aloud, Benjamin Fiore notes several techniques that would have appealed to the ears of the original listeners.[30] Anaphora is the use of several words in a sentence that begin with the same letter or prefix. An example in English would be to describe something as excellent, exceptional, and extraordinary. Sometimes anaphora takes the form of repeated prepositions.

Epiphora is the use of words with similar endings, somewhat like rhyming poems. In 1 Timothy 2:1 Paul writes, "First of all, then, I urge that supplications, prayers, intercessions, and thanksgivings be made for everyone . . ." The four terms used for prayer are arranged in an *abab* rhyming scheme. In the Greek, "supplications" and "intercessions" sound very much alike, as do "prayers" and "thanksgivings." This poetic device would have appealed to listeners and could have served as a memory device.

Sometimes the biblical writers use repetition for effect, repeating a word or phrase several times. In recent history the speeches of Martin Luther King Jr. employed repetition very effectively. The phrase "I have a dream" is but one famous example. Another poetic device is wordplay, using the same word with different meanings, much like modern-day puns. In 2 Timothy 2:9 Paul refers to his being chained and then adds that the word of God is not chained.

In addition to these poetic devices, exhortations employ a broad range of hortatory devices: declarations, comparisons, examples, explanations, applications, concluding calls to action, sufferings, and appeals to common knowledge. They also employ several rhetorical techniques, such as hyperbole, antithesis, paradox, and irony.[31]

4. One final technique, which is sometimes employed quite effectively, is overhearing. The pastoral epistles are but one example. Paul's words, while addressed to Timothy, are obviously intended for a wider audience.[32] A more sophisticated example of this technique is found in James 5:1-11. In the first six verses James really lets the rich have it. He speaks harshly of a judgment to come and of divine punishment. Then, beginning in verse seven, he encourages the poor believers. James clearly is writing to the second group. So why the harsh words to the rich? By addressing people who are not even present, James allows the abused believers to overhear what will eventually be the fate of their abusers.

The poetic and rhetorical techniques that we have just surveyed demand a unique approach to preaching, as well as competent interpretation.

How Can the Sermon Say and Do the Same?

It may well be that the preacher needs to explain some concepts regarding the literary forms of topoi and admonitions. The majority of churchgoers (as well as a good number of preachers) have never heard of topoi. The term "admonition" is familiar enough, but many read into it a harshness that is not necessarily warranted. Any explanation the preacher might choose to provide need not introduce technical terms. The preacher may want to explain that despite their confrontational nature, these parenetic forms are grounded in care and concern. Of course, the preacher will want to model this point, not just talk about it. Such modeling relates to the mood of the sermon.

Sermonic Mood

Everything we have considered thus far has a direct bearing on the mood of the sermon. In this section we will consider each point separately, beginning with the harsh yet caring nature of topoi and admonitions.

It has been said that the purpose of preaching is "to afflict the comfortable, and comfort the afflicted." There is some truth to this old proverb in regard to preaching these parenetic forms. The mood of the sermon needs to be prophetic and challenging as well as pastoral. Preachers who enjoy stepping on toes need to consider the caring motivation out of which the New Testament writers exhort Christlike living. Preachers who disdain confronting sin need to consider the directness of the New Testament writers regarding the moral demands of the faith. Balance is the key.

A couple of techniques may prove helpful. The preacher could point out the balance within the text while modeling it in the delivery of the sermon. Michael Quicke, in a sermon from 1 John 2:1-6, addresses John's candid command to stop sinning:

> If you are in any way serious about the message of God, then you need to understand that there must be a confessing. It must be specific. It must be directed to those areas of your lives where the shortcomings are so painful that they're even now causing such disaster in some of those things where the Lord calls you to be strong and good for him. And so John gently ("my dear children") but with great strength ("I write this to you that you will *not* sin") says *stop it*.[33]

Quicke's application is quite specific and demanding, yet the tone is clearly pastoral. Quicke points out the gentle concern of John and models it in his sermon.

Another approach available to the preacher is to use "we" language—first person plural pronouns. In the example just cited, the pronouns confront the listeners in the second person ("you"). Consider the different mood that could be established by substituting "we" language for "you" language:

> If we are in any way serious about the message of God, then we need to understand that there must be

a confessing. It must be specific. It must be directed to those areas of our lives where the shortcomings are so painful that they're even now causing such disaster in some of those things where the Lord calls us to be strong and good for him. And so John gently ("my dear children") but with great strength ("I write this to you that you will *not* sin") says *stop it*.

The first-person pronouns help establish a mood of pastoral concern, while the direct address honors the prophetic content of the text.

Some preachers attempt to achieve this balance by using humor to offset the confrontational aspects of the sermon—a long stretch of direct application followed up by some anecdote to relieve the tension of the moment. Humor is certainly a valid part of a preacher's repertoire, but it should not be used just because the preacher is uncomfortable with confrontation. The pastoral diplomacy evident in the content and the delivery of the sermon helps listeners identify the spirit in which something is said, whereas humor might prove to be counterproductive.

Another area related directly to the mood of the sermon is the concreteness of New Testament admonitions and topoi. Using personal examples, illustrations, and stories can help make the sermon a more powerful reality for the hearers in much the same way these techniques aided the original hearing.

In his sermon "The Saints: Dogged Blunderers toward Heaven" Carroll E. Simcox begins by telling the story of a saintly songwriter he had known personally:

> At the time, our children were very young, just four and two, and Father John Henry Hopkins was very old; but it was a sight never to be forgotten to see him enchanting them with the manual tricks he could play with a handkerchief. He was not only musically but spiritually fit to compose a song of the saints of God because he knew from the inside what being a saint feels like.[34]

The personal experience and the lifelike qualities of Father Hopkins doing magic tricks with the kids places the sermon in the context of real-life experiences to which the congregation can relate.

Another technique for concretizing the subject of the sermon is to use brief images (in this case a jigsaw puzzle), as illustrated in the following excerpt:

> You can almost hear Paul in the background cajoling his Corinthian congregation, "Were you baptized in the name of your factions?" "Did your factions go to Calvary for you?" When we dispute too much in the church, not speaking the truth in love, Paul's voice rings like a haunting refrain, "Is Christ divided?" Has Jesus become some giant jigsaw puzzle we'll never be able to work?[35]

Another option for the preacher is to provide a brief illustration, as William Willimon does in the closing of his sermon "Living Sacrifice":

> I know a sophomore. Came here last year all buttoned down, sure of himself. Your average, high-SAT-scoring, hyperachieving freshman. He got turned upside down, inside out one evening here at the Chapel. Messed him up for good, as far as I can tell. Gave up a sophomore summer in Vail or Los Alamos to build houses for poor people in Americus, Georgia. To most of the rest of the campus, that's called odd. Here in the Chapel, we call it normal.[36]

These techniques serve to clarify biblical concepts, providing images of what these concepts might look like if lived out. Another aspect of admonitions and topoi that affect the mood of the sermon is their poetic nature. Preachers need to be poetic themselves to do justice to this aspect of these forms. There are a number of ways to bring out the poetry hidden within the Greek (see the discussion in chapter 10). Some preachers choose to write their manuscripts in a poetic format with sentence structures that evidence meter and a concern for poetic flow:

So, the writer drew a picture to prod them along.
The picture is of an amphitheater.
The contestants are on the field, and they are Christians like you and me.
The "race" is the struggle to be faithful to Christ,
    to work for justice,
        show compassion,
        bring healing,
            speak a word of witness.
And the stands are cheering this kind of persistence.[37]

Richard F. Wilson places the prophetic words of Paul in Romans 12:1-2 alongside the poetic prose of Ecclesiastes 3, and allows the two passages to influence each other.[38] Hal Missourie Warheim's sermon "Lovers" reads like a poetic short story about living "east of Eden" and longing for the "city of lovers."[39] Whatever strategy or strategies the preacher chooses, the sermon needs to respect the mood of the text. But what about the movement?

Sermonic Movement

The highly developed structure of a topos certainly provides the preacher with a structural option for the sermon. Such an option is just that, however, and not a requirement, since form-sensitive preaching always respects the mood, but not necessarily the movement. Still, the structural movement within a topos could be followed. For example, in Romans 13:1-4 Paul writes about the believers' relationship to the government. Following the typical structure of a topos he begins with the injunction ("be subject to the governing authorities," v. 1), followed by the reasons ("there is no authority except from God," v. 1, and "whoever resists authority resists what God has appointed," v. 2), and closes with a discussion ("do what is good," v. 3). This structure can be seen in varying degrees throughout the New Testament. A sermon on a topos could follow this structure as well—beginning with the injunction, stating the reasons why it should be followed, and closing with a discussion of what that means for the listeners.

Admonitions, however, have no clearly defined structures. They may be strung together in a series or may occur in isolation. Where no structure exists, the preacher is obviously free to import a structure, though whatever sermon form is used ought to be compatible with the mood of the text. In Romans 12:9-21 Paul seems to have joined together a whole host of loosely related admonitions for living the Christian life. One metaphorical structure that could be imported would be that of a physician writing out a prescription, with the directions that Paul gives treated as prescriptions for how to live. This image would be enhanced by the preacher's pointing out the prescriptive (as opposed to descriptive) nature of parenesis. Another possibility might be an episodic sermon, which consists of separate episodes or vignettes "implicitly connected, but which then find explicit closure" in the conclusion. This kind of sermon typically develops around a metaphor rather than in linear fashion.[40]

Whatever structure is chosen must be true to the content of the text and the mood. The sermon that we will consider comes from a topos in James that appears "to be organized around paraenetical sayings rather than based upon an argument or a rhetorical structure."[41] Rather than following the movement of the text, the sermon employs a different structure. Yet it captures the mood of the text quite well. The sermon is by Donald Musser, who serves on the religion faculty at Stetson University.[42]

"Struggling with Our Mortality"

by Donald W. Musser

James 4:13-16

When we are young, we live as though we are immortal. We act as though we are without limits. We dream of breaking through impossible barriers, streaking beyond the established norms for humankind. Anything is within our reach. We believe that if you dream with desire, if you want it hard enough, if you work hard enough, if you concentrate your energies enough, you will achieve your goal, you will reach your destiny. A bookshelf of self-help manuals undergird our belief. A dozen health-and-wealth preachers inspire us to press beyond our limits to become winners. Wily entrepreneurs sell us $29.95 videotapes containing an assured formula to guarantee material immortality.

[The topic of the sermon is identified right from the start, even with the first line. Specific evidence is produced to show that we think of ourselves as invulnerable. In the next section, however, Musser identifies the concrete challenges of our presuppositions.]

And then, when we are lounging in our Lazyboy recliner, guzzling a can of RC Cola and munching on boiled peanuts, watching Robert Tilden's [*sic*] "Success for Life," a phone call explodes our very American myth into a thousand pieces. Oh, it may not actually be a phone call. But something awakens you from a deep slumber of innocence and naïveté to news that changes you forever: news of twisted wreckage and mangled bodies, a chilling message that a heart attack has slain a friend, or the agonizing announcement that your parents or children are parting in divorce. News that ties your stomach in knots and sets your heart pulsating out of control.

I vividly remember the day twenty-five years ago that I awoke to my own mortality. Having received a dramatic call from God to turn away from a career as a chemical engineer to prepare myself for the teaching and preaching of the gospel, I had resigned from a lucrative job with the Exxon Corporation and U-hauled with my bride of less than a year to the mother of all Southern Baptist seminaries. (A yankee by birth, I went to Southern Baptist Theological Seminary by the grace of God.) Shortly after completing my first year of study, and on the day after my twenty-third birthday, I entered Kentucky Baptist Hospital where a clavicular biopsy and a battery of blood tests revealed that I had lymphoma, an inoperable cancer of the lymph glands. Innocence and naïveté and unbridled idealism died that day. The ancient words of the writer of James became for me a personal and existential reality: "You are like a puff of smoke, which appears for a moment and then disappears" (James 4:14b). I have not disappeared yet. I learned in that valley of the shadow how fragile life is. Daily, I give gratitude for the chemotherapy that killed the cancer cells and to the Grace that has kept the smoldering invader in remission for a quarter century. To be sure, the illusion of immortality beckons me no longer.

[A detailed account of a personal experience further helps to make the preacher's point clear. He does not stop there, however. In the section that follows he points to other examples of mortality.]

All of us, some early in life (like the passionate teenagers who find themselves pregnant at sixteen) and others later (like the privileged and pampered college freshman who has never washed or ironed her own clothes) awaken to the fact that we do not command the universe. We live in an imperfect world where the threads of drudgery and sorrow are woven into the fabric of life. We learn that reality is laced with tragedy; that the powers of death fester in every human achievement, threatening to swallow every breath of life. How do we live in a world that bears within it the dissolution of every achievement? How do we cope when we set our sights high, only to have some inane, unplanned catastrophe dash our hopes? How do we understand our mortality? At least three paths are open to us: the path of illusion, the path of despair, and the path of the gospel.

[The sermon will consider three different responses to mortality. The scheme is more existential than textual, although the mood of the text is definitely respected.]

The path of illusion effectively denies our mortality: We live as though we will never die, as though we can't die. Nothing illustrates this more clearly than the cult of youth that pervades our culture. Teens believe they are immortal. If they were honest with us, every teen in this congregation could tell us of harrowing experiences within the past month where they could have been maimed or killed or had their reputation ruined. But adults should not agree with this assertion so smugly. On every hand adults battle the aging process. We hide the gray with Grecian Formula; we gulp megavitamins; we sweat with Richard Simmons; we eschew biscuits and gravy and gnaw on carrots and broccoli. If we are affluent, we spend thousands to streamline the wrinkles in our faces and to suck the celluloid [*sic*] from our thighs and buttocks. We groan our way to the spa wearing a T-shirt that announces, "I may grow older, but I'll never grow up."

[Specific examples are cited that illustrate our obsession with immortality and youth. The preacher's humorous approach allows him to make his point, while avoiding the pall of condemnation. The humor, however, does not extinguish the confrontational mood. The use of first person plural pronouns also facilitates making the point.]

The denial of our mortality appears prominently in the pseudo-sophisticated subtleties that characterize the New

Age that has been embraced by young and old in middle-class America. For New Agers, mortality is an illusion. Your mistake is that you think you will die. Actually, you have immortality within you: Like Jonathan Livingston Seagull, you can find within yourself intimations of immortality and the energy to ascend to new realities far beyond your imagination. Just believe it; just do it. You are without limits.

[The first path is described using imagery from a well-known piece of literature. For those unfamiliar with the somewhat older story, the contemporary New Age movement is also mentioned. This sermon is exceptionally clear and relevant.]

Unlike Jonathan, who flies freely and unhindered into fantastic new worlds created by the imagination, some of us choose the path of despair. A dark realism enfolds us. We refuse to commit ourselves to any large and distant goals. We choose not to throw ourselves into life because we fear we will be trampled by intruding evil. Our model is not Jonathan but rather Albert Camus's character Sisyphus, who pushes a boulder up a mountain, only to have it thunder down the other side. And he plods dutifully down the mountain to push it up again, endlessly repeating a meaningless task. Life for the despairing is but cycles of mundane activities. We live in a gray fog where nothing ultimately matters, where no truths exist, where no morals subsist. Therefore, we set no goals, strive for no ends, plan for no contingencies. Illusion and denial are not our lot: despair and apathy are our cup of ashes. Ecclesiastes is all the Scripture we have: "Vanity of vanities, all is vanity," we cry out. Our valley of shadows has no exit. Some of us anesthetize our despairing souls with alcohol or hype ourselves momentarily with marijuana or crack cocaine.

[The second inappropriate approach to immortality is discussed, again using an image from literature. The sentence structures are truly poetic.]

The Bible challenges both the paths of limitless immortality of Jonathan Livingston Seagull and the meaningless despair and apathy of Sisyphus. When Jonathan concludes that divinity is ours, and from the myth of our unlimited illusions we think we are masters of our own fates, declaring that "today or tomorrow we will travel to a certain city, where we will stay a year and go into business and make a lot of money," the Bible rages back: "You don't even know what your life tomorrow will be!" When, on the other hand, we slouch into despair with Sisyphus and grouse about what a bummer everything is, the Bible reminds us that a gracious God loves us. When we have given up all hope, a touch or a smile or a card reminds us that some kind Power beyond has touched us.

[In the above paragraph and the one to come Musser introduces the biblical challenge to the approaches of the world. He is very direct and concrete, yet poetic as well.]

The Bible provides us with a third path to life: a way between an illusory utopia that resides only in our imaginations and a senseless existence that reduces us to couch potatoes, drowning out reality with reruns of the "Andy Griffith Show." The Bible provides a vision of a middle way between illusion and despair. It declares that life has limits, while at the same time affirming that marvelous possibilities lie within ourselves and the world. It pronounces that life has focus and purpose when seen from the point of view of God, though not without tragedy and misfortune. The gospel finds a place for a life full of laughter tinged with a cup of tears, for ecstasies that touch eternity and despondency that occasionally knows no solace.

The way of the gospel begins with the admonition of James that "what you should say is this: 'If the Lord is willing,'" we will accomplish this or do that. The writer emphasizes the claim that we are dependent creatures of a Creator God who has made us. We did not will our lives; we had nothing to do with our coming into being: We are by the gracious gift of a

Power beyond us. Life has been given to us as a gift. It is not our own creation. We do not own it or deserve it or control it. We are but stewards of life. Not only is life a gift; it is also a mystery. Like the Spirit of God, life comes into being and flickers out at times that we cannot calculate precisely. God is the giver of life and the taker of life. And life is fragile. In a moment it can end like a mist that evaporates into the atmosphere.

[This section of direct application confronts the congregation with the truth, but it does so in a loving way. The use of first person pronouns helps to set the content within a pastoral context.]

The Christian model for life is not found in the fantastic illusions of Jonathan Livingston Seagull nor in the gloomy despair of Sisyphus, but in the realistic hope of our Pioneer on the path of faith, Jesus Christ. In his teaching about the Kingdom of God he gave us a pattern for living triumphantly in a world that sometimes smiles upon us and sometimes slaps us up the side of the head. In the grotesque and twisted pain of the cross, he enabled us to see that God is with us in a world ridiculed by grievous trials and agonies. And in his resurrection from the dead, God has sanctified the Christ-like way as a path for us.

We often struggle with our mortality by either creating the illusion that we are immortal or by throwing up our hands in despair and renouncing any meaning or hope in life. In the gospel we find a third path. On the gospel path we follow neither Jonathan Livingston Seagull nor Sisyphus but rather Jesus, whose crucifixion recognizes the cruel horrors of life and whose resurrection declares the victory of God over death.

Can we walk the path of Christ today? Can we crucify our mortal struggles and surrender our pride, apathy, and self-delusion, and walk in the hope of resurrection faith with him? These are the questions that face us in our struggle with mortality. The answers are ours to give. And the answers will make all the difference.

[Musser has explored the disappointments and agonies of life in concrete fashion throughout the message. The biblical answers have been examined in all of their realism, but Musser ends by looking to the crucifixion and resurrection of Jesus as signs of hope.]

Exercises

Answer the following nine questions for the admonitions or topoi included in each passage: Romans 13:8-10; 1 Thessalonians 5:12-22; James 2:14-26.

1. Is this text an admonition or a topos? If a topos, does it follow the typical structure associated with topoi?

2. What impact does the context have on understanding the passage? How is the teaching of the passage culturally conditioned?

3. What is the writer admonishing the people to do? In what ways is the advice confrontational? What signs of compassion are evident in the passage? What is the relevance of the writer's relationship to the recipients?

4. What poetic devices can you identify in this passage?

5. What is the mood of the text? What musical instruments might best accompany the text? What colors and/or textures does the mood of the text suggest to you? What adjectives and adverbs best describe it?

6. What concrete images come to your mind that might help listeners identify with the teaching of the passage?

7. What is the text saying?

8. What is the text doing?

9. How could a sermon say and do the same?

Sermon Resources

William J. Carl III, "Unplanned Dissonance" [1 Corinthians 1:10-17], in *Preaching Biblically,* ed. Don M. Wardlaw

(Westminster, 1983), pp. 129-35. Included in the Wardlaw volume as a sample sermon of what it means to preach following the structure of the text. Preacher's own reflections on the text and the sermon also included. Uses some wonderful imagery.

Donald W. Musser, "Struggling with Our Mortality" [James 4:13-16], in *Best Sermons 6*, ed. James W. Cox (Harper and Row, 1993), pp. 202-6. Complete sermon included in this chapter.

Michael Quicke, "Come Alive with 1 John—Stop Sinning!" [1 John 2:1-6], in *Best Sermons 6*, pp. 53-62. Directly addresses the balance between confrontation and comfort in the text. Probably a bit long for most American congregations.

Carroll E. Simcox, "The Saints: Dogged Blunderers toward Heaven" [Hebrews 12:1-2], in *Best Sermons 4*, ed. James W. Cox (Harper and Row, 1991), pp. 118-23. Exceptionally poetic and literate. Concrete imagery, direct application. Captures pastoral aspects of the text.

Hal Missourie Warheim, "Lovers" [1 John 4:7-8], in *Best Sermons 2*, ed. James W. Cox (Harper and Row, 1989), pp. 267-76. Truly poetic sermon. Captivating dialogue and narrative keeps listeners' attention. Poetic and imaginative.

William H. Willimon, "Living Sacrifice" [Romans 12:1-8], in *Preaching to Strangers*, pp. 29-37. Confrontational like the text. Contemporary in application with engaging images.

Richard F. Wilson, "Rhythms" [Ecclesiastes 3:1-15; Romans 12:1-2], in *Best Sermons 5*, ed. James W. Cox (Harper and Row, 1990), pp. 79-85. Juxtaposes the poetry of Ecclesiastes and the admonitions of Romans 12. Full of imagery and pastoral concern.

Robert D. Young, "Keep Up the Good Work" [Hebrews 12:1-2], in *Be Brief about It* (Westminster, 1980), pp. 135-42. An example of brevity in preaching. Imagery and poetry also noteworthy.

CHAPTER 12

Poetry and Hymns: The Gospel in Verse

Poetry. The word evokes all sorts of terms and feelings. Terms like iambic pentameter, couplet, stanza, rhyme, sonnet. Feelings evoked in poems created by figures as diverse as Dr. Seuss and Robert Browning, both great poets in their own right.

Bible. This word evokes all sorts of thoughts and experiences as well. Again terms come to mind, such as genealogies, chapter and verse, dogma, and beatitudes. A host of adjectives also come to mind, such as strange, ancient, wonderful, bizarre, comforting, alarming, and familiar. We think about the stories in the Bible, from Adam and Eve in the front of the book to the New Jerusalem in the back. A lot of things come to mind in connection with the Bible, but poetry is probably not one of them. Yet the New Testament (and the entire Bible, for that matter) overflows with poetry.

The Bible and poetry: like Romeo and Juliet, their chances of getting together seem slim. Is it possible to learn to read the New Testament as poetry in order to help our listeners hear it as poetry? Is it possible to preach such poetry without destroying it at the same time? These are some of the questions we will consider in this chapter.

What Is the Text Saying?

Responsible interpretation and preaching of biblical poetry must respect its artistry. To do that, the preacher needs to hear the music behind the words. Listen for a moment to the world of poetry and some of its tunes. In A. A. Milne's classic *The House at Pooh Corner*, Winnie the Pooh has just finished sharing a poem with Piglet about their new friend Tigger:

"And that's the whole poem," he said. "Do you like it, Piglet?"

"All except the shillings," said Piglet. "I don't think they ought to be there."

"They wanted to come in after the pounds," explained Pooh, "so I let them. It is the best way to write poetry, letting things come."

"Oh, I didn't know," said Piglet.[1]

Another example is drawn from the movie *Dead Poet's Society*. Robin Williams, who plays Professor Keating, is teaching the first session of a course in poetry. He asks one of the students to open the textbook and begin reading:

"Understanding Poetry," by Dr. J. Evans Pritchard, Ph.D. To fully understand poetry we must first be fluent with its meter, rhyme, and figures of speech, then ask two questions. One, How artfully have the objectives of the poem been rendered? And two, How important is that objective? Question one rates the poem's perfection. Question two rates its importance. And once these questions have been answered, determining the poem's greatness becomes a relatively simple matter.

Professor Keating responds with one word: "excrement." He goes on to reveal the absurdity of such a scheme. "We're not laying pipe. We're talking about poetry," he declares. "Now I want you to rip out that page." He has them rip out the entire introduction and then adds, "This is a battle, a war. And the casualties could be your hearts and souls. . . . You will learn to savor words and language."

Now consider a piece of New Testament poetry:

If I speak in the tongues of mortals and of angels,
    but do not have love,
        I am a noisy gong,
        or a clanging cymbal.
And if I have prophetic powers,
and understand all mysteries and all knowledge,
and if I have all faith, so as to remove mountains,
    but do not have love,
        I am nothing.
If I give away all my possessions,
And if I hand over my body so that I may boast,
    but do not have love,
        I gain nothing.[2]

Poetry—letting things come, savoring words and language, the tongues of mortals and of angels. These phrases capture the essence of poetry. When preaching biblical poetry, the preacher must be sensitive to the mood and the nuance of the text, to its rhythms and flavors, to its words and flow.[3] As Karl Rahner reminds us, the most sublime and moving passages of Scripture are invariably those embedded in "a pregnant word of human poetry."[4] Although the task of reading biblical poetry shares much in common with reading nonbiblical poetry, certain differences obviously exist. Interpreting New Testament poetry even differs from interpreting an Old Testament psalm.[5] Good Bible study aids can help the preacher take these differences into account in the process of interpretation.

Initially, however, the interpreter needs to be able to identify biblical poetry. Several forms exist, all of which were most likely used in worship in the early church, much like our responsive readings, hymns, and prayers today.

New Testament poetry includes numerous *hymns* and

hymn fragments, the chief of which is found embedded in a longer passage, Philippians 2:1-11: "who, though he was in the form of God, did not regard equality with God as something to be exploited . . ."[6] Verses 5-11 most likely constitute a hymn of the early church. Other hymns in the New Testament include Colossians 1:15-20; Ephesians 2:14-16; 1 Timothy 3:16; and 1 Peter 3:18-22, just to name a few.[7] Other hymns in the New Testament include Colossians 1:15-20, 1 Timothy 3:16, and 1 Peter 3:18-22, just to name a few. An excellent new resource for interpreting and preaching the hymns of the New Testament is *A Symphony of New Testament Hymns* by Robert Karris (Liturgical Press, 1996). Karris shows that the Pauline corpus of hymns is larger than one might think.

New Testament poetry also includes *prayers* for fellow believers in which Paul (or some other writer) waxes eloquent, apparently quoting some well-known poetic prayer or composing one himself. Ephesians 1:17-19 is one example. Consider this excerpt: ". . . so that, with the eyes of your heart enlightened, you may know what is the hope to which he has called you, what are the riches of his glorious inheritance among the saints. . . ." This too is poetry.

Although they are generally treated separately, *blessings, doxologies,* and *confessions* have a poetic nature as well. Some of these are vertical blessings (which are addressed heavenward), such as, "Now to him who by the power at work within us is able to accomplish abundantly far more than all we can ask or imagine . . ." (Ephesians 3:20-21). Vertical blessings would also include the beatitudes of Jesus ("Blessed are . . ."). Horizontal blessings, those addressed to fellow believers, include typical Pauline blessings, such as "now may our Lord Jesus Christ and God our Father, who loved us and through grace gave us eternal comfort and good hope" (2 Thessalonians 2:16-17).

Lastly, New Testament poetry includes *poetic prose,* when, for instance, the writer suddenly breaks into poetry. Paul's treatment of love in 1 Corinthians 13 or his hope amid trials in 2 Corinthians 4:8-10 are good examples:

> We are afflicted in every way, but not crushed;
> Perplexed, but not driven to despair;
> Persecuted, but not forsaken;
> Struck down, but not destroyed;
> Always carrying in the body the death of Jesus,
> So that the life of Jesus may also be made visible in our bodies.[8]

Sometimes Paul borrows poetry from the Old Testament, such as when he quotes Isaiah 54:1 in Galatians 4:27:

> Rejoice, you childless one,
> you who bear no children,
>   burst into song and shout, you
> who endure no birthpangs . . .[9]

We must seek to understand *how* poetry works if our sermons are to do what the text does.

What Is the Text Doing?

Poetry affects us differently than other forms of communication do, and it makes use of several rhetorical strategies that accomplish this. Following is a discussion of four such strategies.

1. It uses concrete imagery rather than generic abstractions. Consider, for example, Anne Sexton's poem entitled "ROWING," in which she describes the irony of her life in the line "I wore rubies and bought tomatoes."[10] Most preachers would say it differently, claims Robert Waznak. They would speak about life's ups and downs, but not in any way that does justice to real-life experiences.[11] Concrete imagery paints pictures. The same concrete imagery is apparent within biblical poetry as well. The apostle Paul could have written, "Without love, speaking in tongues is meaningless." Instead, he chose the beauty of poetic prose.[12]

2. Poetry places a heavy premium on word choice. Walter Brueggemann speaks of poetry as a corrective for a "prose world." By the term "prose" he means a world that is "organized in settled formulae, so that even pastoral prayers and love letters sound like memos." He calls for preachers to employ poetic language, the kind that moves like a fastball, "that jumps at the right moment, that breaks open old worlds with surprise, abrasion, and pace."[13]

3. Poetry plays with "sustained rhythm,"[14] what might be called the movement of metaphors. Quite often, however, this rhythm can only be sensed in an oral reading of a text. Some preachers never experience the rhythm of a text because they fail to read it aloud prior to the preaching moment. Reading the text orally in the earliest stages of preparation can help unleash the poetic beauty of a passage, the music behind the text.

4. Poetry is most of all an evocative type of literature. Although the poetry of the New Testament may have been used to teach converts about the faith,[15] biblical poetry is primarily addressed to the affective faculty. "Poems change what we think and feel not by piling up facts we did not know or by persuading us through arguments, but by making finely tuned adjustments at deep and critical places in our imaginations."[16] Poetry stimulates our imagination.[17] In much the same way that stories cause us to identify with the characters and thus be challenged by them, biblical poetry produces in us some kind of "ultimate cry or hunger" that eventually all will be right with our world.[18]

How Can the Sermon Say and Do the Same?

As is the case with the majority of New Testament forms, textual movement does not seem to play as large a role as textual mood, though that may vary from text to text.

Sermonic Mood

Determining the mood of a poetic passage is relatively easy. Poetic texts tend to wear their emotions on their sleeves. These passages produce beautiful music, and so must the sermon. The preacher obviously needs to make use of concrete imagery rather than vague abstractions. If the text is about social injustice, for example, the preacher might describe the government housing project in Baltimore where children were afflicted by lead poisoning, a project that was recently torn down. The term "social injustice" is one thing, but a vivid description is quite another.[19] For example, in a sermon from Philippians 2:5-11, Ronald Allen tells about a graduating seminary student and his desire to return to his homeland, Sri Lanka:

> "Why are you going back to that danger?"
> "I have seen the Lord of glory," he said.
> "What can those two-bit caesars do to me?"
> When we confess him,
>   his victory is our victory
>   and no matter what our circumstances
>   it makes all the difference in the world.
> And your calling, Wyatt,
>   is to make that clear:
>   Jesus is Lord.
>   Lord over cocaine.
>   Lord over IBM.
>   Lord over Ronald Reagan.
>   Lord over the church.[20]

Attention to word choice is also crucial. Rather than using a thesaurus to produce alliterated outlines, the preacher needs to search for words to use in the sermon, words that do something to listeners. "The difference between the right word and the almost right word," wrote Mark Twain, "is the difference between lightning and the lightning bug." Preachers must work with their words in order to make words work for them.[21] Preaching biblical poetry demands a poetic use of words. James Zug's sermon "The Inevitable Encounter" is not only printed in poetic form but also makes use of poetic language. Consider this excerpt:

> For nights and days on end he followed . . .
>   as though he had been paid to do so.
> My initial reaction was that of curiosity.
>   Who would want to follow me?
>   And why?
>   *Coincidence!*
>   *Mere coincidence,* I said!
> But soon I was aware that his pursuit
>   was not mere idle chance.
> I found that I could not elude him!
>   Every path and street I traveled . . . he knew.[22]

Above all else, the sermon must seek to be evocative, generating feelings in listeners, just as the original poem generated feelings in its recipients. Such a sermon will cause listeners "to wrestle with the images and moods generated by the poetic experience."[23] There is a difference between explaining what a poem means and breaking into poetry.[24]

Incorporating poetry in the sermon itself can be useful, but is not necessary. A contrived effort can result in tortured poetry and bad preaching. Reading poetry, however, is a wonderful exercise for preachers, even when none of it actually gets used in the sermon. Why? "Because [poetry] says what cannot be said. . . . Preachers have to talk constantly about God, whom they have never seen, to people who are in no better condition than we are on that score. Poetry helps us do that best."[25]

Nourished by healthy doses of poetry, the preacher might be inspired to find words and metaphors that stimulate the imagination. Biblical poetry should not be preached as "propositional theology."[26] It is more open-ended than that. Poetic preaching is more akin to a stained-glass window than a

conventional pane of glass.[27] There is more artistry involved.
Preachers should search for contemporary images and stories that touch people the way the biblical images and stories
do. Kathleen Norris, in her book *The Cloister Walk*, offers a
wonderfully poetic description of a baptismal service:

> Today, we are baptizing our little nephew. He's seven
> months old, chubby, thoroughly healthy. . . . We've
> planned the ceremony for late in the afternoon of Epiph-
> any, at home. . . .
> The baby's tired and cranky, he has no way of knowing
> that we are passing through hell. We renounce the forces
> of evil, and he cries out. As the godmother, I am holding
> him, and he's fussy, squirming; I have to hold on tight:
> Our words wash over you, and you brush them away.
> The candle catches your eye, your mother's hair and fin-
> gers transparent in its light. You want the candle, you want
> the food your mother has become for you, you want to go
> down into this night at her breast. Poor little baby, water
> on your chin, chrism on your forehead, dried milk on your
> chin. Poor, dear little baby; hold on.[28]

What a great image for a sermon from Ephesians 4:1-6, a
passage believed by some to have been used originally as
baptismal liturgy.[29]

As we have seen, some preachers even write their sermon
manuscripts in poetic structure, in hopes that such a format
will affect the mood of the preaching event itself.[30] Anyone
who has ever read poetry aloud (which is really the only way
to read it) knows the value of cadence and rhythm.

Sermonic Movement

As a general rule, textual movement does not play a large
role in preaching such passages, although the rhythm of a
poetic text might offer some suggestions for movement
within the sermon. The rhythms of the text could serve as
clues for the rhythms of the sermon. Some texts reach a
crescendo at midpoint, others near the end. The sermon

could do the same by carefully constructing the materials to be included and their arrangement. Some sermons I have heard included all the components they needed for effective preaching (vivid images, concise exposition, timely application, colorful stories, and so forth), but not necessarily in the best order. What makes one order of presentation better than another is not always easy to describe, though it is typically easy to identify when executed.[31] The ebb and flow of a poetic passage sometimes suggests an ebb and flow for the sermon.

The rate of delivery and the use of pregnant pauses can also enhance the rhythm of the sermon. Delivery is one of the often overlooked aspects of preaching.

Ultimately, preachers who would preach from the poetry of the Bible must learn to view their world poetically. As Elizabeth Barrett Browning reminds us:

Earth's crammed with heaven,
And every common bush afire with God:
But only he who sees, takes off his shoes
The rest sit 'round it and pluck blackberries.[32]

As an example of poetic preaching, we will look at a sermon that I preached recently at a church in Iowa where I was serving as interim pastor. The church was composed of some wonderful people, but there were groups within it that were creating tension. The occasion for this sermon was Palm Sunday, and one of the lectionary readings was Philippians 2:1-11.

"Special Music in the Early Church"

by Mike Graves

Philippians 2:1-11

The church at Philippi—what a wonderful church. No real doctrinal problems. Nobody eating meat sacrificed to idols or bragging about spiritual gifts, as in Corinth. Nobody slipping back into Judaism, giving up on the faith, as in Galatia. Nobody questioning the preacher's motives, as in Thessalonica. What a great church! Nobody squabbling over the organ's being too loud during services. No spats over the color of hymnals. No fights over the carpet for the sanctuary.

[From the very beginning I want the listeners to think of the ancient church settings in contemporary ways and vice versa. Although much has changed, much remains the same.]

Or maybe it was something like that. Oh, I probably shouldn't even mention it. It was a little thing. They really were a great church, no *real* problems. Still, Paul did devote all this space to a call for unity. Why did he do it? Why did he address the need for harmony if everything was hunky-dory?

You did hear it, didn't you? "Make my joy complete: be of the same mind, having the same love, being in full accord and of one mind. Do nothing from selfish ambition or conceit, but in humility regard others as better than yourselves. Let each of you look not to your own interests, but to the interests of others" (vv. 2-4). What gives? Was this the perfect church or not? *NOT!* There's no such thing. They didn't have any big problems, but they did have some problems.

It's only hinted at, but it's there. Chapter 4, verse 2: "I urge

Euodia and I urge Syntyche to be of the same mind in the Lord." "The same mind" is precisely the same phrase used here in chapter 2.

The church at Philippi had no major problems. They were not facing any theological heresies. There had been no church scandals—treasurer absconding with funds and making his way to the Mediterranean to retire in some condo. The problem at Philippi may have been nothing more than pettiness. But pettiness may be the biggest problem a church can face. These two women were at odds about something. Who knows what. So Paul calls them by name, and he expects this letter to be read in church. If I had been reading it, I would have been tempted to skip this part. You know, "And then Paul closes with the usual stuff, sincerely yours, et cetera, et cetera."

[Now the similarities between the ancient world and ours become more personal. The sermon will begin to explore the differences in worship between then and now.]

I've never been to worship where the preacher called out the names of folks in the church who were at odds. I've heard names mentioned for prayer, but not the names of bickering women. Takes a lot of nerve for a preacher to do that. Or a lot of stupidity. Then again, maybe not in this case. Paul wasn't there. I bet he was glad of that. This was a letter to be read in his absence, read as a sermon of sorts.

Interesting, how letters work. They allow for direct, face-to-face communication without actually being face-to-face. Isn't that convenient? Did you ever get a letter from someone telling you off? If they'd said those things to your face, you would have interrupted, yelled back, argued, said, "I don't have to take this." You'd walk away. But not with a letter. Oh, you can throw it away. But first you read it, don't you? Every single line, even though you don't want to hear it.

[A contemporary analogy is employed to illustrate how letters

worked in an oral culture. This will help listeners to eventually understand how hymns worked as well.]

The same was true of Paul's letter. And Paul's letter was part of the worship service. If they'd printed bulletins, it might have come right after the choral anthem and the offering. Or maybe after the announcements and the shaking of hands. Can you see Paul having everybody stand and shake hands with three people around them?

[Comic relief allows the listeners to think about obvious differences in our worship services today. Next the sermon will teach about the basic structure of ancient worship. This insight is crucial in order to grasp how Paul's use of a hymn would have affected his listeners.]

No, of course not. Early church worship was different from our services today, at least in some ways. They met in homes and things were more casual, though not as casual as you might suspect. There were customary elements of worship. Attention was given to prayer, to the "public reading of scripture" (1 Timothy 4:13), to baptism, and to the Lord's Supper. There were other elements of worship, of course. There was the singing of "psalms and hymns and spiritual songs" (Colossians 3:16), what some today call "special music." But the early church knew there was no such thing. All music is special in worship. Last, there was the reading of apostolic letters, especially from Paul, especially at Philippi, a church that Paul had founded. This was Paul's favorite church.

If you were Paul, what would you say? He began with a wonderful line: "I thank my God every time I remember you" (Philippians 1:3). His memories were many. He wrote of praying for them, of being in prison and yet being hopeful, and then decided to address the issue. But how?

In typical fashion, Paul addressed it head-on. He spoke positively of four needed qualities: "be of the same mind, having the same love, being in full accord and of one mind"

(v. 2). He spoke negatively of three undesirable qualities: "do nothing from selfish ambition," "[do nothing from] conceit," "[do not look] to your own interests" (vv. 3-4). What else could he say? He pushed back from the table and stretched. He walked around the room. He had said it all in a sense. Perhaps he thought hard about calling the women by name right here. What else could he possibly say at this point?

[Contemporary trends in preaching have moved away from explaining the text as I have done, but form-sensitive preaching not only does what the text is doing but says what it is saying as well.]

Then his foot began tapping, and he started humming. There was a hymn he couldn't shake loose. Maybe it had been playing on the radio when he awoke that morning. He sang the words, then began to listen, really listen. It was one of the great Christ hymns. It was a piece of music seeking to be heard, "special music" indeed: "Let the same mind be in you that was in Christ Jesus,

who, though he was in the form of God,
did not regard equality with God as something to be exploited,
but emptied himself . . ."

Paul would refer to a hymn. And that's just what he did. Not all translations capture it, but verses 5-11 are a hymn. We don't know if Paul wrote it or borrowed it, but he certainly used it. As he wrote, he hummed. And as he hummed, he wrote. He only hoped those women would be humming when they heard it.

[Now the idea of how Paul might have used this hymn is before us. This is the point to which the sermon has been moving all along.]

I know people in a church in Texas who had been best friends, two couples who bowled together, played dominoes, ate pizza, rented movies, attended church together. Deep, strong friendship. Now they won't even speak to each other. One couple has dropped out of church. The fellowship hall needed new chairs. The committee recommended the plastic kind you stack four or five high. But at the business meeting some wanted to know why folding chairs wouldn't work, being easier to store and all, maybe even cheaper. Some said they were actually more expensive. Others said they weren't. Some said the plastic ones were more durable. Others said they got brittle and cracked. These two couples went to battle against each other over it. One couple dropped out of church.

[A specific example is drawn from a church I once attended. The story is not about my listeners, and yet the concreteness draws them into it.]

Can you imagine what would have happened, if, before they quit coming, the former pastor had written a letter to the church urging them to put aside their petty differences? I can't really be sure, of course. But what if a letter had been read, and what if that pastor threw in one line from a hymn that all of them had sung in worship together? Who knows?

Maybe that's why Paul quoted from a hymn, to remind them of their worship together. But why this one? This hymn is considered one of the most majestic passages in the Bible— a classic hymn. In fact, tradition has it that this text should be read on Palm Sunday because, more than any other hymn, it reminds us of God's wonderful gift in the sacrifice of Christ.

But why would Paul use such a rich theological hymn for such a petty disagreement? Why roll out the big guns over such a small argument? Maybe because it's when we are forced to look at the awesome gift of God's giving his son that our pettiness becomes insignificant. Maybe alongside triumphal entry and loud hosannas arguments among Christians begin to look silly.

[The liturgical context is pointed out to explain the rich traditions associated with this passage, but also to begin the move toward the direct application that follows.]

This church is one of the finest I have ever been associated with. It has wonderful facilities and wonderful people, but it has a few tensions too. No major problems. No major debts.

But some tensions among persons. Paul says to be united, to love one another. And just in case we don't hear those words, he sings it out in this rich hymn about Christ.

It's the same for the hymn we sang earlier in worship, "Joyful, Joyful, We Adore Thee." The tune is by Beethoven. It is adapted from the finale of his *Ninth Symphony*, which is considered by many to be the most beautiful piece of music ever written.

Do you know the story of this hymn? Beethoven wrote it inspired by a poem by Schiller about the joy we can have in relation to God and each other. Years later Henry Van Dyke, a preacher, wrote the words we now sing. Listen to that third stanza again:

Thou art giving and forgiving,
Ever blessing, ever blest,
Well-spring of the joy of living,
Ocean-depth of happy rest!
Thou our Father, Christ our Brother—
All who live in love are Thine;
Teach us how to love each other,
Lift us to the joy divine.

All kinds of stories have sprung up around the life of Beethoven. There was a children's story released on CD and then made into a children's book—*Beethoven Lives Upstairs*. Great book! They even made a movie this year, *Immortal, Beloved*. Did you see it? It tells the story of when, as a young man, Beethoven fell in love with this beautiful young lady. They agreed to meet one afternoon. Perhaps this would even be the time to propose marriage, but Beethoven was delayed. By the time he showed up, she was gone, and, as it turned out, the two never spoke to each other again.

Years later, after Beethoven's death, she learned that he had sent a letter explaining his delay and asking her to wait for him. But she never received it. She never got the letter.

But we did, this letter of Paul's. This call to unity. We got it, didn't we?

[Reference is made to the Beethoven piece used earlier in our own worship service. A contemporary story about Beethoven is then used to close the sermon, reminding us of what Paul's letter and hymn was intended to accomplish among us.]

Exercises

Answer the following six questions for the poetry in each passage: 2 Corinthians 4:8-10; Ephesians 3:20-21; Colossians 1:15-20.

1. Which poetic form is included in the text: hymn, prayer, blessing, confession, doxology, or poetic prose? What does this form tell you about the meaning of the text?

2. What images come to mind as you read the text aloud? Do new images emerge with repeated readings? What kinds of rhythm do you notice?

3. What concrete imagery does the text employ? What concrete images and/or contemporary stories might be used in a sermon on this text?

4. How does the poetry of the text affect you? What is the mood? What kinds of musical instruments might convey the mood(s)? Does the text suggest certain colors and/or textures?

5. What textual movements can you identify? How could they be used in the composition of the sermon?

6. What is the text saying? What is the text doing? How could a sermon say and do the same?

Sermon Resources

Ronald J. Allen, "The Difference" [Philippians 2:5-11], in *Preaching as a Social Act,* ed. Arthur Van Seters (Abingdon, 1988), pp. 187-96. Based on the hymn, uses a poetic format. Filled with imagery and contemporary material.

Fred B. Craddock, "Doxology" [Romans 11:33-36], in his book *As One without Authority* (Abingdon, 1971), pp. 163-68. A powerful sermon that utilizes personification to bring the idea of doxology alive. Exceptionally creative.

Charles W. Scriven, "God's Grief" [Isaiah 53:3-5; Philippians 2:5-8; Colossians 1:15], in *Best Sermons 1*, ed. James W. Cox (Harper and Row, 1988), pp. 163-70. Uses two New Testament hymns.

James R. Zug, "The Inevitable Encounter" [Psalm 139; Ephesians 1:9-10], in *Best Sermons 2*, ed. James W. Cox (Harper and Row, 1989), pp. 43-52. Poetic format. Makes use of a dream to convey the message. Very creative.

CHAPTER 13

Apocalypse:
The Curious Visions of John

Consider two different worlds and their inhabitants. First, the modern world. Crowded malls and January white sales. Ragged hands holding ragged cardboard signs that read, "Will work for food." Chrysler minivans and Boeing 747s. Super bowls and world series. Turmoil in the Middle East. PCs, VCRs, and CDs. Skyscrapers. The suburbs.

Second, the world of apocalyptic. A great red dragon with seven heads. Bottomless pits. Awful plagues. A conquering warrior mounted on a white horse. Thunder and lightning. Swords and famine. The apocalyptic world of first-century Christians.

The first sounds so familiar. It is where we live. The second sounds so outlandish, like some kind of sci-fi thriller from Ray Bradbury or Stephen Spielberg. What could these two worlds possibly have in common? More specifically, how can the modern preacher relate these two worlds to each other while doing justice to both? How do you preach from apocalyptic literature? For that matter, what is apocalyptic literature?

The best known piece of apocalyptic literature in the New

Testament is the book of Revelation, an eclectic blending of many forms: prophetic oracles, commissioning visions, dirges, hymns, vice and virtue lists, letters, and more. In fact, the whole "book" is enclosed within a letter format with some uniquely narrative features throughout.[1] The purpose of apocalyptic, according to recent biblical scholarship, is "to interpret present, earthly circumstances in light of the supernatural world and of the future, and to influence both the understanding and the behavior of the audience by means of divine authority."[2] Or as Bruce Malina notes, the purpose of such writings in antiquity was to deal with the problems of the present in much the same way science fiction does today,[3] thus making apocalyptic literature more "diagnostic" than "predictive."[4] Simply put, dragons and swords have more to do with our modern world of minivans than we realize.

Apocalyptic literature addresses our contemporary "thoughts, attitudes, and feelings by the use of effective symbols and a narrative plot that invites imaginative participation."[5] Interestingly, it is the strangeness of Revelation that has long kept so many at bay, while millions have flocked to see the *Star Wars* series or *E.T.* The power of apocalyptic literature, like a good sci-fi flick itself, has the capacity to bring these two worlds together. Once they do, this world will never be the same again.

Bringing these two worlds together begins with sound biblical interpretation, but it also involves more than that. Certain homiletical challenges are also present. So we need to consider the preliminary questions of sermon composition.

What Is the Text Saying?

As with any biblical text, the answer to this question involves understanding the literary form used, among other exegetical issues. This is especially true for apocalyptic literature, since it is so widely misunderstood. People today are familiar with proverbs; they occur not only in the Bible but in comic strips as well. Narratives are not limited to the pages of the Scriptures but are commonplace in movies and novels. Apocalyptic seems so outlandish, so strange. What does it mean?

The central message of apocalyptic literature was the ultimate triumph of God's goodness over the evils of the present.[6] Revelation sought to overcome the dissonance between what was and what ought to be, the tension between the persecution that first-century Christians were facing and the divine justice they longed for.[7] "Their experience of hunger, deprivation, pestilence, and war undermined their belief in God's good creation."[8] Those things affect us the same way today. That is why Revelation must be preached.

There are other apocalyptic passages, however, within the New Testament. For instance, the gospels use apocalyptic language, some of it as obvious as Jesus declaring that "you will see the Son of Man seated at the right hand of the Power . . ." (Mark 14:62). Some of it is disguised, as when our Lord speaks of a coming reward: "Blessed are you who are hungry now, for you will be filled" (Luke 6:21). This too is an apocalyptic saying, since it is related to both the end times and now.

The Gospels also contain pronouncements of holy law, eschatological correlatives ("For just as Jonah became a sign to the people of Nineveh, so the Son of Man will be to this generation" [Luke 11:30]), and end-time prophecies that describe earthquakes and the darkening of the sun, among other phenomena.[9] Some of the New Testament epistle writers also employ these apocalyptic features.[10] Revelation, however, is the primary apocalyptic document of the New Testament, and it is the focus of this chapter.

What Is the Text Doing?

Having determined what a text is saying, the interpreter must determine what the text is doing. Specifically, this involves determining the strategy the text uses to communicate biblical truth. How does apocalyptic work? What techniques does it use?

Revelation seeks not only to stir imaginative experience but also to stir readers to action. It accomplishes the latter by means of the former.[11] In other words, the bizarre storylike features of apocalyptic literature are the very elements intended to stir the hearers-readers to action. The wonderfully imaginative visions and scenes of Revelation not only stir the imagination, they also engage us. Bruce Metzger points out that while the Psalms appeal to our emotions and Romans appeals to our intellect, Revelation appeals primarily to our imagination. Revelation "contains a series of word pictures, as though a number of slides were being shown upon a great screen. As we watch we allow ourselves to be carried along by impressions created by these pictures."[12] But how specifically does the apocalyptic genre do that? Let me identify five strategies and devices that are used.

1. It seeks to encourage believers in the face of catastrophe by reminding them of what they are facing. The tension between what is and what ought to be is intensified, then the hearers are led to experience the conviction that what ought to be is, even if it does not seem to be so. Revelation seeks "to create that tension for readers unaware of it, to heighten it for those who felt it already, and then to overcome it in an act of literary imagination."[13] It is important to remember that these first-century Christians were undergoing severe persecution, including martyrdom.

2. Revelation employs the imaginative world of symbols to engage its hearers-readers. Revelation does not use reasoning or debate; rather, it evokes hope through the power of its symbols.[14] Although they are foreign to today's readers, the symbols were obvious to early Christians. Most of them were borrowed from the Old Testament and the surrounding culture.[15]

3. Revelation's use of symbol is couched within a unique

form of narrative. Unlike the parabolic narratives Jesus used, apocalyptic is practically devoid of "concrete particularity." "The images are . . . distortions and intensifications of everyday reality, 'unreal,' in a word, mystical."[16] Apocalyptic literature deals with life in cosmic proportions. "Instead of being the narrative of 'our' community, it becomes as well the story of 'the kingdoms of the world.'"[17]

4. Repetition plays an important part in apocalyptic literature. The seven seals, followed by the seven trumpets, followed by . . . well, you get the idea. Revelation piles images one on top of the next to herald the same message over and over, producing an overwhelming effect.[18]

5. The language of apocalyptic literature is not so much informational as expressive and evocative. Revelation is more concerned with evoking hope than mere mental acknowledgement. It is poetic in the truest sense of the word, which may help explain why it was Emily Dickinson's favorite book of the Bible. The language of Revelation touches its hearers very deeply.[19]

How Can the Sermon Say and Do the Same?

How can the preacher employ the textual strategies in the sermon? What are the practical implications of the techniques just mentioned, especially in relation to mood and movement?

Sermonic Mood

The preacher first needs to create a tension between what is and what ought to be. In a world filled with injustice, that will not be hard to do, though our situation today hardly compares to the martyrdom of those early Christians. Still, ours is not a perfect world. Suffering and injustice are commonplace, though there is a difference between theodicy in general and a systemic, evil attack on the innocent.

The preacher needs to heighten feelings of despair. Then the sermon can announce a coming justice. Remember, apocalyptic literature frequently employs radical mood swings. In the final analysis the message must not be overly optimistic or overly pessimistic, but realistic. A good example of this is found in the final scene of *Schindler's List*. Viewers find themselves rejoicing that so many innocent Jews have been saved. Oskar Schindler stands there with all those fortunate persons. But just before the credits are shown, a surreal scene portrays the actors and their historical counterparts placing rocks on the graves where so many other innocent people were buried. Preaching the apocalyptic themes in our day requires a similar balance—feelings of despair mingled with appropriate feelings of hope.

Many North American Christian congregations today include persons of some wealth, some power, some respect in the community. (How unlike John's audience!) What does apocalyptic literature say to people who are well off at the expense of others? Thomas Long reminds us that while the message may be one of hope for the oppressed, it can also be a word of warning to those who are too comfortable. Long notes, "This is why the Book of Revelation prefaces its vision with letters to the churches, including letters of warning to congregations like Sardis, who has the appearance of life but is really dead, and Laodicea, who is neither cold nor hot."[20] The coming justice may be bad news to some of our listeners.

Second, the sermon needs to employ symbols with which the listeners are familiar. The apocalyptic symbols in Revelation were drawn largely from the Old Testament. Even those symbols may be unfamiliar in our biblically illiterate times, presenting us with a unique challenge.

Perhaps the biggest struggle the preacher faces in preaching from Revelation is the strangeness of the literary form. From an apologetic standpoint David Buttrick dismisses apocalyptic imagery altogether, while trying to hold on to its message. He says that Hal Lindsey may sell, but modern churchgoers dismiss what Lindsey writes as nonsense.[21] Buttrick's point is well taken, but I disagree with him on two counts. First, the message cannot be separated from the form; and second, apocalyptic forms have never been more popular, even among the highly educated.

Mythology has resurfaced powerfully in North America's fascination with science-fiction literature and movies. Movies such as *Star Trek* have fans from several generations and now *Star Wars* has been released again. Apocalyptic still appeals to people today, though many do not see any connection between reading Revelation in a church sanctuary and viewing the latest sci-fi flick in a movie theater.

In their original setting, apocalyptic forms worked because of their familiarity. If today's preacher has to explain the symbols, some of the evocative power of apocalyptic has been lost already, though explanations do not have to be pedantic. *Preaching through the Apocalypse,* a recent work devoted solely to preaching from Revelation, warns against overexplaining the text, to which I add a hearty amen. I recently retold some of Revelation's stories to my children, without any explanation. In fact, I did not even say that the story I was telling (Revelation 12) was a biblical story. Still, they got it. My five-year-old daughter immediately proceeded to interpret it for all of us. She was right on target. This is not to say that some matters will not need to be explained. Some will, but how? One obvious strategy might be to briefly explain apocalyptic material using some modern analogies.[22] In our culture the preacher might point to political cartoons. Everyone knows what donkeys and elephants stand for in the newspapers. Or the preacher might refer to the popularity of science-fiction literature and how it actually serves to critique the present. Whatever strategy it employs, the sermon must use recognizable symbols. The use of stories can be especially helpful for experiencing the power of the text's symbols.[23]

Third, the sermon must deal with issues of cosmic proportions, not minor daily trials or inconvenient obstacles. The first-century believers to whom Revelation was addressed were facing martyrdom, not flat tires. Using stories might be helpful, though the preacher must resist the temptation to address only minor trials. The stories must deal with life-and-death issues on a grand scale. As Long notes, apocalyptic literature speaks to times of ultimate despair, "when the police dogs are being released toward the marchers on the bridge into Selma, when the knock of the secret police is heard at the door and the church is hiding an attic full of Jews, when the diagnosis is melanoma and there is nothing more that the physicians can do."[24]

One such story is about the Russian poet Anna Akhmatova, who lived during Stalin's purges. Standing in the long lines outside one of the prisons, she and others waited to leave letters and packages for loved ones that they hoped were still alive. A woman recognized her as the accomplished poet and asked, "Can you describe this?" She replied, "I can." Akhmatova's poetic description, which emerged later, was a form of apocalyptic. "Just the act of describing can be defiance, in the face of terror; it allows the powerless a glimpse into another reality, one in which words and images (not guns and prisons) have power."[25]

Fourth, evocative language will help the sermon communicate more than the facts: "Here's what they were facing . . ." Expressive language can describe the historical context as well as our own, and at the same time evoke something in the listeners. Expressive language enables the sermon to "present again" the struggles that the early Christians faced and help us to identify with our own.

Sermonic Movement

The one aspect inherent in apocalyptic literature that directly affects movement is repetition. The preacher needs to capitalize on the power of repetition. One contemporary story or image piled on top of another can be very effective in eliciting despair or hope, both of which are essential in preaching from Revelation. A series of stories of injustice to begin the sermon can be overwhelming. The mere mention of Bosnia or the latest global hot spot can conjure up images in the minds of listeners. Where is God in the face of all of this? Once those feelings have been aroused, the preacher may then pile up images of hope and confidence in the ultimate reign of God.

For instance, in Revelation 12 John tells the story of a dragon seeking to devour a newborn infant. The characters themselves are obvious enough, even if multifaceted: the woman is Israel/Mary, the infant is Christ, her offspring is the church, the dragon is Herod/Nero/Domitian/Satan. The plot or movement of the text comes from ancient combat myths. These myths typically involved a rebellion by some evil force, a temporary reign by that evil force, the eventual defeat of evil by a good ruler, and a storybook ending. John's message is plain: the persecution that Christians faced at the hands of the Romans would not last forever. Christ would conquer.

The sermon itself can begin by generating feelings of despair that were experienced by John's readers. There are several corollaries to the story, both ancient and contemporary: the Greek myth of the birth of Apollos, the Old Testament account of Israel's exodus from Egypt, tales of chivalry from King Arthur's England, Prince Charming's rescue of Sleeping Beauty, and Luke Skywalker's battle with Darth Vader in *Star Wars*, just to name a few. The preacher can show how in every culture there have been stories like the one John tells because people have always longed to know that justice will ultimately win out. Contemporary examples of injustice can add to the impact of the message.

The sermon can then move to resolution, showing that a day is coming when justice will be served, when evil will be vanquished, and Christ's bride will live happily ever after. In other words, the movement within the text can be regenerated to some degree, though that is optional. Mood is more important.

As an example of form-sensitive preaching from apocalyptic literature, we will look at a sermon by Thomas H. Troeger, who teaches preaching at Iliff School of Theology.[26]

"Overhearing Love's Music in a Brutal World"

by Thomas H. Troeger

Revelation 7:15-17

You are on a trip;
    and have just settled into a motor lodge for the night.
        The sign out front reads:
            "Free Cable Television in Every Room."

The people next door have already turned on their set.
    The words of the movie they are watching
    are only vaguely intelligible.

But you can tell from the soundtrack,
    It is a picture of romance and love,
        something to pull on the heartstrings.

You switch on your own television to the news network.
    There is no sound.
        You look at the screen anyway,
            hoping the sound will come on
                once the set warms up.

[Troeger begins by directly involving the listeners, using the second-person, "you." In addition, listeners are engaged by the every-dayness of the story. Notice also the poetic language and format.]

Soldiers with semi-automatic rifles are leading four
    handcuffed men into a bare room with a plain table
    and a microphone.
From the television set on the other side of the wall
    you hear a surge of romantic music
        and the voices of the actors

speaking passionately to each other.
You catch bits of phrases here and there:
"... I promise you ..."
"... and no more shall we ..."
"... but only love ..."
The voices fade.

All you hear is misty music.

[The preacher employs competing images. The sermon will evoke
outrage and despair but also hope for a happy ending.]

Meanwhile,
    the handcuffed prisoners and their guards
        disappear from your silent screen.
        You see the newscaster
        followed by
            the next on-the-scene report:
Seagulls and fish are covered with sticky black oil.
    People in raincoats are raking and shoveling the beach,
        which is also covered with the same viscous sludge.

            Ta ta ta taaaa!
            Ta ta ta taaaa!

You distinctly hear the sound of Mendelssohn's "Wedding
March."
    The movie in the next room must be ending.
    The trumpets are making their famous triumphal call:

        Ta ta ta taaaa!
        Ta ta ta taaaa!

While you watch a shore worker
    pick up a large dead bird covered with oil,
    you imagine the grand wedding procession on the other set,
    the bride in white,
        the smiling groom.

The newscast images on your television insist on one
    reality while the music coming through the wall

keeps awakening a different scene.

You hear someone in the next room click off the television.
  You watch in silence the face of the news announcer
  mouthing words you cannot hear.
      You decide the sound is never going to come on.
      You turn off the set and get ready for bed.

But you find a strange thing happening in your mind.
Usually when you click off the set,
  the images fade from consciousness.
      Then you begin to think about the day that is past
      and what faces you tomorrow.

But things are different tonight.

The images of the handcuffed people and the oil-covered
  creatures do not fade from your mind.
      You find they are held there by the love music
      that keeps replaying itself in your head.
The music that you thought was a sentimental intrusion
  upon the real world of the news show
      has done something that broadcast words
      have never accomplished.
The music has amplified the dissonance
  between the brutality of the world
      and the hopes of the human heart for a life of
      tenderness,
      fidelity,
      love.

Even if the movie was a Hollywood concoction,
  there is no denying those yearnings of the heart
      that it has stirred.
If you had heard the love music entirely on its own,
  or
If you had watched the news entirely on its own,
  the effect would have been different.
Then you would have entered one reality or the other.
  You would have accepted each on its own terms.

But now it is the juxtaposition
    of the two worlds
        that is haunting your imagination.
The contrast between the news images and the soundtrack
    has broken the grip that the talk of the broadcasters
        usually holds upon you.
Instead of concluding,
    "That's the way the world is,"
        you find yourself thinking:
        "The world does not have to be that way.
        The heart knows other possibilities."

[Troeger has directly explained the scene he has just painted. He clarifies the dissonance that we just experienced during the newscast.]

As you go to bed and the music continues to echo in your memory,
    you find yourself praying for those handcuffed people
        whose names you did not even hear
            and for those fish and birds suffocated in oil.

That moment of prayer
    awakened by the music of love
        brings you close to the spirit of John,
            the writer of the book of Revelation.

[Now the sermon shifts to the book of Revelation, pointing out the correlations and explaining the context of John's writing.]

Although he had no television,
    like you, he had an imagination
        that filled with images
            and with the sound of remembered music.
Also like you, he knew the brutality of the world.
    The Roman authorities had exiled him to the island of
Patmos
        because of his Christian witness.
        He was one of the more fortunate believers:
        at least he had not been executed.
Nevertheless, exile is cruel and unusual punishment.

There he was on a rocky island,
   thirty-seven miles from the mainland,
     a man of passionate faith,
     now torn from the community
     whose worship and life had sustained him.

John looked out from the cliffs of Patmos,
   and the world appeared as violent to him
     as it does to us when we watch the evening news.

He saw the Roman ships sailing by,
   soldiers and chariots crowded upon the decks.
     But the soundtrack that played in his head
       was the not the martial music of imperial Rome.

Instead,
   he heard the hymns of praise
     that he remembered from the worship of his
        community.
Perhaps he forgot some of the words
or sometimes had difficulty recalling exactly how the tune
went.
   But what he never forgot
     was the music within the music,
       the assurance of faith
         that the brutality of the world
           is not
             the final
              and triumphant
              reality of life.

The news from the mainland was bad.
   Christians needed shelter from persecution,
   they needed food and drink,
   they needed guidance when they were on the run,
   they needed comfort as they wept for those who had been
   slaughtered.
Thinking of these desperate people
   and imagining all of those who were yet to suffer

before the kingdom of God was fully realized,
　John recalled a hymn,
　　or perhaps he composed it himself,
drawing inspiration from well-known verses
out of the Psalms, Isaiah, and Ezekiel:

　　Therefore are they before the throne of God,
　　　[whom they] serve day and night within
　　　　[God's] holy temple;
　　and [God] who sits upon the throne
　　　　will shelter them with [God's own] presence.
　They shall hunger no more, neither thirst any more;
　　the sun shall not strike them,
　　　nor any scorching heat.
　For the Lamb in the midst of the throne will be
　　　their shepherd,
　　and [God] will guide them to springs of living water;
　and God will wipe away every tear from their eyes.
　　　　　　　　　　(RSV, altered to be inclusive)

*[Before quoting the hymn that John includes, Troeger explains very
briefly that it is a hymn and that John may have borrowed it or
composed it himself. Sometimes even the most poetic of sermons
must explain certain important points.]*

The music of that hymn,
　like the love music
　　coming through the thin wall of the motor lodge
　　　stirred a vision in John
　　　　that was utterly different
　　　　from the Roman ships that passed
　　　　　before him.
His vision was a countervision to the vast worldly power
　that had exiled him
　　and that was threatening the churches on the mainland.
John saw an alternative world,
　another reality,
　a different way of being.
And from that vision he drew strength for himself

and for the churches he loved
who were facing horrors they could not escape.
Like the music of love accompanying the news broadcast,
John's hymn is a reminder of the yearnings of the human
heart.
And yet it is much more than that:
the hymn is a declaration that
the world
will not always be
the way
the world
is now.

*[Troeger will now move to direct application. Several issues of
contemporary significance are addressed. These are not daily little
trials but serious matters.]*

Look at the world before your eyes,
but listen to John's hymn
and let his vision rise in your heart.
Look at the battered women and children.
"[God] who sits upon the throne
will shelter them with [God's own] presence."
Since God will shelter them,
we who claim God's name
will also provide shelter.
Look at the hollow eyes of a people needing bread.
"They shall hunger no more,
neither thirst any more."
Since God will feed them,
we who claim God's name
will also offer food.

Look at the people lost to drugs.
"For the Lamb in the midst of the throne
will be their shepherd,
and he will guide them
to springs of living water."
Since Christ will guide them,

we who claim to follow Christ
will point them to our savior.

Look at those who are mourning.
"God will wipe away every tear from their eyes."
Since God will comfort them,
we who claim God's name
will also give comfort.

Do not wait for the sound of the world
to go dead on your television
or to grow quiet in your head.
The world is intrusive and insistent.
Instead,
listen with John
and sing with John
until your song, your prayer, and your
action are one.
Then through your life others will hear John's hymn.
The world will lose its iron grip on their lives.
And they will be empowered
to sing and act in unison
with all those who declare:

"Blessing
and glory
and wisdom
and thanksgiving
and honor
and power
and might
be to our God for ever
and ever! Amen."
(7:12)

*[The sermon ends in praise. Having begun by heightening our
anxiety, it ends with a word of encouragement. God will reign and
God is worthy of our praise.]*

Exercises

Answer the following nine questions for each apocalyptic passage: Revelation 6:1-17; 13:1-10; 19:11-16.

1. How does the text stimulate your imagination?
2. What kinds of symbols are employed?
3. What is the mood of the text? What musical instruments might best accompany the text? What colors and/or textures help to describe the mood of the text? What adjectives and adverbs come to mind?
4. Is repetition a key to understanding the passage? How does the text build up to a crescendo?
5. What is the basic plot of the text?
6. What kind of textual movement is evident? What clues within the text indicate movement?
7. What contemporary issues of injustice does the text address?
8. What is the text saying? What is the text doing?
9. How could a sermon say and do the same?

Sermon Resources

Ronald J. Allen, "With Eyes of Fire" [Revelation 1:12-16], in *Preaching through the Apocalypse* (Chalice, 1992), pp. 50-61. Evocative and poetic. Good examples of preaching responsibly from Revelation.

Amanda J. Burr, "Now That's a Horse of a Different Color," in *Preaching through the Apocalypse,* pp. 91-96. A much more detailed sermon in terms of explanation. Wonderful job of applying the text to the world today.

Donald Chatfield, "The Pilgrim's River" [Revelation 22], in *Dinner with Jesus* (Zondervan, 1988), pp. 55-63. Highly imaginative style and creative storytelling.

Joel Eidsness, "Lament for the City of Man" [Revelation 17-18], in *Biblical Sermons,* ed. Haddon W. Robinson (Baker, 1989), pp. 241-53. Evocative language and wonderful contemporary images.

H. Stephen Shoemaker, "Washed" [Revelation 7:9-17], in *Best Sermons 1*, ed. James W. Cox (Harper and Row, 1988), pp. 15-22. Tries to respect the dreamlike quality of the text while using contemporary images.

Thomas H. Troeger, "Imagine" [Revelation 7:9-17], in *Biblical Preaching Journal* (spring 1992): 16-17. Brief but very creative approach to apocalyptic preaching. Uses current and specific imagery.

Thomas H. Troeger, "Overhearing Love's Music in a Brutal World" [Revelation 7:15-17], in *Preaching through the Apocalypse*, pp. 97-105. Complete manuscript included in the chapter.

Notes

Chapter 1 / First Movement

1. Fred Craddock, *As One without Authority* (Nashville: Abingdon, 1971), p. 143. Robert D. Young, *Be Brief about It* (Philadelphia: Westminster, 1980), p. 55, notes that even preachers who were not traditional in their sermon styles were predictable, usually employing the same sermon structure week after week.

2. Craddock, *As One without Authority*, pp. 143-144.

3. H. Grady Davis, *Design for Preaching* (Philadelphia: Fortress Press, 1958). Other pioneers in the area of preaching related to literary forms are Amos Wilder, *Early Christian Rhetoric* (London: SCM, 1964), pp. 12-13, and David James Randolph, *The Renewal of Preaching* (Philadelphia: Fortress, 1969), p. 100.

4. See Eugene L. Lowry, *The Homiletical Plot* (Atlanta: John Knox, 1980), as well as his *How to Preach a Parable* (Nashville: Abingdon, 1989). Lowry also has a comprehensive textbook forthcoming entitled *The Sermon: Dancing the Edge of Mystery* (Nashville: Abingdon, 1997).

5. Don M. Wardlaw, "Introduction: The Need for New Shapes," in *Preaching Biblically* (Philadelphia: Westminster, 1983), p. 16.

6. This emphasis on form relates directly to what William Beardslee refers to as a literary criticism that is more akin to Aristotle's *Poetics* than his *Rhetoric*. The latter views the form as a vehicle for content; the former views form as integral to the content. William Beardslee, *Literary Criticism of the New Testament* (Philadelphia: Fortress, 1970), pp. 3-4.

7. Various schemes of New Testament genres have been offered. For example, see Sidney Greidanus, *The Modern Preacher and the Ancient Text* (Grand Rapids: Eerdmans, 1988), pp. 22-23,

and W. Randolph Tate, *Biblical Interpretation* (Peabody, Mass.: Hendrickson, 1991), p. 107.

8. Tate, *Biblical Interpretation*, pp. 65-71.

9. Donald L. Hamilton, *Homiletical Handbook* (Nashville: Broadman, 1992), p. 178. Hamilton acknowledges the possibility of more narrative structures at times but seems to prefer a more propositional approach. See also *Reclaiming the Prophetic Mantle*, ed. George L. Klein (Nashville: Broadman, 1992), pp. 19-126, which also favors propositional approaches to sermon structure, and *Handbook of Contemporary Preaching*, ed. Michael Duduit (Nashville: Broadman, 1992), pp. 247-389, which contains a mixture of propositional and representational approaches to preaching from various literary forms. This propositional approach is also found within the older work *Biblical Preaching: An Expositor's Treasury*, ed. James W. Cox (Philadelphia: Westminster, 1983).

10. Ben Witherington III, *Paul's Narrative Thought World* (Louisville: Westminster/John Knox, 1994).

11. See Sidney Greidanus, *The Modern Preacher and the Ancient Text* (Grand Rapids: Eerdmans, 1988), p. 20.

12. James L. Bailey and Lyle D. Vander Broek, *Literary Forms in the New Testament: A Handbook* (Louisville: Westminster/John Knox, 1992).

13. I have tried to combine insights from rhetorical criticism with recent trends in homiletics. I use the term "rhetorical criticism" to encompass some of the positive features also gleaned from form and literary criticism. See Burton L. Mack, *Rhetoric and the New Testament* (Minneapolis: Fortress, 1990), pp. 9-17. Also see George A. Kennedy, *New Testament Interpretation through Rhetorical Criticism* (Chapel Hill: University of North Carolina Press, 1984), especially chapter 1.

14. Grant Lovejoy, "Shaping Sermons by the Literary Form of the Text," in *Biblical Hermeneutics*, ed. Bruce Corley, Steve Lemke, and Grant Lovejoy (Nashville: Broadman and Holman, 1996), pp. 357-359, discusses four reasons why sermons ought to be shaped by the form of the text: the variety of forms in the Bible, the relation between form and content, the balance between information and experience, and the variety needed in the church's preaching. These relate to the premises that follow.

15. Fred Craddock, *Preaching* (Nashville: Abingdon, 1985), p. 123.

16. Charles B. Bugg, "Back to the Bible: Toward a New Description of Expository Preaching," *Review and Expositor* 90 (summer 1993): 416. He adds, "The Word of God both says something

and does something, and sensitive preachers pay attention to both event and experience."

17. The New Testment uses the term "bowels," which "expresses the total personality at the deepest level" (Helmut Koester, σπλάγνον in *Theological Dictionary of the New Testament*, vol. 7 (Grand Rapids: Eerdmans, 1971), pp. 553-557.

18. Orality in the Scriptures was not limited to narratives and speeches. New Testament epistles had an oral quality as well as an aural quality; that is, they were expected to be read aloud (Colossians 4:16). See David E. Aune, *The New Testament in Its Literary Environment* (Philadelphia: Westminster, 1987), pp. 158-159.

19. H. Grady Davis, *Design for Preaching* (Philadelphia: Fortress, 1958), p. 163, notes that sermons are like music in the live performance, not in the score.

20. Nicholas Lash, *Theology on the Way to Emmaus* (London: SCM, 1986), p. 37. Emphasis his.

21. Ibid., pp. 40-41.

22. Richard F. Ward, *Speaking from the Heart* (Nashville: Abingdon, 1992), pp. 76-77. With both uses of this word, Ward borrows from the works of others (Dwight Conquergood, "Communication as Performance," in *The Jensen Lectures: Contemporary Studies*, ed. John I. Sisco, nd), (Tampa: University of South Florida), p. 27; and Alla Bozarth-Campbell, *The Word's Body* (Tuscaloosa: University of Alabama Press, 1979), p. 2.).

23. Eugene L. Lowry, "The Narrative Quality of Experience as a Bridge to Preaching," in *Journeys toward Narrative Preaching*, ed. Wayne Bradley Robinson (New York: Pilgrim, 1990), pp. 72-73.

24. Note the musical metaphor of composition as opposed to the more traditional metaphors that have been used over the years. For example, in the nineteenth century legal analogies of putting together a case and preaching for a verdict were popular. In the twentieth century architectural metaphors have been popular, such as J. Randall Nichols, *Building the Word* (San Francisco: Harper and Row, 1980).

25. Long treats both of these items briefly, along with some other possible options. *Preaching and Literary Forms*, pp. 128-135.

26. Fred B. Craddock, "The Tunes of Preaching," *Leadership* (spring 1987): 64.

27. For instance, see Evans E. Crawford, *The Hum: Call and Response in African American Preaching* (Nashville: Abingdon, 1995); Henry Mitchell, *Black Preaching* (Nashville: Abingdon, 1990) and *Celebration and Experience in Preaching* (Nashville: Abingdon,

1990); Jon Michael Spenser, *Sacred Symphony: The Chanted Sermon of the Black Preacher* (Greenwood, 1987).

28. Long, *Preaching and Literary Forms*, p. 134.

29. William J. Carl III, "Shaping Sermons by the Structure of the Text," in *Preaching Biblically*, p. 124.

30. Craddock, "The Tunes of Preaching," p. 68.

Chapter 2 / Second Movement

1. P.T. Forsyth, *Positive Preaching and the Modern Mind* (London: Independent Press Ltd., 1907), p. 62.

2. The use of present-tense verbs is intentional. Answering the first question, of course, involves determining what the text meant before determining what it means, but present-tense verbs serve as a reminder that the text still speaks, and in the case of the second question, that the text still acts. These questions have been posed in various forms and combinations by several scholars, including David Buttrick, "Interpretation and Preaching," *Interpretation* 35 (January 1981): 50-54; Thomas Troeger, "Shaping Sermons by the Encounter of Text with Preacher," in *Preaching Biblically*, ed. Don M. Wardlaw (Philadelphia: Westminster, 1983), p. 154; Fred Craddock, *Preaching* (Nashville: Abingdon, 1985), pp. 122-124.

3. Jerry Camery-Hoggatt, *Speaking of God* (Peabody, Mass.: Hendrickson, 1995), p. 173, correctly reminds us that attention to form is only one of the many exegetical issues that must be addressed in sermon preparation.

4. James L. Bailey and Lyle D. Vander Broek's *Literary Forms in the New Testament: A Handbook* is without equal. See also W. Randolph Tate, *Biblical Interpretation* (Peabody, Mass.: Hendrickson, 1991), especially chapters 4-6 on the role of literary forms; Ronald J. Allen, *Contemporary Biblical Interpretation for Preaching* (Valley Forge: Judson, 1984), who discusses several critical methodologies of interpretation.

5. Interview with Joel Nederhood, "Do We Really Have to Compete with TV?" *Leadership* (summer 1992): 16.

6. John H. Elliott, *A Home for the Homeless: A Sociological Exegesis of 1 Peter* (Philadelphia: Fortress, 1981), pp. 10-11, defines his own methodology as examining the "strategy" of the biblical writer. Referring to more than just the communication of ideas, Elliott means the "deliberate design of a document," which was intended to have an effect on the hearers-readers.

7. M. Eugene Boring, "Rhetoric, Righteousness, and the Sermon

on the Mount," in *Listening to the Word,* ed. Gail R. O'Day and Thomas G. Long (Nashville: Abingdon, 1993), p. 53.

8. Craddock's sermon is available through the tape series *Preaching Today,* 465 Gundersen Drive, Carol Stream, IL 60188.

9. Compliment with an *i* respects the fact that the poet's text and the film's script are not incomplete. Complement with an *e* implies the completing of something that is missing. This is crucial in preaching as well. The biblical texts are not incomplete, needing to be completed by the sermon. Form-sensitive sermon structure seeks to compliment the text.

10. Søren Kierkegaard notes the ecclesiological dimensions of worship in one of his parables. He proposes that in worship, God—not the congregation—is audience. Those in the pews are the players, the ministers prompting them with their lines. *Parables of Kierkegaard,* ed. Thomas C. Oden (Princeton, N.J.: Princeton University Press, 1978), pp. 89-90.

11. David James Randolph, *The Renewal of Preaching* (Philadelphia: Fortress, 1969), p. 124, writes that the biblical forms themselves should serve as the "substratum from which sermonic structures are to be molded." He adds that "the preacher must decide in each case which of the structures best carries forth the intention and mood of the text."

12. Don Wardlaw, "Shaping Sermons by the Context of the Text," in *Preaching Biblically,* p. 67, notes the importance of "word choice and manner of expression" for determining a text's mood. Of course, a sermon's mood is also dependent on the delivery of the preacher. Tone of voice, cadence, pausing, and other factors contribute as well.

13. Those familiar with the history of sermon forms may recall the term "organic" as used by H. Grady Davis, *Design for Preaching* (Philadelphia: Fortress, 1958), pp. 139-162. In contrast to his usage, I mean to imply that the form for the sermon is quite possibly inherent within the text itself.

14. Eugene Lowry, *Living with the Lectionary* (Nashville: Abingdon, 1992), p. 80.

15. Fred Craddock, *Preaching* (Nashville: Abingdon, 1985), p. 178. David L. Bartlett, "Texts Shaping Sermons," in *Listening to the Word,* p. 149, writes that "the rhetorical purpose of the text is a more crucial control on the form of the sermon than the text's genre and structure." I would agree, omitting the reference to "genre." A text's genre is more than its structure. It conveys a mood or impact as well.

16. Randolph, *The Renewal of Preaching,* p. 123.

17. See Craig Loscalzo, "Rhetoric," in *Concise Encyclopedia of Preaching*, ed. William H. Willimon and Richard Lischer (Louisville: Westminster/John Knox, 1995), pp. 409-416.

Chapter 3 / Third Movement

1. Richard Bartlett, "Texts Shaping Sermons," in *Listening to the Word*, ed. Gail R. O'Day and Thomas G. Long (Nashville: Abingdon, 1993), p. 150.

2. Thomas G. Long, "When the Preacher Is a Teacher," *Journal for Preachers* 16 (Lent 1993): 21-22. Citing from George Lindbeck's work, *The Nature of Doctrine* (Philadelphia: Westminster, 1984), Long notes that there are various ways of conveying information and thereby teaching. Another helpful work in this area is Clark M. Williamson and Ronald J. Allen, *The Teaching Minister* (Louisville: Westminster/John Knox, 1991).

3. A new book in honor of David Buttrick which addresses the neglect of theology in homiletics is Edward Farley and Thomas G. Long, eds., *Preaching as a Theological Task* (Louisville: Westminster/John Knox Press, 1996).

4. Eugene Lowry, "The Revolution of Sermonic Shape," in *Listening to the Word*, p. 111.

5. Lowry notes, "One should no more label a narrative sermon as *mere story* than one would name a traditional sermon *mere logic* "("The Revolution in Sermonic Shape," p. 112.). Emphasis his.

6. It is true that the New Testament and even Jewish rabbinical schools employed Greco-Roman rhetoric, but the insistence on three Roman numerals for preaching is totally foreign to the biblical texts.

7. Thomas Long, "And How Shall They Hear? The Listener in Contemporary Preaching," *Listening to the Word*, p. 173.

8. Robin Meyers, *With Ears to Hear: Preaching as Self-Persuasion* (Cleveland: Pilgrim, 1993), p. 3. The theological debate that arose between Karl Barth and Emil Brunner continues today in some measure among preachers. See Long, "And How Shall They Hear?" pp. 174ff., who discusses this debate and its implications for today.

9. Tertullian, *Liber de Praescriptionibus Adversus Haereticos*, chapter 7, cited by Christopher Morse, *Not Every Spirit* (Valley Forge: Trinity Press International, 1994), p. 14.

10. Some of the more pertinent studies include Bernard Fine, "Conclusion-Drawing, Communicator Credibility, and Anxiety as Factors in Opinion Change," *Journal of Abnormal and Social*

Psychology 54 (May 1957): 369-74; Paul Heinberg, "Factors Related to an Individual's Ability to Perceive Implications of Dialogues," *Speech Monographs* 28 (November 1961): 274-81; Carl Hovland and Wallace Mandell, "An Experimental Comparison of Conclusion-Drawing by the Communicator and by the Audience," *Journal of Abnormal and Social Psychology* 47 (July 1952): 581-88; Stewart Tubbs, "Explicit Versus Implicit Conclusions and Audience Commitment," *Speech Monographs* 35 (March 1968): 14-19.

11. For more on inductive preaching, see Fred Craddock, *As One without Authority* (Nashville: Abingdon, 1971); Lucy Rose, "The Parameters of Narrative Preaching," in *Journeys toward Narrative Preaching*, ed. Wayne Bradley Robinson (New York: Pilgrim, 1990), pp. 23-41.

12. See the new work by Leonora Tubbs Tisdale, *Preaching as Local Theology and Folk Art* (Minneapolis: Fortress, 1997).

13. P.T. Forsyth, *Positive Preaching and the Modern Mind* (London: Independent Press Ltd., 1907), pp. 68-69.

14. Gene E. Bartlett, *The Audacity of Preaching* (New York: Harper and Brothers, 1962), p. 45.

15. See Robert Jewett, *Saint Paul at the Movies* (Louisville: Westminster/John Knox, 1993), pp. 31-42.

Chapter 4/Parables

1. Stanley Hauerwas and William H. Willimon, *Resident Aliens* (Nashville: Abingdon, 1989), pp. 54-55.

2. Ronald J. Sider and Michael A. King, *Preaching about Life in a Threatening World* (Philadelphia: Westminster, 1987), p. 27. Jesus' use of the everyday does not lead us to see the sacred and the secular as two different realities; rather, the secular has been invaded by the sacred, and thus nothing is secular anymore. See David M. Granskou, *Preaching on the Parables* (Philadelphia: Fortress, 1972), pp. 2-3.

3. Robert E. C. Browne, *The Ministry of the Word* (Philadelphia: Fortress, 1958), p. 39, quoted in Thomas G. Long, *The Witness of Preaching* (Louisville: Westminster/John Knox, 1989), p. 167.

4. C. H. Dodd, *The Parables of the Kingdom*, rev. ed. (New York: Scribner's, 1961), p. 5.

5. Bernard Brandon Scott, *Hear Then the Parable: A Commentary on the Parables of Jesus* (Minneapolis: Fortress, 1989), p. 8.

6. Ibid., pp. 8-62.

7. Much has been made of the difference between Jesus' parables and later rabbinic parables, some asserting that

the rabbinic usage was more pedantic and illustrative than aesthetic and engaging. For instance, see *Parable and Story in Judaism
and Christianity*, ed. Clemens Thoma and Michael Wyschogrod
(New York: Paulist, 1989).

8. Dodd's definition recognizes two basic types: similes and
metaphors. Robert Funk, *Language, Hermeneutic, and Word of God*
(New York: Harper and Row, 1966), pp. 136ff., lists three basic
types of parables: simile (A is like B), metaphor (A is B), and parable proper (an extended story about A that allows listeners to
make application to B). Dan O. Via, *The Parables* (Philadelphia:
Fortress, 1967), p. 11, lists three types as well, but a different
three: similitude (one-to-one comparison), example story (clear
illustrative examples), and true parable (rich metaphor that invites participation). James L. Bailey and Lyle D. Vander Broek,
Literary Forms in the New Testament: A Handbook (Louisville: West-
minster/John Knox, 1992), pp. 107-108, list four possible types:
figure of speech (short saying typically having only one verb), similitude (more than one verb, but not a story), parable proper
(extended vignette), and example story. It should be noted that
some scholars reject the idea of example stories altogether. An interesting popular twist on the types of parables can be found in
Thomas Long, *Preaching and the Literary Forms of the Bible* (Philadelphia: Fortress, 1989), pp. 95-98.

9. Funk, *Language, Hermeneutic, and Word of God*, p. 147.

10. David Stern, "Jesus' Parables from the Perspective of Rabbinic Literature," in *Parable and Story in Judaism and Christianity*,
p. 49.

11. N. T. Wright, *The New Testament and the People of God* (Fortress, 1992), p. 77.

12. Dodd, *The Parables of the Kingdom*, p. 159. See also Scott,
Hear Then the Parable, p. 37.

13. Joachim Jeremias, *The Parables of Jesus*, rev. ed. (New York:
Scribner's, 1963), p. 12-13.

14. Funk, *Language, Hermeneutic, and Word of God*, p. 160.

15. Ibid., p. 161. The examples given are mine.

16. Long, *Literary Forms*, p. 97.

17. Ibid., pp. 100-101.

18. John W. Sider, *Interpreting the Parables* (Grand Rapids: Zondervan, 1995), pp. 157-160. See also Scott, *Hear Then the Parable*,
pp. 198-200.

19. Rudolf Bultmann, *History of the Synoptic Tradition*, 2d ed.,
trans. John Marsh (Oxford: Basil Blackwell, 1968), pp. 188-192.

20. Birger Gerhardsson, "If We Do Not Cut the Parables Out of Their Frames," *New Testament Studies* 37 (July 1991): 331.

21. Frank Kermode, *The Genesis of Secrecy: On the Interpretation of Narrative* (Cambridge, Mass.: Harvard University Press, 1979), pp. 29-47. Kermode tackles that delicate question of why Jesus spoke in parables—Mark's ἵνα ("in order that" or "so that") versus Matthew's ὅτι ("because").

22. Granskou, *Preaching on the Parables*, p. 2.

23. Funk, *Language, Hermeneutic, and Word of God*, pp. 155-156.

24. Philip Sellew, "Interior Monologue as a Narrative Device in the Parables of Luke," *Journal of Biblical Literature* 111 (1992): 239-53.

25. Long, *Literary Forms*, p. 99.

26. Bultmann, *History of the Synoptic Tradition*, p. 191.

27. Ibid., p. 189.

28. Richard A. Jensen, *Thinking in Story: Preaching in a Post-Literate Age* (Lima, Ohio: CSS, 1993), pp. 45-66. See also Pierre Babin, *The New Era in Religious Communication*, trans. David Smith (Minneapolis: Fortress, 1991).

29. For practical helps on preaching the gospel in story, see Thomas E. Boomershine, *Story Journey* (Nashville: Abingdon, 1988). Although chapter 4 of his work is the only one exclusively concerned with a parable, the whole book offers very helpful advice.

30. Sider, *Interpreting the Parables*, pp. 29-35.

31. Douglas E. Oakman, "Was Jesus a Peasant? Implications for Reading the Samaritan Story (Luke 10:30-35)," *Biblical Theology Bulletin* 22 (Fall 1992): 117-25.

32. I have preached a sermon using this imagery, the idea for which came from Eduard Richard Riegert, "'Parabolic' Sermons," *Lutheran Quarterly* 26 (1974): 24-31.

33. Sallie McFague, *Speaking in Parables* (Philadelphia: Fortress, 1975), p. 78. Emphasis mine.

34. Eugene L. Lowry, "Down the Up Staircase," *Preaching Today*. This tape series is published by *Christianity Today* and is available by writing 465 Gundersen Drive, Carol Stream, IL 60188.

35. R. Wayne Stacy, "Living with the Limits," *Pulpit Digest* (July/August 1993): 35-36. Emphasis his.

36. Riegert, "'Parabolic' Sermons," p. 24.

37. Eugene L. Lowry, *How to Preach a Parable* (Nashville: Abingdon, 1989), pp. 31-41.

38. Lowry, *The Homiletical Plot* (Atlanta: John Knox, 1980).

39. Lowry, "Down the Up Staircase," *Preaching Today* tape series.

Chapter 5/Aphorisms

1. William A. Beardslee, "Uses of the Proverb in the Synoptic Gospels," *Interpretation* 24 (January 1970): 61. Since Beardslee made his observation, considerable attention has been given to the subject of aphorisms. See *Foundations and Facets Forum* 1 (March 1985) and (June 1985).

2. Beardslee, *Literary Criticism in the New Testament* (Philadelphia: Fortress, 1970), p. 34. Beardslee notes that "the proverb is a distinctively wisdom form, . . . the parable arises from that tradition."

3. John Dominic Crossan, *In Fragments: The Aphorisms of Jesus* (San Francisco: Harper and Row, 1983), pp. 330-341.

4. Alyce M. McKenzie, *Preaching Proverbs: Wisdom for the Pulpit* (Louisville: Westminster/John Knox, 1996), p. xiii. I am especially grateful to McKenzie for allowing me to see an early draft of this book.

5. Tex Sample, *Ministry in an Oral Culture—Living with Will Rogers, Uncle Remus, and Minnie Pearl* (Louisville: Westminster/John Knox, 1994), p. 6. Emphasis his. Sample later notes that one of the important differences between a primary oral culture and a secondary oral culture such as ours is that the latter uses a written language, but operates with a strong sense of the oral (p. 9).

6. Beardslee, *Literary Criticism*, p. 30.

7. Crossan distinguishes between aphoristic sayings, aphoristic compounds (two aphorisms joined together), and aphoristic clusters (three or more), pp. 120ff., 153ff.

8. The terms "proverb" and "aphorism" are often used interchangeably, as is the case in this chapter. James L. Bailey and Lyle D. Vander Broek, *Literary Forms in the New Testament: A Handbook* (Louisville: Westminster/John Knox, 1992), p. 99, note that technically a proverb is a form of speech not attributed to a specific person, whereas an aphorism is ascribed to a certain person. In the case of Jesus, when he quotes what was originally a proverb, it becomes an aphorism. In a broad sense, any brief saying of Jesus functions as an aphorism.

9. Ibid., pp. 103-104, offers significant help with these issues.

10. Ibid., pp. 99-100. Bailey and Vander Broek offer these examples, though the translation used here is the NRSV.

11. Vernon K. Robbins, "Picking Up the Fragments," *Foundations and Facets Forum* 1 (June 1985): 31. Robbins discusses the

"old and new quest of the historical Jesus," incorporating "socio-rhetorical" analysis into the process of interpretation.

12. Bailey and Vander Broek, *Literary Forms*, p. 100.

13. Thomas G. Long, *Preaching and the Literary Forms of the Bible* (Philadelphia: Fortress, 1989), pp. 56-57.

14. Beardslee, *Literary Criticism*, p. 31.

15. J. H. Moulton, *A Grammar of New Testament Greek*, vol. 1, *Prolegomena* (Edinburgh: T. and T. Clark, 1930), p. 172, notes that imperatives may vary from permission to the strongest command.

16. Bailey and Vander Broek, *Literary Forms*, pp. 100-101.

17. Ibid., p. 102.

18. Long, *Preaching and the Literary Forms* p. 59.

19. Ibid., p. 58.

20. C. H. Dodd originated this phrase in relation to parables, but it also fits with proverbial literature such as aphorisms.

21. Beardslee, "Uses of the Proverb," p. 61.

22. Bailey and Vander Broek, *Literary Forms*, p. 102.

23. Ibid., p. 103.

24. Paul Ricoeur, "Biblical Hermeneutics," *Semeia* 4 (1975): 113, quoted in Long, *Preaching and the Literary Forms*, p. 57. See also Beardslee, *Literary Criticism*, p. 32. For an interesting study of the relation between Old Testament proverbs and parallels in the parables of Jesus, see Beardslee, "Uses of the Proverb," p. 65.

25. McKenzie, *Preaching Proverbs*, p. xv.

26. Bailey and Vander Broek, *Literary Forms*, p. 100.

27. J. Daniel Baumann, *An Introduction to Contemporary Preaching* (Grand Rapids: Baker, 1972), pp. 247-251, discusses three types of sermons in regard to application: direct, indirect, and none at all. Baumann adds, "We may seriously question whether the latter is a sermon in any purist sense" (p. 247). See also Harold Freeman, *Variety in Biblical Preaching* (Waco: Word, 1987), pp. 30-37, as well as his extensive notes.

28. Kenneth L. Gibble, "Mr. Witmer's Gift," in *Once upon a Wonder: Imaginings from the Gospels* (Nashville: Upper Room, 1992), pp. 82-85.

29. The best works on inductive preaching are Fred Craddock, *As One without Authority* (Nashville: Abingdon, 1971) and Lucy Rose, "The Parameters of Narrative Preaching," in *Journeys toward Narrative Preaching*, ed. Wayne Bradley Robinson (New York: Pilgrim, 1990), pp. 24-47.

30. Bailey and Vander Broek, *Literary Forms*, p. 100.

31. Robert John Versteeg, "Consider the Monkeys," in *Best Sermons*

4, ed. James W. Cox (San Francisco: Harper and Row, 1991), pp. 253-257.

32. Thomas G. Long, *The Witness of Preaching* (Louisville: Westminster/John Knox, 1989), p. 166.

33. Ibid., p. 167.

34. Long, *Preaching and the Literary Forms*, p. 65.

35. David Buttrick, *Homiletic: Moves and Structures* (Philadelphia: Fortress, 1987), p. 26, proposes several smaller "moves" within a sermon rather than the traditional three longer "points."

36. "A Second Look" appeared in *Preaching* (March/April 1988): 23-25.

Chapter 6/Pronouncement Stories

1. This illustration and all the others here were adapted from Vernon K. Robbins, "The Chreia," in *Greco-Roman Literature and the New Testament*, ed. David E. Aune (Atlanta: Scholars Press, 1988), p. 1.

2. Martin Luther King Jr., "I See the Promised Land," in *I Have A Dream: Writings and Speeches That Changed the World*, ed. James M. Washington (San Francisco: HarperCollins, 1992), p. 203.

3. Richard N. Soulen, *Handbook of Biblical Criticism*, 2d ed. (Atlanta: John Knox, 1981), p. 41. See also Robbins, "The Chreia," p. 2, who refers to these accounts as a "particular type of reminiscence."

4. James L. Bailey and Lyle D. Vander Broek, *Literary Forms in the New Testament* (Louisville: Westminster/John Knox, 1992), p. 114.

5. Vernon K. Robbins, "Apophthegm," in *Anchor Bible Dictionary*, vol. 1, ed. David Noel Freedman (New York: Doubleday, 1992), pp. 307-309. For a helpful overview of the different approaches over the years see Vernon K. Robbins, "Chreia and Pronouncement Story in Synoptic Studies," in *Patterns of Persuasion*, ed. Burton L. Mack and Vernon K. Robbins (Sonoma, Calif.: Polebridge, 1989), pp. 1-22.

6. Rudolf Bultmann emphasized speech as opposed to action. See his *History of the Synoptic Tradition*, trans. John Marsh (Oxford: Basil Blackwell, 1963), pp. 49ff. Vernon K. Robbins, "Pronouncement Stories from a Rhetorical Perspective," *Foundations and Facets Forum* 4 (June 1988): 4, believes this emphasis on the saying to the exclusion of the story probably resulted from the overwhelming number of proverbial statements in the Gospels

that do not need a context. For more on New Testament proverbs see chapter 5, "Aphorisms: The Proverbial Sayings of Jesus."

7. This development was due in part to an examination of
Greco-Roman forms. Prior to this, some scholars tended to view
the form as consisting of written versions of early sermons
within the Christian community.

8. Robert C. Tannehill, "Introduction: The Pronouncement
Story and Its Types," *Semeia* 20 (1981): 1.

9. Robbins, "Pronouncement Stories," p. 3. See also Miriam
Dean-Otting and Vernon K. Robbins, "Biblical Sources for Pronouncement Stories in the Gospels," *Semeia* 64 (1994): 95-116.

10. Robert C. Tannehill, "Varieties of Synoptic Pronouncement
Stories," *Semeia* 20 (1981): 102-16. Tannehill does list the possibility of another type (description stories), but notes only one possible example in the New Testament (Luke 14:15-24).

11. Edwin K. Broadhead, "Form and Function in the Passion
Story: The Issue of Genre Reconsidered," *Journal for the Study of
the New Testament* 61 (1996): 18.

12. Robbins, "Apophthegm." He notes that eleven well-
known stories have been agreed on by all as representative of
the form, but that many other hybrids and types bring the total
to about one hundred.

13. For example, see several of the volumes in the Interpretation series (Westminster/John Knox), Word Biblical Commentary series (Word), and the New Interpreter's Bible series
(Abingdon). In the latter see Robert C. Tannehill, "The Gospels
and Narrative Literature," in *NIB*, vol. 8 (Nashville: Abingdon,
1995), pp. 56-70.

14. Robert C. Tannehill, "Attitudinal Shift in Synoptic Pro-
nouncement Stories," in *Orientation by Disorientation: Studies in
Literary Criticism and Biblical Criticism*, ed. Richard A. Spencer
(Pittsburgh: Pickwick, 1980), p. 183.

15. Bailey and Vander Broek, *Literary Forms*, p. 114.

16. Ibid.

17. Ibid., p. 116.

18. Tannehill, "Varieties of Synoptic Pronouncement Stories,"
p. 117.

19. Tannehill, "Introduction: The Pronouncement Story and
Its Types," pp. 3-4.

20. Ibid., p. 3.

21. Ibid.

22. Ibid., pp. 3-4. In addition to position, the saying is typically

concise, that is, brief and yet powerful, "Attitudinal Shift in Synoptic Pronouncement Stories," p. 186.

23. Tannehill, "Varieties of Synoptic Pronouncement Stories,"
p. 104.

24. Tannehill, "Introduction: The Pronouncement Story and
Its Types," p. 7.

25. Tannehill, "Varieties of Synoptic Pronouncement Stories,"
p. 105.

26. Tannehill, "Introduction: The Pronouncement Story and
Its Types," pp. 7-8.

27. Tannehill, "Varieties of Synoptic Pronouncement Stories,"
p. 105.

28. Tannehill, "Introduction: The Pronouncement Story and
Its Types," p. 8.

29. Tannehill, "Varieties of Synoptic Pronouncement Stories,"
pp. 109-110.

30. Tannehill, "Introduction: The Pronouncement Story and
Its Types," p. 9.

31. Tannehill, "Varieties of Synoptic Pronouncement Stories,"
p. 112.

32. Ibid.

33. Ibid., pp. 115-116.

34. Tannehill, "Attitudinal Shift in Synoptic Pronouncement
Stories," p. 184.

35. See James Sanders and his discussion of prophetic versus
constitutive hermeneutics in *God Has a Story Too: Sermons in Context* (Philadelphia: Fortress, 1979), pp. 1-27, esp. pp. 18-21.

36. Broadhead, "Form and Function in the Passion Story,"
p. 21.

37. Tannehill, "Attitudinal Shift in Synoptic Pronouncement
Stories," p. 195. For more on narrative retelling see Richard L.
Thulin, "Retelling Biblical Narratives as the Foundation for
Preaching," and Michael E. Williams, "Preaching as Storytel-
ling," in *Journeys toward Narrative Preaching*, ed. Wayne Bradley
Robinson (New York: Pilgrim, 1990), pp. 7-22, 106-129; H.
Stephen Shoemaker, *Retelling the Biblical Story* (Nashville: Broad-
man, 1985), pp. 148-180.

38. Kenneth Burke, *A Rhetoric of Motives*, 2d ed. (Berkeley: University of California, 1969), pp. 21, 62. Significant amounts have
been written about Burke's theories as related to preaching, especially by Craig Loscalzo. See his article, "Burke, Burke, Still the
Lurk," *Homiletic* 14 (winter 1989): 5-8.

39. See J. Daniel Baumann, *An Introduction to Contemporary Preaching* (Grand Rapids: Baker, 1972), pp. 226-227.

40. Kenneth L. Gibble, *The Preacher as Jacob* (Minneapolis: Seabury, 1985), p. 72.

41. William H. Willimon, "Love in Action," in *Best Sermons 3*, ed. James W. Cox (San Francisco: Harper and Row, 1990), p. 201.

42. Fred B. Craddock, *As One without Authority* (Abingdon, 1971), p. 59.

43. Tannehill, "Attitudinal Shift in Synoptic Pronouncement Stories," pp. 194-195.

44. Eugene L. Lowry, "Swept Upstream," in *A New Hearing*, ed. Richard L. Eslinger (Nashville: Abingdon, 1987), p. 92.

45. Lowry, *How to Preach a Parable* (Nashville: Abingdon, 1989).

46. It really should come as no surprise that inductive preaching would be so compatible with these Gospel stories, since all stories (biblical and otherwise) are inductive by their very nature.

47. Beverly Roberts Gaventa, "The Discipleship of Extravagance," *Princeton Seminary Bulletin* 15 (1994): 53. Emphasis hers.

48. Thomas G. Long, "Figs Out of Season," in *Preaching Biblically*, ed. Don M. Wardlaw (Philadelphia: Westminster, 1983), pp. 94-100. Long's sermon includes parenthetical notes of his own that I will incorporate into my own reflections.

49. A. M. Hunter, *The Gospel according to Saint Mark: A Commentary* (London: Collier, 1962).

Chapter 7 / Miracle Stories

1. James L. Bailey and Lyle D. Vander Broek, *Literary Forms in the New Testament* (Louisville: Westminster/John Knox, 1992), p. 137.

2. Hans Dieter Betz, "The Early Christian Miracle Story: Some Observations on the Form Critical Problem," *Semeia* 11 (1978): 70.

3. Ronald J. Allen, *Our Eyes Can Be Opened: Preaching the Miracle Stories of the Synoptic Gospels* (Washington, D.C.: University Press of America, 1982), pp. 1-6, 9-28, notes a variety of ways that miracle stories have been interpreted in recent years. His approach is to consider them as stories, much as I am doing in this chapter.

4. Ibid.

5. Jarl Fossum, "Understanding Jesus' Miracles," *Bible Review* 10 (April 1994): 18, lists some of these.

6. Rudolf Bultmann, *Jesus* (Tübingen: Mohr, 1926), p. 146, quoted in Fossum, "Understanding Jesus' Miracles," p. 23.

7. Fossum, "Understanding Jesus' Miracles," p. 18. See also

Rudolf Bultmann, *History of the Synoptic Tradition*, trans. John
Marsh (Oxford: Basil Blackwell, 1963), p. 228, and N. T. Wright,
Who Was Jesus? (Grand Rapids: Eerdmans, 1992), pp. 80-81.

8. Wright, *Who Was Jesus?* pp. 80-81.

9. Harold E. Remus, "Miracle (NT)," *Anchor Bible Dictionary,*
vol. 4, ed. David Noel Freedman (New York: Doubleday, 1992),
pp. 856-869.

10. For example, see Bailey and Vander Broek, *Literary Forms,*
p. 143; Betz,"The Early Christian Miracle Story," p. 71; Robert
Tomson Fortna, *The Gospel of Signs* (Cambridge: Cambridge University Press, 1970), pp. 1-25; Harold Remus, "Does Terminology
Distinguish Early Christian from Pagan Miracles?" *Journal of Biblical Literature* 101 (1982): 531-551.

11. W. Nicol, *The Semeia in the Fourth Gospel,* Supplements to
Novum Testamentum, vol. 32 (Leiden: E. J. Brill, 1972), pp. 41-43.

12. Bailey and Vander Broek, *Literary Forms,* pp. 137-39. Their
listing combines the lists of Gerd Theissen, *The Miracle Stories of
the Early Christian Tradition,* trans. F. McDonagh (Philadelphia:
Fortress, 1983) and Antoinette Clark Wire, "The Structure of the
Gospel Miracle Stories and Their Tellers," *Semeia* 11 (1978): 83-
113.

13. Fossum, "Understanding Jesus' Miracles," p. 18.

14. Remus, "Miracle (NT)," p. 859.

15. Ibid.

16. Bailey and Vander Broek, *Literary Forms,* p. 139.

17. Paul J. Achtemeier, "The Lucan Perspective on the Miracles of Jesus: A Preliminary Sketch," *Journal of Biblical Literature*
94 (1975): 549.

18. Bailey and Vander Broek, *Literary Forms,* p. 139.

19. Remus, "Miracle (NT)," p. 857.

20. For another view, see David Buttrick, "Interpretation and
Preaching," *Interpretation* 35 (January 1981): 51, who states that
miracle stories "were designed to evoke a 'wow!' from listeners."

21. Wire, "The Structure of the Gospel Miracle Stories," pp. 88-
89.

22. Theissen, *The Miracle Stories of the Early Christian Tradition,*
pp. 89-90.

23. Ibid.

24. Ibid., p. 90.

25. I am indebted to Fred Craddock for this observation made
at a pastor's conference on preaching.

26. Wire, "The Structure of the Gospel Miracle Stories," p. 94.

Notes

275

27. Theissen, *The Miracle Stories of the Early Christian Tradition,* pp. 107, 111-112.

28. Wire, "The Structure of the Gospel Miracle Stories," p. 96.

29. Ibid., pp. 99-100; Bailey and Vander Broek, *Literary Forms,* p. 138.

30. Wire, "The Structure of the Gospel Miracle Stories," pp. 107-108.

31. Ibid., p. 98.

32. Theissen, *The Miracle Stories of the Early Christian Tradition,* p. 106.

33. Ibid., p. 103.

34. Ibid., p. 106.

35. Ibid., pp. 99-101.

36. Ibid., p. 99.

37. Fossum, "Understanding Jesus' Miracles," p. 21.

38. Theissen, *The Miracle Stories of the Early Christian Tradition,* p. 94.

39. Ibid., pp. 94-95. See also Bailey and Vander Broek, *Literary Forms,* pp. 138-139.

40. Wire, "The Structure of the Gospel Miracle Stories," p. 109.

41. Kenneth L. Gibble, "Graveyard Maniac," *Pulpit Digest* (September/October 1990): 35.

42. Leander E. Keck, "Limited Resources, Unlimited Possibilities," in *How to Preach a Parable,* by Eugene Lowry (Nashville: Abingdon, 1989), p. 83.

43. Michael Hough, "For Those Who Trust in God," in *Best Sermons 5,* ed. James W. Cox (San Francisco: HarperCollins, 1992), p. 86.

44. R. Wayne Stacy, "The Kingdom of the Forgotten Son," unpublished sermon manuscript from the pulpit ministry of First Baptist Church, Raleigh, North Carolina. Used by permission.

45. Wire, "The Structure of the Gospel Miracle Stories," p. 109.

46. Kenneth Gibble, "Graveyard Maniac," p. 39.

47. Walter Wink, *Unmasking the Powers* (Philadelphia: Fortress, 1986), pp. 48-49.

48. For an imaginative consideration of how to capture the fairy-tale kind of mood in provision stories, see Frederick Buechner, *Telling the Truth: The Gospel as Tragedy, Comedy, and Fairy Tale* (New York: Harper and Row, 1977), pp. 73-98.

49. R. Wayne Stacy, unpublished sermon manuscript from the pulpit ministry of First Baptist Church, Raleigh, North Carolina. Used by permission.

50. Jim Scarborough, "What to Do When the Boat Is Sinking," *Pulpit Digest* (July/August 1992): 36.

51. William Hethcock, "That We May Receive Our Sight," in *Best Sermons 3*, ed. James W. Cox (San Francisco: Harper and Row, 1990), pp. 101-102.

52. Eugene Lowry, *How to Preach a Parable* (Nashville: Abingdon, 1989).

53. Lowry, "Cries from the Graveyard," in *Daemonic Imagination*, ed. Robert Detweiler and William G. Doty (Atlanta: Scholars Press, 1990), pp. 27-39.

Chapter 8/Johannine Discourse

1. Fred Craddock, *John*, Knox Preaching Guides (Atlanta: John Knox, 1982), pp. 1-2; Gail R. O'Day, *The Word Disclosed: John's Story and Narrative Preaching* (St. Louis: CBP, 1987), p. 9.

2. O'Day, *The Word Disclosed*, p. 14.

3. Robert Tomson Fortna, *The Fourth Gospel and Its Predecessor* (Philadelphia: Fortress, 1988), pp. 1-8.

4. For an interesting look at the literary role played by Nicodemus in John's Gospel, see Jouette M. Bassler, "Mixed Signals: Nicodemus in the Fourth Gospel," *Journal of Biblical Literature* 108 (December 1989): 635-46. Bassler offers many fine insights that can be readily incorporated into sermonic material.

5. Craddock, *John*, p. 46.

6. David E. Aune, *The New Testament in Its Literary Environment* (Philadelphia: Westminster, 1987), pp. 51-52.

7. C. H. Dodd, *The Interpretation of the Fourth Gospel* (Cambridge: Cambridge University Press, 1958), p. 133.

8. O'Day, *The Word Disclosed*, p. 15.

9. Raymond E. Brown, *John*, vol. 1, *The Anchor Bible* (New York: Doubleday, 1966), p. cxxxii; Rudolf Schnackenburg, *The Gospel according to St. John*, trans. Kevin Smith (Freiburg: Herder and Herder, 1968), p. 112.

10. I mention *The Brothers Karamazov* because of an article by Thomas Rogers, who teaches Russian at Brigham Young University, and who discusses the brilliant literary features of John's Gospel: "The Gospel of John as Literature," *Brigham Young University Studies* 28 (summer 1988): 67-80.

11. R. Alan Culpepper, *Anatomy of the Fourth Gospel* (Philadelphia: Fortress, 1983), p. 4.

12. It is typical to think of the Samaritan as a promiscuous woman living with some guy, but in the first-century world women did not even have the right to file for divorce.

13. Culpepper, *Anatomy of the Fourth Gospel*, pp. 190-198, discusses these at length.

14. The first twelve chapters are typically designated as the "book of signs" in John's Gospel. The seven signs in John's Gospel are roughly equivalent to the miracle stories in the Synoptics. (See chapter 7, "Miracle Stories: The Supernatural Identity of Jesus.")

15. Kim E. Dewey, "*Paroimiai* in the Gospel of John," *Semeia* 17 (1980): 81-100. She notes that the term "embraces a range of literary forms, devices, and concepts, including: riddle, proverb, parable, metaphor, allegory, irony, paradox, enigma, aporia, and so on" (p. 82).

16. Culpepper, *Anatomy of the Fourth Gospel*, p. 152. See also E. Richard, "Expressions of Double Meaning and Their Function in the Gospel of John," *New Testament Studies* 31 (1985): 98.

17. Richard, "Expressions of Double Meaning and Their Function," p. 97, notes that the Fourth Gospel uses a variety of double meaning patterns. He notes six distinct types. See also David W. Wead, *The Literary Devices in John's Gospel* (Basel: Friedrich Reinhardt, 1970), pp. 30-46.

18. Paul D. Duke, *Irony in the Fourth Gospel* (Atlanta: John Knox, 1985), p. 29. Culpepper, *Anatomy of the Fourth Gospel*, p. 176, notes, however, that the most common form of Johannine irony does not occur in dialogue with Jesus but in unanswered questions. In these unanswered questions, characters unknowingly speak the truth or at least hint at it. For example, Nathanael says to Philip, "Can anything good come out of Nazareth?" (John 1:46).

19. D. C. Muecke, *The Compass of Irony* (London: Methuen, 1969), p. 14, quoted in *Irony in the Fourth Gospel*, p. 13. See also Culpepper, *Anatomy of the Fourth Gospel*, pp. 166-167.

20. Culpepper, *Anatomy of the Fourth Gospel*, p. 168.

21. Richard, "Expressions of Double Meaning and Their Function," p. 107.

22. Culpepper, *Anatomy of the Fourth Gospel*, p. 164.

23. Aune, *New Testament in Its Literary Environment*, p. 52; Culpepper, *Anatomy of the Fourth Gospel*, p. 153; Dodd, *Interpretation of the Fourth Gospel*, pp. 134, 42; Gail R. O'Day, *John*, The New Interpreter's Bible (Nashville: Abingdon, 1995), p. 494. Jesus is much more aware of his divine nature in the Fourth Gospel than in the Synoptics. Most scholars agree this reflects what was probably the homiletical language of the Johannine community. See James L. Bailey and Lyle D. Vander Broek, *Literary Forms in the*

New Testament: A Handbook (Louisville: Westminster/John Knox, 1992), p. 172, for a summary of this scholarship.

24. Culpepper, *Anatomy of the Fourth Gospel*, p. 165.

25. Ibid., p. 164.

26. O'Day, *John*, p. 494, notes that John's literary techniques demand readers to work, and yet John frequently comments on a story to ensure comprehension (for example, John 7:39; 8:27; 11:51-52). For an extended treatment of implicit commentary, see Culpepper, *Anatomy of the Fourth Gospel*, chapter 6.

27. Robert Kysar, "The Promises and Perils of Preaching on the Gospel of John," *Dialog* 19 (summer 1980): 216.

28. Rogers,"The Gospel of John as Literature," p. 68.

29. Craddock, *John*, pp. 4-5.

30. Tom Thatcher, "A New Look at Asides in the Fourth Gospel," *Bibliotheca Sacra* 151 (October/December, 1994): 430.

31. Richard Lischer, "Acknowledgment," in *Best Sermons 5*, ed. James W. Cox (San Francisco: HarperCollins, 1992), p. 17.

32. Eugene L. Lowry, "Strangers in the Night," in *Journeys toward Narrative Preaching*, ed. Wayne Bradley Robinson (New York: Pilgrim, 1990), p. 79.

33. Lowry, *How to Preach a Parable* (Nashville: Abingdon, 1989), pp. 115-141.

34. Ibid., p. 133.

35. Bailey and Vander Broek, *Literary Forms in the New Testament*, p. 177.

36. Wead, *Literary Devices in John's Gospel*, p. 30, for instance, cautions against pressing double meanings one way or another. That they have two meanings allows for two possible responses.

37. For a thoughtful critique of these trends in worship, see Marva Dawn, *Reaching Out without Dumbing Down* (Grand Rapids: Eerdmans, 1995); Philip Kenneson, "Selling [Out] the Church in the Marketplace of Desire," *Modern Theology* 9 (October 1993): 319-348.

38. Kysar, "Promises and Perils of Preaching on the Gospel of John," pp. 217-18.

39. D. A. Carson, "Understanding Misunderstandings in the Fourth Gospel," *Tyndale Bulletin* 33 (1982): 73.

40. M. deJonge, "Nicodemus and Jesus: Some Observations on Misunderstanding and Understanding in the Fourth Gospel," *Bulletin of the John Rylands Library* 53 (spring 1971): 359.

41. C. Michael Fuhrman, "The Tragicomedy of the Gospel," in *Best Sermons 4*, ed. James W. Cox (San Francisco: HarperCollins, 1991), pp. 69-76.

42. Cindy Witt, "A Marriage Made in Heaven," in *Best Sermons* 2, ed. James W. Cox (San Francisco: Harper and Row, 1989), pp. 125-131.

43. Barbara Brown Taylor, *The Preaching Life* (Boston: Cowley, 1993), pp. 100-106.

Chapter 9 / Adventure Narratives

1. William H. Willimon, *Acts*, Interpretation (Atltanta: John Knox, 1988), p. vii.

2. Henry J. Cadbury, *The Making of Luke-Acts* (New York: Macmillan, 1927), p. 136.

3. Mark Allan Powell, *What Are They Saying about Acts?* (New York: Paulist, 1991), p. 9.

4. David E. Aune, *The New Testament in Its Literary Environment* (Philadelphia: Westminster, 1987), p. 77.

5. Charles H. Talbert, *What Is a Gospel?* (Philadelphia: Fortress, 1977), pp. 107-9. See also his work *Literary Patterns, Theological Themes, and the Genre of Luke-Acts* (Missoula, Mont.: Society of Biblical Literature Scholars Press, 1974).

6. Richard Pervo, *Profit with Delight* (Philadelphia: Fortress, 1987), pp. 12-57. Pervo's thesis seems to emphasize the "delight" aspects of Acts more than the "profit" aspects. For a briefer account of Pervo's approach to Acts as novel, see his *Luke's Story of Paul* (Fortress, 1990).

7. For example, see Aune, *New Testament in Its Literary Environment*, pp. 77-80.

8. Mikeal Parsons and Richard Pervo, *Rethinking the Unity of Luke and Acts* (Minneapolis: Fortress, 1993).

9. Ibid., pp. 7-44. See also J. Dawsey, "The Literary Unity of Luke-Acts: Questions of Style—A Task for Literary Critics," *New Testament Studies* 35 (1989): 48-66; Martin Dibelius, *Studies in the Acts of the Apostles* (New York: Scribner's, 1956), p. 2; Richard Pervo, "Must Luke and Acts Belong to the Same Genre?" Society of Biblical Literature Scholars Press 28 (1989): 309-316; 7-44.

10. Powell, *What Are They Saying about Acts?* p. 96.

11. Ernst Haenchen, "The Book of Acts as Source Material for the History of Early Christianity," in *Studies in Luke-Acts*, ed. Leander Keck and J. Louis Martyn (Nashville: Abingdon, 1966), p. 260.

12. Haenchen, *The Acts of the Apostles* (Philadelphia: Westminster, 1971), pp. 90-91.

13. Aune, *New Testament in Its Literary Environment*, p. 83; W. Ward Gasque, "A Fruitful Field: Recent Study of the Acts of the

Apostles," *Interpretation* 42 (April 1988): 129; Beverly Roberts
Gaventa, "Toward a Theology of Acts: Reading and Rereading,"
Interpretation 42 (April 1988): 149-52; I. Howard Marshall, *Luke:
Historian and Theologian* (Exeter: Paternoster, 1970), pp. 18-52.

14. Even Aune, *New Testament in Its Literary Environment*, p. 80,
who disagrees with Pervo's identification of Acts as an ancient
form of the novel, agrees that Acts is an edifying and entertaining work that is not to be taken as literal history.

15. Ibid., pp. 120-131.

16. For more on how the speeches function in Acts, see
Marion L. Soards, *The Speeches in Acts* (Louisville: Westmin-
ster/John Knox, 1994). My colleague David May has rightly
noted that although these speeches make up only 20 percent of
Acts, that 20 percent is larger than Jude, Philippians, Titus, and
so forth. In addition, the speeches are a major source of kerygma.

17. Pervo, "Must Luke and Acts Belong to the Same Genre?"
pp. 18-57.

18. To the contrary, J. M. Gilchrist, "The Historicity of Paul's
Shipwreck," *Journal for the Study of the New Testament* 61 (1996):
29-51, affirms the historicity of this account and others in Acts,
and goes so far as to encourage archaeologists to find the wreckage.

19. Eckhard Plümacher, *Lukas als hellenistischer Schriftsteller*
(Göttingen: Vandenhoeck and Ruprecht, 1972), pp. 80-136, cited
by Aune, *New Testament in Its Literary Environment*, p. 129.

20. Pervo, "Must Luke and Acts Belong to the Same Genre?"
p. 18.

21. Ibid., p. 22.

22. Ibid.

23. Ibid., p. 34.

24. Richard S. Ascough, "Narrative Technique and Generic
Designation: Crowd Scenes in Luke-Acts and in Chariton,"
Catholic Biblical Quarterly 58 (1996): 78-79.

25. Pervo, "Must Luke and Acts Belong to the Same Genre?"
p. 42.

26. Aune, *New Testament in Its Literary Environment*, p. 123.

27. Vernon K. Robbins, "By Land and by Sea: The We-Pas-
sages and Ancient Sea Voyages," in *Perspectives on Luke-Acts*, ed.
Charles Talbert (Danville, Pa.: Association of Baptist Professors
of Religion, 1978), pp. 215-16.

28. Pervo, "Must Luke and Acts Belong to the Same Genre?"
p. 51. See also Robbins, "By Land and by Sea," pp. 232-233.

29. Robbins, "By Land and by Sea," p. 233.

30. Aune, *New Testament in Its Literary Environment*, pp. 129-130.

31. Robbins, "By Land and by Sea," p. 217. Robbins contends that interpreting the "we" passages as only indicating Luke's presence on these journeys can be traced to Irenaeus but that the evidence does not support that view (pp. 228-229). Aune, *New Testament in Its Literary Environment*, p. 123, however, does interpret the first person as indicating Luke's involvement on the journeys.

32. Robbins, "By Land and by Sea," p. 234.

33. Aune, *New Testament in Its Literary Environment*, p. 128.

34. Paul Ricoeur, *Interpretation Theory: Discourse and the Surplus of Meaning* (Fort Worth: Texas Christian University Press, 1976), pp. 25-32, cited by Ronald Allen, *Contemporary Biblical Interpretation for Preaching* (Valley Forge: Judson, 1984), pp. 131-134.

35. Allen, *Contemporary Biblical Interpretation*, p. 133.

36. Leonard Griffith, "Christianity at Its Best," in *Best Sermons 2*, ed. James W. Cox (San Francisco: Harper and Row, 1989), p. 215.

37. William H. Willimon, "'Eyewitnesses and Ministers of the Word': Preaching in Acts," *Interpretation* 42 (April 1988): 159.

38. Haenchen, "The Book of Acts," p. 259.

39. Willimon, "Eyewitnesses and Ministers," p. 160.

40. William H. Willimon and Stanley Hauerwas, *Preaching to Strangers* (Louisville: Westminster/John Knox, 1992), pp. 17-25.

Chapter 10/Vice and Virtue Lists

1. Abraham J. Malherbe, *Moral Exhortation: A Greco-Roman Sourcebook* (Philadelphia: Westminster, 1986), pp. 121-122.

2. David E. Aune, *The New Testament in Its Literary Environment* (Philadelphia: Westminster, 1987), p. 219.

3. Malherbe, *Moral Exhortation*, pp. 129-134; James L. Bailey and Lyle D. Vander Broek, *Literary Forms in the New Testament* (Louisville: Westminster/John Knox, 1992), pp. 38-42.

4. Bailey and Vander Broek, *Literary Forms*, p. 62.

5. David G. Bradley, "The *Topos* as a Form in the Pauline Paraenesis," *Journal of Biblical Literature* 72 (1953): 239.

6. Bailey and Vander Broek, *Literary Forms*, p. 62.

7. Leo G. Perdue, "Paraenesis and the Epistle of James," *Zeitschrift für die Neutestamentliche Wissenschaft* 72 (1981): 251.

8. Bailey and Vander Broek, *Literary Forms*, p. 62.

9. Ibid., p. 65.

10. J. N. Sevenster, "Education or Conversion: Epictetus and

the Gospels," *Novum Testamentum* 8 (1966): 247, cited by Neil J. McEleney, "The Vice Lists of the Pastoral Epistles," *Catholic Biblical Quarterly* 36, no. 2 (1974): 217.

11. Victor Paul Furnish, *Theology and Ethics in Paul* (Nashville: Abingdon, 1968), p. 84.

12. Eduard Lohse, *Die Briefe an die Kolosser und an Philemon* (Göttingen: Vandenhoeck and Ruprecht, 1968), p. 223, cited by W. C. Coetzer, "The Literary Genre of Paranesis in the Pauline Letters," *Theologica Evangelica* 17, no. 3 (1984): 36.

13. S. Wibbing, *Die Tugend- und Lasterkataloge im Neuen Testament: und ihre Traditions Geschichte unter besonderer Beruck-sichtigung der Qumran-Texte* (Berlin: A. Töpelmann, 1959), p. 81, cited by McEleney, "Vice Lists," p. 206.

14. John T. Fitzgerald, "Virtue/Vice Lists," in *Anchor Bible Dictionary*, vol. 6, ed. David Noel Freedman (New York: Doubleday, 1992), p. 857-859.

15. McEleney, "Vice Lists," p. 203, identifies twelve virtue lists, while Aune, *New Testament in Its Literary Environment*, p. 195, lists twenty, and G. Mussies, *Dio Chrysostom and the New Testament* (London: E. J. Brill, 1972), pp. 172-173, lists twenty-one catalogues of virtues.

16. Mussies, *Dio Chrysostom*, p. 67, lists ten catalogues of sins, nine catalogues of sinners, and one catalogue of both (Romans 1:29-31). Aune, *New Testament in Its Literary Environment*, p. 195, counts twenty-three vice lists in the New Testament, two of which are in the gospels, not the epistles. McEleney, "Vice Lists," p. 203, identifies twenty-one lists of vices, two of which are in the gospels as well (Matthew 15:19 and Mark 7:21-22).

17. Mussies, *Dio Chrysostom*, pp. 67, 172-173.

18. Furnish, *Theology and Ethics*, p. 86.

19. Burton Scott Easton, "New Testament Ethical Lists," *Journal of Biblical Literature* 51 (1932): 5. See also Wayne A. Meeks, *The Origins of Christian Morality* (New Haven: Yale University, 1993), pp. 67-68.

20. Ibid.

21. Ibid., p. 12.

22. Furnish, *Theology and Ethics*, p. 87.

23. McEleney, "Vice Lists," p. 207.

24. Aune, *New Testament in Its Literary Environment*, pp. 194-195.

25. Bailey and Vander Broek, *Literary Forms*, p. 66.

26. Amos Wilder, *Early Christian Rhetoric* (London: SCM, 1964), p. 64.

27. Bailey and Vander Broek, p. 66.

28. McEleney, "Vice Lists," p. 214.

29. Thanks to my colleague David May for these possible parallels.

30. Robert P. Mills, "Wayside Sacraments," *Best Sermons 5*, ed. James W. Cox (San Francisco: Harper and Row, 1992), p. 273.

31. Wilder, *Early Christian Rhetoric*, p. 64.

32. Thomas Edward McComiskey, *Reading Scripture in Public* (Grand Rapids: Baker, 1991). McComiskey discusses the reading of biblical poetry in some detail, and although his focus is largely on parallelism, his exercises can be applied to other poetic passages.

33. Gerard Mussies, "Catalogues of Sins and Virtues Personified," in *Studies in Gnosticism and Hellenistic Religions*, ed. R. Van Den Broek and M. J. Vermaseren (London: E. J. Brill, 1981), pp. 315-335.

34. For an example of responsible use of personification within a sermon, see Fred Craddock, *As One without Authority* (Nashville: Abingdon, 1971), pp. 163-68. Although the sermon is actually based on a liturgical fragment (see chapter 12, "Poetry and Hymns: The Gospel in Verse"), the personification is quite admirable.

35. Thomas G. Long, *The Witness of Preaching* (Louisville: Westminster/John Knox, 1989), pp. 165-172.

36. Easton, p. 21.

37. This sermon is taken from *Best Sermons 2*, ed. James W. Cox (San Francisco: Harper and Row, 1989), pp. 199-206.

Chapter 11/Admonitions and Topoi

1. Abraham J. Malherbe, *Moral Exhortation, A Greco-Roman Sourcebook* (Philadelphia: Westminster, 1986), pp. 121-22.

2. James L. Bailey and Lyle D. Vander Broek, *Literary Forms in the New Testament* (Louisville: Westminster/John Knox, 1992), p. 62.

3. David E. Aune, *The New Testament in Its Literary Environment* (Philadelphia: Westminster, 1987), p. 191.

4. Benjamin Fiore, "Parenesis and Protreptic," in *Anchor Bible Dictionary*, vol. 5, ed. David Noel Freedman (New York: Doubleday, 1992), p. 163.

5. Bailey and Vander Broek, *Literary Forms*, p. 62.

6. Stanley K. Stowers, *Letter Writing in Greco-Roman Antiquity* (Philadelphia: Westminster, 1986), p. 96. See also Malherbe, *Moral Exhortation*, p. 124.

7. Fiore, "Parenesis and Protreptic," p. 164.

8. Abraham J. Malherbe, "Exhortation in First Thessalonians," *Novum Testamentum* 25 (1983): 238.

9. Benjamin Fiore, *The Function of Personal Example in the So-cratic and Pastoral Epistles* (Rome: Biblical Institute Press, 1986), pp. 14-15. Emphasis mine.

10. Malherbe, *Moral Exhortation*, p. 124. See also Stowers, *Letter Writing*, p. 96. The genre/form of James has been highly debated over the years. For more information, see Peter Davids, *Commentary on James*, New International Greek Testament Commentary (Grand Rapids: Eerdmans, 1982), pp. 22-28; Martin Dibelius, *James*, rev. Heinrich Greeven, Hermeneia (Minneapolis: Fortress, 1975), pp. 1-7; Malherbe, *Moral Exhortation*, p. 124; and Stowers, *Letter Writing*, p. 97.

11. Bailey and Vander Broek, *Literary Forms*, p. 62.

12. Ibid.

13. Fiore, "Parenesis and Protreptic," p. 164.

14. David G. Bradley, "The *Topos* as a Form in the Pauline Paraenesis," *Journal of Biblical Literature* 72 (1953): 240.

15. Ibid., pp. 244-245.

16. Terrence Y. Mullins, "Topos as a New Testament Form," *Journal of Biblical Literature* 99 (1980): 547. In addition to these three essentials, some topoi also employed analogous situations and refutations.

17. For more on hymns see chapter 12, "Poetry and Hymns: The Gospel in Verse."

18. Fiore, "Parenesis and Protreptic," pp. 163-164, believes that the highly developed topoi of Paul are probably original with him, whereas the brief admonitions scattered throughout the epistles may have been borrowed.

19. Bradley, "The *Topos* as a Form," pp. 239-240.

20. Bailey and Vander Broek, *Literary Forms*, p. 63. See also David M. Scholer, "Unseasonable Thoughts on the State of Biblical Hermeneutics: Reflections of a New Testament Exegete," *American Baptist Quarterly* 2 (June 1983): 139-140, who proposes eight guidelines for distinguishing eternal principles from cultural references; and Edward Farly, "Preaching the Bible and Preaching the Gospel," *Theology Today* 51 (April 1994): 90-103, who questions the prevailing paradigm of exegesis for preaching.

21. Bailey and Vander Broek, pp. 62-63. See also Mullins, "Topos as a New Testament Form," p. 547.

22. J. H. Moulton, *A Grammar of New Testament Greek*, vol. 1, *Prolegomena* (Edinburgh: T. and T. Clark, 1930), p. 172.

23. Fiore, "Parenesis and Protreptic," p. 164.

24. Ibid.

25. Aune, p. 208, notes that parenesis can function as call to something new (deliberative) or as reminder (epideictic). See also Luke T. Johnson, *The Writings of the New Testament* (Philadelphia: Fortress, 1986), pp. 261-262, who discusses parenesis as involving "the interplay of three elements": memory (recalling that which the listeners already know), model (following the writer's own example), and maxim (short, pithy sayings).

26. Malherbe, *Moral Exhortation*, p. 125. See also Fiore, "Parenesis and Protreptic," p. 164; Stowers, *Letter Writing*, p. 96.

27. Fiore, "Parenesis and Protreptic."

28. There is considerable debate among scholars as to whether these sections in James (for example, 2:1-13 and 2:14-26) are a narrative version of topoi or an admonition. See Davids, *Commentary on James*, pp. 22-28; Dibelius, *James*, pp. 1-7.

29. Dibelius, *James*, p. 4.

30. Benjamin Fiore, *The Function of Personal Example*, pp. 12-13.

31. Fiore, "Parenesis and Protreptic," pp. 163-164.

32. Stowers, *Letter Writing*, p. 97.

33. Michael Quicke, "Come Alive with 1 John—Stop Sinning!" in *Best Sermons* 6, ed. James W. Cox (New York: HarperCollins, 1993), pp. 56-57. Emphasis his.

34. Carroll E. Simcox, "The Saints: Dogged Blunderers toward Heaven," in *Best Sermons 4*, ed. James W. Cox (San Francisco: Harper and Row, 1991), p. 118.

35. William J. Carl III, "Unplanned Dissonance," in *Preaching Biblically*, ed. Don M. Wardlaw (Philadelphia: Westminster, 1983), p. 134.

36. William H. Willimon and Stanley Hauerwas, *Preaching to Strangers*, p. 36.

37. Robert Young, "Keep Up the Good Work," in his book *Be Brief About It* (Philadelphia: Westminster, 1980), p. 136.

38. Richard F. Wilson, "Rhythms," in *Best Sermons 5*, ed. James W. Cox (San Francisco: Harper and Row, 1992), pp. 79-85.

39. Hal Missourie Warheim, "Lovers," in *Best Sermons 2*, ed. James W. Cox (San Francisco: Harper and Row, 1989), pp. 267-276.

40. Eugene L. Lowry, "Narrative Preaching," in *Concise Encyclopedia of Preaching*, ed. William H. Willimon and Richard Lischer (Louisville: Westminster/John Knox, 1995), p. 343.

41. Bailey and Vander Broek, *Literary Forms*, p. 196.

42. Donald W. Musser, "Struggling with Our Mortality," in

Best Sermons 6, ed. James W. Cox (San Francisco: Harper and Row, 1993), pp. 202-206.

Chapter 12/Poetry and Hymns

1. A. A. Milne, *The House at Pooh Corner* (New York: E. P. Dutton, 1928), pp. 32-33.

2. The structural arrangement is mine. Amos Wilder, *Early Christian Rhetoric* (London: SCM, 1964), p. 115, prefers to label passages such as 1 Corinthians 13 as liturgical, not poetic in the technical sense of the word. For an interesting discussion of the literary form of 1 Corinthians 13, see James G. Sigountos, "The Genre of 1 Corinthians 13," *New Testament Studies* 40 (1994): 246-260.

3. Some preachers resist the notion of preaching poetry entirely. For them it would trivialize the poetic mood of the passage. But as Thomas Long notes, that does not have to be the case. *Preaching and the Literary Forms of the Bible* (Philadelphia: Fortress, 1989), pp. 43-44.

4. Karl Rahner, "Priest and Poet," in *The Word: Readings in Theology,* quoted in Robert P. Waznak, "The Preacher and the Poet," *Worship* 60 (January 1986): 46.

5. Although parallelism has been hailed as the trademark of all biblical poetry, New Testament poetry includes a variety of styles. See James Kugel, *The Idea of Biblical Poetry* (New Haven: Yale University Press, 1981), pp. 1-3; Northrop Frye, *The Great Code: The Bible and Literature* (New York: Harcourt Brace Jovanovich, 1982), pp. 209-210.

6. James L. Bailey and Lyle D. Vander Broek, *Literary Forms in the New Testament* (Louisville: Westminster/John Knox, 1992), pp. 72-82, discuss these forms in some detail. See also W. Hulitt Gloer, "Homologies and Hymns in the New Testament: Form, Content and Criteria for Identification," *Perspectives in Religious Studies* 11 (summer 1984): 115-32. Gloer makes some helpful distinctions for the interpreter, and he shows the liturgical and confessional nature of these forms.

7. Jack T. Sanders, *The New Testament Christological Hymns* (Cambridge: Cambridge University Press, 1971), pp. 9-25. For a more recent treatment of the hymnic qualities of Ephesians 2, see Ralph P. Martin, "Reconciliation and Unity in Ephesians," *Review and Expositor* 93 (spring 1996): 210-217.

8. Bailey and Vander Broek, *Literary Forms*, p. 78, offer this arrangement and example.

9. Ibid., p. 77.

10. Anne Sexton, "ROWING," *The Awful Rowing toward God* (Boston: Houghton Mifflin, 1975), pp. 1-2.

11. Waznak, "The Preacher and the Poet," p. 52. Waznak quotes Sexton's poem in its entirety to teach several lessons that preachers can learn from poets.

12. Bailey and Vander Broek, *Literary Forms*, p. 77.

13. Walter Brueggemann, *Finally Comes the Poet: Daring Speech for Proclamation* (Minneapolis: Fortress, 1989), p. 3.

14. Bailey and Vander Broek, *Literary Forms*, p. 77.

15. Gloer, "Homologies and Hymns in the New Testament," p. 118.

16. Long, p. 45.

17. Bailey and Vander Broek, *Literary Forms*, p. 77.

18. Wilder, *Early Christian Rhetoric*, p. 98.

19. Fred Craddock, *Preaching* (Nashville: Abingdon, 1985), pp. 200-203, offers a good discussion on the use of description.

20. Ronald Allen, "The Difference" [Philippians 2:5-11], in *Preaching as a Social Act*, ed. Arthur Van Seters (Nashville: Abingdon, 1988), p. 193.

21. Robert D. Young, *Be Brief about It* (Philadelphia: Westminster, 1980), especially chapter 2, "Adopt a Poetry Model."

22. James R. Zug, "The Inevitable Encounter," [Psalm 139; Ephesians 1:9-10], in *Best Sermons 2*, ed. James W. Cox (San Francisco: Harper and Row, 1989), p. 44.

23. Bailey and Vander Broek, *Literary Forms*, p. 81.

24. John Mason Stapleton, *Preaching in Demonstration of the Spirit and Power* (Philadelphia: Fortress, 1988), p. 59.

25. Gerard Sloyan, *Worshipful Preaching* (Philadelphia: Fortress, 1984), p. 28.

26. Bailey and Vander Broek, *Literary Forms*, p. 81.

27. George Santayana, *Interpretation of Poetry and Religion* (New York: Harper, 1957), pp. 255-256.

28. Kathleen Norris, *The Cloister Walk* (New York: Riverhead, 1996), p. 89.

29. Andrew T. Lincoln, *Paradise Now and Not Yet* (Cambridge: Cambridge University Press, 1981), pp. 135-136. Thanks to my colleague Molly Marshall for pointing this out to me.

30. Peter Marshall used to write his sermons in this fashion. For a contemporary example, see Ronald Allen's sermon, "When the Universe Has Two Centers," in *Preaching Biblically*, ed. Don M. Wardlaw (Philadelphia: Westminster, 1983), pp. 44-56. The sermon features parenthetical notes throughout that explain Allen's strategy. For practical help of a general nature, see Patricia

Wilson-Kastner, *Imagery for Preaching* (Minneapolis: Fortress, 1989), pp. 47-61. In contrast, see Walter Kaiser Jr., *Toward an Exegetical Theology* (Grand Rapids: Baker, 1981), pp. 170-173, who imports rhetorical outline structures into Old Testament poetry.

31. This strategic arrangement relates to the rhetorical aspects of homiletical theory. Thus, form-sensitive preaching must consider the rhetorical strategies not only within the text but also within the composition of the sermon itself.

32. "Aurora Leigh," in *The Poetical Works of Elizabeth Barrett Browning* (New York: Macmillan, 1897), p. 466.

Chapter 13/Apocalypse

1. James Bailey and Lyle Vander Broek, *Literary Forms in the New Testament* (Louisville: Westminster/John Knox, 1992), pp. 202-5. Elisabeth Schüssler Fiorenza, *The Book of Revelation: Justice and Judgment* (Philadelphia: Fortress, 1985), pp. 166-70, notes how Revelation is uniquely liturgical, mythical (that is, the staging of a battle between good and evil), and prophetic at the same time and all within the form of a letter.

2. Adela Yarbro Collins, "Introduction: Early Christian Apocalypticism," *Semeia* 36 (1986): 7.

3. Bruce J. Malina, *On the Genre and Message of Revelation* (Peabody, Mass.: Hendrickson, 1995), pp. 25-30.

4. Bernard Brandon Scott, *Hollywood Dreams and Biblical Stories* (Minneapolis: Fortress, 1994), p. 213.

5. Adela Yarbro Collins, *Crisis and Catharsis: The Power of the Apocalypse* (Philadelphia: Westminster, 1984), p. 145.

6. William A. Beardslee, *Literary Criticism of the New Testament* (Philadelphia: Fortress, 1970), p. 54.

7. Collins, *Crisis and Catharsis*, p. 141.

8. Fiorenza, *Book of Revelation*, p. 194.

9. Bailey and Vander Broek, *Literary Forms*, pp. 122-29, discuss these at some length, including how to interpret such forms.

10. Ibid., pp. 54-62.

11. Fiorenza, *Book of Revelation*, p. 187.

12. Bruce M. Metzger, *Breaking the Code: Understanding the Book of Revelation* (Nashville: Abingdon, 1993), p. 11.

13. Collins, *Crisis and Catharsis*, pp. 141, 154.

14. Fiorenza, *Book of Revelation*, p. 187.

15. Beardslee, *Literary Criticism*, p. 59.

16. Ibid., p. 57. Of course, many of Jesus' parables themselves are apocalyptic in nature.

17. Ibid., p. 54.

18. Ibid., p. 59. The recapitulation theory of interpretation affects every aspect of understanding Revelation, even the millennial question. Even if we do not agree with the recapitulation theory as a whole, the importance of repetition as a literary device in the Apocalypse is hard to deny. Recapitulation, however, is more than just repetition; it also includes intensification.

19. Collins, *Crisis and Catharsis*, p. 144.

20. Thomas G. Long, "Preaching Apocalyptic Literature," *Review and Expositor* 90 (summer 1993): 379-80. Long notes three possible strategies for preaching from apocalyptic texts: as a vision of worship, as a warning, and as hope for those whose lives have been torn apart.

21. David Buttrick, *Preaching Jesus Christ* (Minneapolis: Fortress, 1988), p. 65.

22. Joseph R. Jeter Jr., "Revelation-Based Preaching: Homiletical Approaches," in *Preaching through the Apocalypse: Sermons from Revelation*, ed. Cornish R. Rogers and Joseph R. Jeter Jr. (St. Louis: Chalice, 1992), pp. 16-18.

23. Ibid., pp. 30-32.

24. Long, "Preaching Apocalyptic Literature," p. 374.

25. This incident is cited in Kathleen Norris, *The Cloister Walk* (New York: Riverhead, 1996), pp. 214-215.

26. Troeger's sermon is from *Preaching through the Apocalypse*, pp. 97-105.